SRI LANKA
BY RAIL

SRI LANKA
BY RAIL

Royston Ellis

Bradt Publications, UK
The Globe Pequot Press, USA

First published in 1994 by Bradt Publications,
41 Nortoft Road, Chalfont St Peter, Bucks SL9 0LA, England.
Published in the USA by The Globe Pequot Press Inc,
6 Business Park Road, PO Box 833, Old Saybrook, CT 06475-0833

British Library Cataloguing in Publication Data
A catalogue record for this book is available from the British Library
ISBN 0 946983 77 1

US Library of Congress Cataloging in Publication Data
A catalogue record for this book is available from the Library of Congress
US ISBN 1-56440-536 2

Maps based on research by Wasantha Siriwardena:
Inside covers Carte Blanche. *Others* Caroline Crump

Cover photographs: Gemunu Amarasinghe
Front left: A line of Buddhist monks climbing Sigiriya Rock
Front right: Steam locomotive No 340 class B1D 4-6-0 built by Robert Stephenson &
Hawthorns, Darlington, 1945, with No 213 class B2B 4-6-0TT, built by Vulcan Foundry,
Newton-le-Willows, 1922, between Kadugannawa and Balana stations on the main line
from Kandy to Colombo.
Back: Broad gauge steam locomotive No 340 class B1D 4-6-0, built 1945, pulling the
Viceroy Special carriages over the Nine Arches Bridge between Domodera and Ella
railway stations, heading towards Nanu Oya. The banker locomotive is No 213 class
B2B 4-6-0TT, built 1922.

Typeset by Concise Artisans
Printed and bound by Guernsey Press

The Author

Royston Ellis is a travel writer and novelist who has lived in Sri Lanka since 1981, from where he contributes features on Indian Ocean countries to major British newspapers, and to magazines worldwide. He is a Life Fellow of the Royal Commonwealth Society and a Member of the Institute of Rail Transport (India). He is the author of 30 books, some under pseudonyms, and of the Bradt guides *India By Rail* and *Guide To Mauritius*.

Acknowledgements

As a regular user of the railways in Sri Lanka I am grateful to the railwaymen, particularly the guards, drivers and stationmasters who are proud of the railways and have always been helpful with information and advice.

The Minister of Transport and Highways, the Hon T Wijayapala Mendis, and the permanent secretary of the Ministry, Mr A R M Jayawardana, gave early encouragement, and the Minister of State for Information and Broadcasting, A J Ranasinghe, was always helpful. Mr P Manatunga, Additional General Manager, Operations, of the Sri Lanka Railways put me on the right track when I had the idea for this book in 1990.

This is by no means an official guide. Indeed, my facts are mostly culled from unofficial (but I hope reliable) sources. In my research I have been aided by my long-time associate and manager, K P Neel Jayantha, and by his colleague, Tissa Samarasekera. For their assistance in many ways I am also grateful to Mathi K Parthipan of *Explore Sri Lanka* magazine, to Hemasiri Fernando and Noel Jayasekera of J F Tours, and to Hugh Ballantyne, leader of the Dorridge Travel rail photo safaris to Sri Lanka and contributor of the section on steam engines.

Extracts from this book have previously appeared in *Explore Sri Lanka*. I have also written about Sri Lanka and her railways (and am thus grateful for the research opportunity) for the *Sunday Times* and *Sunday Observer* of Sri Lanka, *The Times* and *The Daily Telegraph* of London, the inflight magazines of Air Lanka, Emirates, Gulf, Thai and Korean airlines, in *International Living* (USA) and *Business Traveller* (Asia Pacific).

To photographer Gemunu Amarasinghe my thanks not only for his atmospheric photographs, some of which provided inspiration for the sketches, but also for his research, enthusiasm and companionship on many rail trips, without which this book would never have been completed.

Any errors, of course, are my own and I would be grateful to hear from readers who discover them, or can let me know of new developments.

Royston Ellis
Bentota, Sri Lanka
1994

Contents

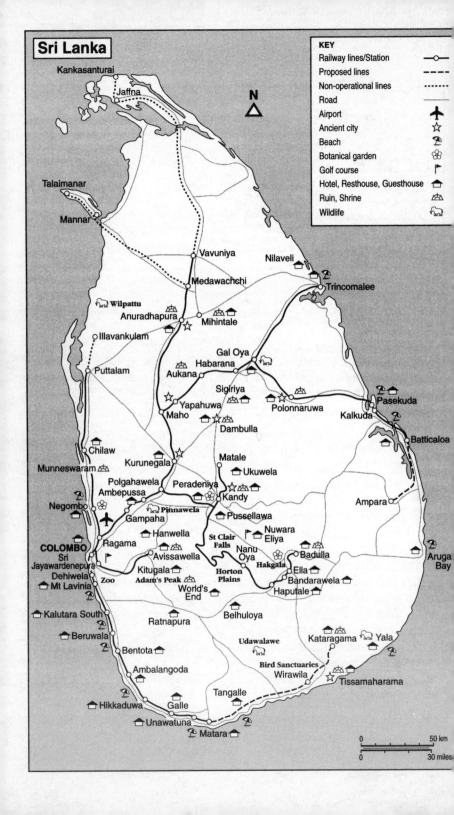

Chapter One

Discovering Sri Lanka by Rail

'Another guide to Sri Lanka?' you might ask as you pick up this book.

Actually this is the *first* guide to seeing Sri Lanka by train to be published for over 80 years. In 1910, an intrepid parson called Henry W Cave explored a railway system which was even smaller than it is now. He managed to write four books based on his travels by rail around what was then Ceylon.

This, too, is a guide based on personal experience gained over several years, not from a short research trip. As well as having taken the night mail to the hill country a dozen times, I have also been a commuter, catching the 3rd class, standing room only, early morning slow train to Colombo. The best and the worst, but both trains give an insight into this delightful (if at times frustrating) country.

This book is for the reader who wants to know, experience and, above all, enjoy Sri Lanka. It is for the budget traveller and the affluent. Independent travellers who fly by scheduled airline and spend time exploring the country, and tourists who pay in advance for charter flight and half board hotel accommodation, can all enjoy rail travel. It is perfect for those who seek in Sri Lanka an enchantment, a lifestyle which — although the country has problems — contains much that is lost to the modern world. Rail travel in Sri Lanka leads to the discovery of far more of this extraordinary island, not just of places but of people, too, than any other means of mass transportation could provide.

Geographically and metaphorically Sri Lanka is at the crossroads of the modern world and ancient Asia, with a railway system built by the British that is a neglected legacy of when the country was Ceylon. The railways lag behind much that is advancing towards the 21st century but the system is the best way to travel throughout the island — and the trains are fun and easy to use.

With not much more than 1,000km of track serving an island of 65,610km^2, and almost 18 million people, the railways are child's play compared with India's. That adds to the attraction: there are no four-hour queues, as in India, to buy tickets, no automatic ticket franking machines as in Europe. Rail journeys in Sri Lanka are short, always scenic and, thanks to pleasant fellow passengers, never dull.

They may be slow but, in the words of one expatriate living in Sri Lanka, 'the roads are such a nightmare of people crossing, children, dogs, carts . . . that trains are infinitely preferable'.

They also happen to be inexpensive: Rs90 (about £1.21 or US$1.83) for a return ticket and reserved seat on the Intercity Express from Colombo, climbing through the hills and rubber plantations for the 120km ride to Kandy, or less than 40 pence or 58 cents for a 2nd class ticket for the 64km journey from Colombo to the beach resort of Bentota.

Foreign travellers in the know are to be seen on the most popular trains, such as the *Ruhunu Kumari* to Galle and the *Podi Menike* to Badulla, but ordinary unnamed expresses and even slow trains have an appeal for everyone who wants to discover the fascination of Sri Lanka.

Of course, at times the system can go wrong and become exasperating. In this book, I have tried to provide information so that the visitor can turn any situation — even a frustrating one — into a rewarding experience. One of the attractions of Sri Lanka's rail service is that fares are low, so you can leave the train at any station that takes your fancy on the way, without losing a lot of money by abandoning your journey. And since all trains have unreserved accommodation, you can jump on any one as you please without having to stick to a fixed itinerary.

If your journey does get delayed, take that as a chance to get to know your fellow travellers, or simply leave the train and explore the countryside around you. You will inevitably find somewhere to stay for a few hundred rupees, and a wayside shop where you can buy something to eat and drink.

The best way to enjoy Sri Lanka by rail is to travel without compulsion. Of course, this sets you apart from other passengers who are all travelling because they have to and with a purpose: to get to their destination as quickly as possible. If you have no set plans, no booked hotel to get to, no one to meet you at the other end, no plane to catch, you are completely free. It is an amazing feeling.

With a light pack, a water bottle, and rupees in your money belt, you can spend a month touring the island by train, letting serendipity influence your journey. Serendipity, of course, is the word for the faculty of making happy and unexpected discoveries by accident and comes from Serendip, an ancient name for Sri Lanka.

Beware

Once, while dozing on the upper berth of a railway sleeping compartment, a kinsman of mine was eaten by a lion. Consequently, whenever I travel by train in parts tropic, I am careful to close the window at night.

Actually, becoming dinner for a lion was one of the hazards 90 years ago when my distant relative was an Indian Railways engineer building a new line in East Africa. Charles Ryall volunteered one night to shoot the lion which had been devouring his labourers. He waited for hours in a stationary carriage, eventually falling asleep. The lion climbed in through the open window and dined on him instead.

Bedding down for the night in Africa or India or in Sri Lanka is not so hazardous now. The animals to beware of are the human kind. I have often seen polite, liberal foreigners succumb to the irrepressible charm of Sri Lankans whose motive is not friendship but fiscal dentistry: to extract money from them painlessly. Why do visitors, when they travel in lands of sun and smiles, forget what mother told them about speaking to strange men?

Always remember that if a stranger makes the first overture, something is in his mind. You may hate being rude to a fellow human being, but by steadfastly declining to join in any kind of conversation, you could save yourself embarrassment later. On the other hand, those lads who approach you when you arrive at a station and want accommodation can be helpful. It is their job.

Travelling in Sri Lanka by train will teach you a lot about people, as well as about yourself. Don't be scared. Sri Lanka is safe if you are not foolish and, if you are foolish, some kindly soul will come to your rescue. You are sure to find rail travel in Sri Lanka much more fun than in India, England, Germany, the USA, or wherever you come from.

If you have any doubts at all, cast them aside. Go to Colombo Fort railway station, look on the departures board for a train, buy a ticket to the end of the line, and step on board. Sri Lanka is now yours to discover and enjoy.

SRI LANKA AT A GLANCE

Location
Southeast of India and 880km north of the Equator

Area
65,610km^2 (25,332 sq miles)

Population
17.6 million, of whom approximately 74% are Sinhalese, 18% Tamil, 7% Moors and the balance Malays, Burghers (descendents of Dutch colonists) and others.

Capital
Sri Jayawardenepura. The commercial capital is Colombo (population 650,000)

Government
The Democratic Socialist Republic of Sri Lanka is governed by an Executive President

Religion
69% Buddist, 15% Hindu, 8% Muslim, 8% Christian

Population distribution
21.5 urban; 78.5% rural

Topography
Flat on the coastal areas and northern half of the island with the central and south central areas being hilly and mountainous

Climate
Tropical in the lowlands with average temperature of 27°C. Cooler in the central hills with an average of 16°C. Monsoon in the southeast May-July; in the northeast December-January. Average rainfall varies from 950mm (37in) to 5,800mm (228in)

Tourism
Around 400,000 visitors annually in 1992 and 1993, mainly from Germany (21.7%), France (10.21%) and UK (8.78%)

Main foreign exchange earner
Garments, emigrants' remittances, tea, tourism.
Sri Lanka is the largest exporter of black tea, with 17.3% of world tea exports, the second largest exporter of desiccated coconut (30% of world exports), the eighth largest exporter of rubber, and the world's largest producer of cinnamon (91% of total world exports)

Annual per capita income
US$444

Labour force
46% agriculture; 29% industry and commerce; 19% services

Rice cultivation season
Maha — September-March
Yala — April-August

Business hours
Government offices: Monday-Friday 0830-1615
Commercial offices: Monday-Friday 0800-1700
Banks: Monday-Friday 0900-1300 or 1500
Shops: Monday-Friday 0800/1000-1800/2000
        Saturday 0800-1200 or 2000
Post offices: Monday-Friday 0830-1700
Saturday 0830-1300

Electricity
230AC

Motor vehicles
Just over one million. Driving is on the left.

Exchange rates (at June 1 1994)
UK£1.00 = Rs74.71   German DM = Rs30.09
US$1.00 = Rs49.53   French franc = Rs8.80
Calculations in this book are based on £1 = Rs74, US$1 = Rs49.

What to Expect
With tracks that are unfenced and used as thoroughfares by livestock
and people — and even as a cool place for an afternoon nap by some
rural folk — and which have not had much maintenance, trains are
obliged to go slowly. Often they are delayed but when you expect one
to be late it may even be early. There are some expresses, particularly
the Intercity train from Kandy to Colombo, that build up so much speed
you will find yourself wishing it would go slower. Then suddenly
it does, making an unscheduled stop for five minutes while it waits
for the train coming towards it on the single line to pass it and clear
the way.

The major trains will be crowded and standing for 12 hours on the
nightmail to the hill country is an experience nobody enjoys. Book a
sleeper in advance instead, or go by observation car in the day, or do it
in stages.

If you board popular trains at an intermediate station, expect to stand,
even in 2nd class. Most of the other passengers who are standing have
probably bought 3rd class tickets because they don't believe in paying
the 2nd class fare if they cannot get a 2nd class seat. If a train only has
3rd class, the seats — if you can get one — with wooden slats are
actually more comfortable than those with benches upholstered in
grimy, sticky plastic (rexine).

Snack vendors travel even the slowest local trains so you need not go hungry, but carry a water bottle (mineral water is available island wide). Some trains have snack bars where you can get a cup of tea or coffee, but no alcohol.

Trains are basically two types, all diesel hauled. There are the expresses which will generally have 2nd as well as 3rd class carriages with a vestibule linking them all. The toilets will be unspeakable (due to lack of water) and, if the train is crowded, unusable too since passengers will be standing in them, oblivious of the pong. Slow, local trains may be the old power sets with wooden bench seats and no vestibule, or the new, sleek orange and grey trains with fibreglass seats, no vestibule or toilet, but a light and airy ambience.

Ticket purchase is simple: you queue and buy a single ticket to your destination. Reserved seats and return tickets are only available on some trains (see Chapter 4, *Good Training*). Railway police check tickets — there is a heavy fine if you don't have one — while the guard (one at each end of the train), dressed smartly in black tunic and white trousers, waves a green flag, blows a whistle, and keeps to his van.

The train doors and windows (which are not barred as in India) will always be open, except at the slightest sign of rain which causes passengers to batten down everything and suffer in an airless, sweaty fug. There are fans, even in 3rd class, unless they have been removed to adorn someone's residence. Doors open inwards and the steps up into the carriages are steep, like a ladder.

Fellow passengers will discuss your presence among them in Sinhala or Tamil but generally will only speak to you if you make the first approach. If you do, the journey will pass much quicker as you will soon be answering the oddest questions and having to decline spontaneous, and genuine, offers of hospitality. Ask questions, too, and everyone will be delighted by your interest.

Entertainment is often provided by travelling singers, drummers, young boys who snap their joints in an alarming manner, and a procession of beggars, some of whom might actually be blind. Unfortunately, as a foreigner (how do those 'blind' ones know?) you will be subjected to special attention. Sri Lankans, who believe they gain merit by giving, keep loose change for such occasions. I keep a newspaper handy to hide behind.

The scenery on every journey — even a short run form, say Colombo to Mount Lavinia — is fantastic. The seascapes will set you dreaming and the lushness of the climb from Polgahawela to Peradeniya (see Chapter 7, *On the Move*) is breathtaking. Glimpses of village life as the train trundles through marketplaces, or saunters past back garden palm groves where girls are twining coconut fibre rope, make you want to know more. Even long stretches of flat, barren land are interesting because of the sudden glimpse of memorable sights such as a saffron-robed monk standing in apparent meditation under a black umbrella in the noonday sun as he waits for the train to pass.

When you arrive at your destination, get out smartly, unless it is a terminus, when you can take your time. You will have to present your ticket to the platform ticket collector. If there is a snack bar — none of them at any station are fit to be called a restaurant — a break there for a cup of tea will allow the crowds and the touts to disappear, and give you a chance to get your bearings.

If you have no idea where to stay, do not worry, someone will help you. If not, seek out the stationmaster: he will usually be able to suggest something, or someone. In touristy towns, touts recommending guesthouses usually get commission for taking you to them.

When you want to eat, choose places where business looks brisk. The variety of food available is wonderful and since much of it is on display, you can choose what takes your fancy. It is not all fiery and those with nervous stomachs need to be more wary of the water and eating unpeeled fruit than of rice and curry.

At night, mosquitoes are common. Coils that you light so they smoulder throughout the night are a good deterrent and are obtainable at town shops. I prefer them to guesthouse mosquito nets which always seem so dirty and claustrophobic, as well as torn so mosquitoes get in anyway.

Your bed will probably only have one sheet as well as a pillow. If you have learned to sleep with a *sarong* (the cotton cloth all Sri Lankan men favour for relaxing) you can cocoon yourself with that. Otherwise, ask for a sheet to cover yourself. If you have a choice between a fan and air conditioning, the fan is better because air conditioning disturbs your acclimatisation.

The weather, unless you are in the hill country, will usually seem humid. It is. So make sure your clothes are cotton, not synthetic material. You don't have to dress formally but you will be more respected in smart casual clothes than in filthy denims or, for women, shorts. Remember, Sri Lankans are conservative, even old fashioned in many ways, and politeness, respect for traditions, and a wholesome appearance is appreciated in foreigners.

The Sri Lankans you will meet come from all walks of life but if they speak English well they will either be of the old school, when Sri Lanka was Ceylon (it changed its name in 1972 after becoming independent in 1948), civil servants, or students from what are known as 'leading' schools. Although Sri Lanka is proud to have a literacy rate of 90% this does not mean everyone reads or understands English since their education would have been in Sinhala or Tamil.

For information about train times, ask at the station, from the ticket clerk or the stationmaster (he is often the same person in smaller stations). Do not rely on information from the guesthouse owner or staff since they probably travel by bus. If you are tempted to take a bus where there is a train, resist the temptation, wait for the train.

For a long journey, if there is no train then you will have to go by bus. However, if there are two of you travelling together, it could be worthwhile to hire your own three-wheeler so you can travel in comparative comfort, stop where you like to take photographs, and have a great, instead of a nerve-racking, time.

There are no rail passes available in Sri Lanka (as with the famous Indrail pass for touring India), although the idea has been considered. You need nothing in advance of your visit to Sri Lanka except a curiosity and a willingness to accept that Sri Lanka is not home and people are sensitive. A little patience helps, too, since communication — as well as your train — may break down.

Is train travel safe? Yes. Trains on single tracks run on a system that prevents one entering a section unless it is clear. Major disasters have been few, much less than the number of road accidents. You will know what I mean about travelling on Sri Lanka's roads when you see how pedestrians and pedal cyclists challenge fate when they launch themselves into oncoming traffic.

Expect a country of contrasts — of fast food franchises and restaurants where the cooking is still done over a wood fire; of bullock carts jostling for road space alongside luxury motorcars. The people and the infrastructure have a long way to go to catch up with the modern world, but the country loses none of its dignity and appeal because of that.

SRI LANKA RAILWAYS AT A GLANCE

The network (as at March 31, 1994)

Main Line
Colombo Maradana — Badulla (290km)

Matale Line
Peradeniya Junction — Matale (34km)

Puttalam Line
Ragama — Puttalam (119km)

Northern Line
Polgahawela — Vavuniya (180km)

Mihintale Line
Mihintale Junction — Mihintale (13km)

Batticaloa Line
Maho — Batticaloa (211km)

Trincomalee Line
Gal Oya Junction — Trincomalee (70km)

Coast Line
Maradana — Matara (158km)

Kelani Valley Line
Maradana — Avissawella (59km)

Track
From Colombo to Polgahawela (72km) and from Colombo to Panadura (28km) the track is double line; the rest of the network is single line. All tracks are broad gauge (5ft 6in) with the Kelani Valley Line recently converted from narrow gauge (2ft 6in) to broad gauge on a dual gauge track.

Origin
First passenger train from Maradana to Ambepussa, October 1865.

Stations:	Over 290 stations
Locomotives:	Approximately 200 diesel; 6 steam
Coaching stock:	Over 1,000
Maximum speed:	50mph
Retiring rooms:	At seven stations

Chapter Two

Planning the Trip

PRELIMINARIES

One of the joys of rail travel in Sri Lanka is that advance arrangements before you arrive are not necessary, nor possible. Only if you plan to go to the hill country or Kandy at peak times will you definitely need a reservation. But since that cannot be done more than ten days in advance, you could do it after you have arrived in Sri Lanka.

Do not plan to take a train the day you arrive, even if your flight is only a short one from India. Allow time to recover from getting to Sri Lanka, and from getting into Colombo from the airport. Actually, the airport arrival procedure is one of the smoothest in the region, but the shock of all that traffic on the road to Colombo, on top of jet lag, will strain your tolerance.

Hotels and guesthouses in Colombo are rarely full (tourists usually head straight for the southwest coast beaches, a gruelling three-hour drive) so the chances of finding accommodation in the city on arrival are good. Or you may prefer to head for Negombo, the nearest beach resort to the airport, and take a train from there to Colombo after you have acclimatised. If you prefer to have a hotel reservation before coming to Sri Lanka, this could be done through the nearest chain hotel, such as the Inter-Continental or Marriott groups (or, in India, the Oberoi or Taj chains), or by fax direct to the hotel of your choice, or on arrival at the airport, at the hotel counters (or the tourist board desk).

Colombo is fortunate in having luxury hotels of superlative quality (and not stuffy) at rates far lower than a hotel in the same chain would cost elsewhere. The advantage of paying to stay at least the first night in a five-star hotel such as the Ceylon Inter-Continental or the Colombo Marriott are manifold. The infrastructure is ideal for the independent traveller, with lots of advice and help available. Those two hotels happen to be within walking distance of Colombo Fort station which is where you will go often. The Taj Samudra and Lanka Oberoi are at the other end of the city's seafront promenade (Galle Face Green) but also have the no-nonsense support a first-time visitor to a strange place needs.

Although they are part of major groups, all Colombo's five-star hotels have identities that are uniquely Sri Lankan. It is possible and practical to make your base (and to leave luggage and receive mail) in one of them while spending a few days at a time on rail safaris, returning when you need to recharge your batteries. Of course, it adds to the cost of a holiday but if your visit is short, a good quality Colombo base is the most convenient.

Even if you only stay in Colombo on your first night, you will then have the advantage of proximity to Fort station and being able to visit it . and find out everything without having to lug your luggage along with you. And you will get a good night's sleep before starting your journeys.

Maps

Since Sri Lanka is so small, even a sketch map as appears in this book is sufficient to plan your rail trip in advance. In the UK, check with Edward Stanford Ltd, 12/14 Long Acre, London WC2E 9LP; tel: 071 836 1321, to see what is available in the way of maps. In the USA, try The Complete Traveller at 199 Madison Avenue, New York, NY 10016; tel: 212 685 9007.

In Sri Lanka you will be offered maps by street pedlars in Colombo and will see some fancy ones in local bookshops. Best, though, are those obtainable through the Survey Department whose head office is at Kirula Road, Colombo 5, with a small sales outlet opposite the main road entrance to the Colombo Hilton.

The compact 52cm × 36cm size map is at a scale of 1:1,000,000, which means 10km to 1cm (10 miles to five-eighths of an inch). All the railway lines are shown, except the new line to Mihintale. The Survey Department's road map of Sri Lanka is much larger (scale of 1:500,000, or 5km to 1cm) and has town plans of Nuwara Eliya, Anuradhapura, Sri Jayawardenepura (the political capital; no railway station), Kandy and Colombo, as well as a distance chart, resthouse locations (see page 163 for what a resthouse is), and railway lines. It costs Rs50.

Tourist Offices

For information about Sri Lanka before you arrive, write to the Ceylon Tourist Board (yes, the country is still marketed as Ceylon — perhaps it is a better image?) at 78 Steuart Place, Colombo 3; tel: 437059. They have a travel information centre on the ground floor of the building, which is on the sea side of the main Galle Road, opposite the Lanka Oberoi Hotel.

There is also an information counter at the airport (tel: 452411), in Kandy (tel: 08 22661), in Bentota (tel: 034 752121) and in Negombo.

The Ceylon Tourist Board offices overseas are:

London
Director, Ceylon Tourist Board
c/o High Commissioner for Sri Lanka in the UK
13 Hyde Park Gardens, London W2 2LU, England
Tel: (071) 262 5009/1841 Fax: (071) 262 7970

Frankfurt
Ceylon Tourist Board
Allerheiligentor 2-4
D-6000 Frankfurt Main 1, Germany
Tel: 069 287734/288216
Fax: 069 288371
Telex: 4170091 CTB 7D

Paris
Assistant Director
Office de Tourisme de Ceylon
19 rue 4 Septembre
75002 Paris, France
Tel: 42604999 Telex: 210577 F OFTC F
Fax: 42860499

Australia
Honorary Director
Ceylon Tourist Board
439 Albany Highway, Victoria Park
Western Australia 6100
Tel: 09 3624579
Telex: AA 94690 TAPRO

Bangkok
Honorary Director
Ceylon Tourist Board
PO Box 316, 1/7 — 1/8 Soi 10
Sukhumvit Road
Bangkok, Thailand
Tel: 251-8062, 251-0803
Telex: 20463 INMARKTH
Fax: 622 2544820

Timetables

Before coming to Sri Lanka, the best source of information about train times and routes is the Thomas Cook Overseas Timetable, published six times yearly by Thomas Cook Publishing, Thorpe Wood, Peterborough PE3 6SB, England; tel: 0733 268943; fax: 0733 505792. It is obtainable from the Thomas Cook office at 45 Berkeley Street, London W1A 1EB, at a cost of £7.25. This has two pages of timetables for main line trains and a tiny map, as well as a note of principal bus services.

In Sri Lanka, a printed timetable booklet is occasionally issued and this can be obtained from one of the booking counters at Colombo Fort railway station for Rs10, if it is still in print. As this book went to press, a new edition was planned to replace the last one, issued in February 1991.

At Colombo Fort station there is an enquiry counter (tel: 434215) which can give departure times from Fort but whose staff are reluctant to divulge more than that. Also at Fort station is a kiosk (with darkened windows) at the station entrance called Railway Tours. This is not an enquiry office but the operating centre for special rail tours and excursions organised by J F Tours, the operators of the Viceroy Special steam engine. The staff are actually more helpful than the real enquiry office if you wander in there by mistake. (Tel: 440048; open 0900-1730, Saturdays 0900-1500.)

Staff on other stations are more helpful than those at Fort when you need train times. At the other Colombo station, Maradana, train departure times are written in ink on a chart by the platform entrance barrier. While station staff will generally be helpful with arrival and departure times at their own station, they won't have much information about times en route.

Of course, there is a valid timetable with all times detailed on it. It is called *Working Timetable* and is issued by the Operating Superintendent's office (Sri Lanka Railway Headquarters, Maradana Road, Colombo 10) but contains the notation 'Private. For Information Of Railway Employees Only'. It is a fascinating document of 210 A4 size pages containing details of train formation as well as schedules such as 'working of explosive van' and which trains carry parcels and where the head guard 'will convey cheques'.

Amendments are issued by the Central Trains Control office at Maradana whenever a special train runs or a new train is introduced to the schedules. Since most of Sri Lanka's rail network is single line this means that any new or special train service affects the existing ones, which consequently have to be retimed as not more than one train can run on a section of the single line at the same time. No wonder timetables are hard to come by!

Special trains run during festive and pilgrimage seasons. The longest pilgrimage season is from January to April when nearly 500,000 people travel to, and from, Hatton station to climb Sri Pada (Adam's Peak). Extra trains between Colombo and Hatton are run then with special bus connections from Hatton station to the mountain.

During the national new year (April 13 and 14), scores of extra trains are run between Colombo and Matara in the south, and special relief trains run to the hill country (April is the season in Nuwara Eliya). Some trains are extended to provide same-train service linking Matara with Anaradhapura or Kandy, via Colombo.

For the *Vesak* season, commemorating Lord Buddha's birth, enlightenment and death, and, centred around the May *poya* (full moon) day, extra services run to Kandy, Anuradhapura and Kalutara. For the *Poson* season, which celebrates the advent of Buddhism in Sri Lanka, and which is marked by the June *poya* day when people travel to Anuradhapura and Mihintale in the north, special trains run from the south and there are extra services to Kurunegala and Maho.

For the Kandy *perahera*, or 'parade of parades', in July or August there are lots of specials for people to go and see the elephants, drummers and dancers. Extra trains are put on the line to Puttalam at the time of the festival of Talawila off the Puttalam lagoon.

A curiosity of the published timetable is its reference to UP and

DOWN trains. All trains *to* Colombo are described as DOWN trains (and consequently all trains *from* Colombo are UP trains) except for trains on the southwest coast line. Trains *to* Colombo from Matara and all stations in between are UP trains, and all trains heading south *from* Colombo are DOWN trains.

The numbering of trains has evolved over the decades and, if there is any logic in the system, it is not immediately apparent. In general, express trains have single or double digit numbers, while slow, local trains have three digit numbers.

Timetables are based on the 24 hour clock, with 2400 meaning arrival at midnight and 0000 meaning departure at that time. Arrival of a train is indicated by 'a' and departure by 'd'. Additional information about a train is contained in the train column under the train number, with a code, such as *nmh* which means 'runs on non-mercantile holiday' (there is a key). Popular train names are abbreviated, eg: ICE means Intercity Express.

How Long

Because the attractions of Sri Lanka are so many, and the flight to get there from anywhere but India is so long, allow as much time as possible to the enjoy the country. The normal period given at the airport for a holiday visit is 30 days, which would be adequate to travel every line, to stay awhile at places that appeal to you, and to spend some time on the beach. If you only have two weeks, or less, you would have to confine your rail travel to the most popular routes: up to Kandy and the hill country and along the west coast to Galle.

Planning the Itinerary

Although trains do not reach everywhere in Sri Lanka, they cover the most interesting parts of the country or give access to the other parts you may want to visit.

Colombo is used as the starting point for all itineraries in this book, although it is possible to join a train at any point en route without a reservation, as long as you have a ticket. If you happen to get on a train without one, see the guard immediately and pay him. If the ticket checkers get you, the fine can be considerable as well as embarrassing.

Rail routes are listed here in order of priority on the basis of what are the most important to try according to the time you have available.

1. Colombo to Kandy and on to the hill country via Nanu Oya (for Nuwara Eliya) to Bandarawela and, possibly, Badulla

2. Colombo along the west coast via Bentota to Galle, on to Matara only if you have plenty of time
3. Colombo northwards to Anuradhapura, with side trips by train to Mihintale and (only to say you have been there) to Vavuniya
4. Colombo to Trincomalee and the beaches of the east
5. Colombo to Avissawella on the Kelani Valley Line, a unique dual broad and narrow gauge railway
6. Kandy to Matale (for road trip to Sigiriya)
7. Colombo via Negombo and Chilaw to Puttalam (for road trip to Anuradhapura)
8. Colombo via Polonnaruwa to Batticaloa

If you are prepared to try the rural buses, too, it is possible to make a circuit or two without travelling up and down the same lines. However, the timing of trains on one line is not always designed to connect with trains on another line (especially at Gal Oya), even if you can find out the times at junctions in advance.

Whatever your rail plans, be sure to include the ride up to Peradeniya, outside Kandy, either by Intercity Express or by hill country train, for its staggering views, and if you have time, continue for the gentle jaunt through hills and tea plantations to Bandarawela.

A possible two-part itinerary covering most of the accessible parts of the island and all rail destinations is given here. You could also stop at intermediate stations and continue the journey another day. In 28 days you would have time to visit the ruins of Anuradhapura and Polonnaruwa, to enjoy Kandy and the hill country, to visit the game park at Yala, and to laze on west or east coast beaches.

Part 1 (allow 10 days)
Colombo to Kandy by train
Kandy to Nanu Oya by train
Nanu Oya to Nuwara Eliya to Nanu Oya by road
Nanu Oya via Bandarawela to Badulla by train
Badulla to Tissamaharama (for Yala and Kataragama) by road
Tissa to Matara by road
Matara via Galle, Hikkaduwa and Bentota to Colombo by train

Part 2 (allow 18 days)
Colombo to Avissawella by train
Avissawella to Ratnapura by road
Ratnapura to Haputale by road

Haputale to Kandy by train
Kandy to Matale by train
Matale via Dambulla and Sigiriya to Polonnaruwa by road
Polonnaruwa to Batticaloa by train
Batticaloa to Gal Oya by train
Gal Oya to Trincomalee by train
Trincomalee to Maho by train
Maho to Anuradhapura by train
Anuradhapura to Mihintale to Anuradhapura by train
Anuradhapura to Vavuniya to Anuradhapura by train
Anuradhapura to Colombo by train
or Anuradhapura to Puttalam by road and then Puttalam via Chilaw and
Negombo to Colombo by train (or stay at Negombo to be close to the
airport for the flight home).

If you have only a day spare for rail travel during a brief stopover in
Colombo, do not despair. There are three opportunities to sample the
uniqueness of the railways and to see some memorable scenery, and
have a great day out.

1. Intercity Express to Kandy and back (150 minutes each way)
2. By express down the west coast to Galle (three hours) for lunch at the
   New Oriental Hotel in Galle Fort, and back to Colombo in the evening
3. By local power-set train on the Kelani Valley Line through paddy
   fields and plantations to Homagama and back, on the dual broad and
   narrow-gauge line.

If you are staying in a beach hotel on the west coast, there is no need to
buy an expensive excursion by sightseeing tour bus, or taxi, for a day's
outing. There are stations close to the beach resorts so you can easily
take a train instead. Even the Viceroy Special makes stops (at Alutgama,
Kalutara) on its two-day excursion to and from Kandy.

When to Go
When you are ready!
   The rule used to be that October to March was the best time to stay on
the west coast (the sea is calm then and the beach broad). April is the
spring season in the hill country and May to September is the time to
be on the east coast beaches around Trincomalee when the sea there
is at its best.
   Recently the seasons have not been so predictable so you could take
a chance at any time of the year and find a climate that suits you
somewhere on the island.

Expect Kandy to be mild (and humid at times) and Nuwara Eliya to be cold at night.

If cost rather than climate is your concern, there is nothing wrong in going in the so-called off-season (May to September, except for the busy peak in July/August at the time of the Kandy *perahera*). Flights are cheaper then, and package holidays sometimes offer an extra week free. Guesthouse accommodation could also be had at lower than peak season rates, depending on demand. Fortunately, even when it rains, especially in the forest hills, Sri Lanka has an attraction that exerts its own special spell. In other words, it's magic then, too.

How to Go

By sea

Getting to Sri Lanka by sea, even from India, is impossible since there are no longer any regular services. The ferry from southern India is suspended and likely to remain so. Occasional cruise liners call and some sponsored ships such as peace or other propaganda vessels with youngsters from many nations pop in, and there are visits by some cargo/passenger vessels. If you are determined to come by sea, the best method seems to be as a crew member.

By air

From Europe the choice is not as wide as it was, since British Airways and Swissair have pulled out their scheduled services and instead serve Colombo through their charter affiliates, Caledonian and Balair. It is possible to buy a low-cost package for a couple of weeks at around £500 from London, which includes flight and accommodation. That is worth it, especially as airport transfers are included. You could spend the first night, and the last, at the hotel and roam around the island by rail at your own expense for the rest of the time.

The national carrier is Air Lanka which gives you a taste of Sri Lanka (their slogan is 'It's a taste of paradise') from the moment you board. You will be greeted by a steward or stewardess with palms together at chest level in the traditional salutation of *ayubowan*, a wish that you enjoy long life. You will almost certainly enjoy the flight if you have a chance to talk to the crew, who are great ambassadors for their country.

Air Lanka was formed in 1979 and has grown to carrying over a million passengers a year. Currently it operates six wide-bodied Lockheed Tristar 1-1011 and two new Airbus 320 aircraft, but fleet changes are underway.

The 29 destinations it serves in 21 countries are:
• London, Amsterdam, Paris, Frankfurt, Zurich, Rome and Vienna;
• Dubai, Abu Dhabi, Muscat, Dhahran, Kuwait, Jeddah and Riyadh;
• Bombay, Karachi, Delhi, Madras, Trivandrum and Tiruchchirappalli;
• Bangkok, Kuala Lumpur, Singapore, Hong Kong, Tokyo and Fukuoka;
• Maldives (Malé).

In Sri Lanka, reservations and reconfirmations can be made by telephone on 421161 or, for all Air Lanka offices, on 073 5555. Offices are at 37 York Street, 10 Sir Baron Jayatilaka Mawatha, 55 Janadhipathi Mawatha, 660 Galle Road and at Colombo International Airport. Fax: 94 73 5122.

A great favourite with passengers to Sri Lanka is Emirates, because of the inflight service, the giveaways (an eyemask is provided in economy which is very useful to wear when you want to sleep on a train), and the inflight entertainment on individual video screens. It does involve a change of aircraft in Dubai but that is an opportunity for superb duty free shopping, with liquor being a good buy. Emirates has six connecting flights a week to Sri Lanka from London Heathrow, four from Manchester and several via Dubai from Frankfurt, Paris, Rome and Zurich.

Airlines serving Colombo from their home base in Europe, without a change of aircraft, are Aeroflot, Balkan, Bulgarian, KLM, LTU and several charter airlines like Condor and Lauda. Colombo is also served from Europe by connecting flights of Kuwait, Royal Jordanian, Saudia and Middle East Airlines.

The quoted price of fares to Sri Lanka from London at press time was £1,937 for first class, £1,272 for business class and £952 for economy class, all one way. Excursion fares were listed from £943. By shopping around flights could be obtained for less but make sure you purchase from a reliable source as overbooking (especially out of Colombo) is rife and holders of deep discounted tickets are the first to be bumped, especially if the return reservation has not actually been registered.

Like thousands of other frequent travellers, I use WEXAS International when I need to buy tickets in the UK (or have them sent to me if I am overseas by courier or airmail). Membership of WEXAS is worthwhile not only for the lower ticket prices on scheduled airlines (no charters are used) but also for its inexpensive insurance schemes. For a round trip to Colombo from London, they quote between £400 and £600 according to routing and season. (WEXAS International, 45-49 Brompton Road, Knightsbridge, London SW3 1DE; tel: 071 589 3315).

There are no direct flights to Colombo from the USA or Canada. Connections could be via Europe, the Middle East or the Orient. No airline currently flies direct from Australia but — as well as by Air Lanka — there are direct flights from Singapore (Singapore Airlines), Hong Kong (Cathay Pacific) and Bangkok (Thai). There is no direct service from Africa, only via the Middle East, Bombay or Singapore.

From India, Indian Airlines fly from Madras and Trivandrum. Avoid leaving or entering India via Tiruchchirappalli (by Air Lanka) as the conduct of customs and immigration officials, and the facilities, are degrading. But at least Air Lanka serves beer, free, on its India services.

Air Lanka and Emirates provide a link with Malé, capital of the Maldives, great if you want a change, or somewhere to go for a few days if your visa has expired.

It can be worthwhile buying air tickets for onward journeys (or even to get back home) in Colombo although fares are not as low as they were, and there is a local tax of 5.3% payable on the rupee purchase price. Savings are possible if your foreign currency changed at the bank yields more than the applicable airline exchange rate. Local travel agents can offer cheaper deals than airline ticket offices, but choose a reputable one.

Reconfirmation of all flight reservations out of Colombo at least 72 hours before departure time is vital. Do it soon after arrival so you don't have to worry about it while touring. It can be done by telephone.

What to Take

Really, hand luggage — that you can carry on the plane with you — is enough. Most of us take far too much on the 'just in case' principle. Not only is Sri Lanka a hot, humid country, it is also a developing one with 200 garment factories. So you won't need much in the way of clothing (cotton T-shirts and trousers and loose fitting dresses) and there are some great shops in Colombo selling western fashions, made in Sri Lanka for export, at a quarter of what they cost in the west. Or you can easily have cotton shirts and slacks made up in a few hours by a village tailor.

If you plan to spend time in the hill country, you will need a sweater but even warm clothes are made in the garment factories so you could buy something fashionable as well as warm in Colombo or in the streets of Nuwara Eliya.

Clothing needs to be practical for travelling every day. Trousers — especially ones like Rohan bags with lots of zippered pockets to stash cash, loo paper and passports — are better than shorts. Women should have loose fitting garments (also with hidden, zippered pockets) for greater comfort. Scanty clothing is fine for the beach but not for a train, unless you want to get sticky, sweaty, dirty, embarrassed and propositioned, since your lack of clothing sends the wrong signals.

You can get practically everything in Sri Lanka but suncream may be expensive and difficult to find, and you should bring prescription medicines. If you want decent matches bring them, too, since the Sri Lanka ones require a special technique to strike them alight (ask a Sri Lankan smoker to show you how).

If you plan on writing lots of airmail letters, bring airmail envelopes; the Sri Lankan product is flimsy with flaps that don't stick.

There is an appalling habit that you will encounter wherever you see children: they will rush up asking for 'school-pen' or 'bon-bon'. Obviously those words have been introduced by previous visitors. If you feel distributing ballpoint pens and sweets encourages cordial relations, just try it.

What to give gracious hosts and their children is often a problem but do not try to solve it by bringing keyrings, bottle openers, etc, from your home country. Cakes (the pastry shops of the Colombo hotels make some superb ones) are always a welcome gift that will delight.

Be disciplined when you come to packing. Spread everything you plan to take with you out on a bed, reduce it by half, check again to see if you really need all the items that remain, then start to pack.

Books, and notebooks, can be bought in Colombo; so can a torch (which you certainly should take) if you lose yours. An essential item is a strong water bottle in which to pour mineral water from the local, plastic bottles. A penknife with bottle opener is useful but may be removed by airline security if you only have hand luggage. A small hand towel is useful. Take whatever gadgetry (Walkman, radio) that you would feel lost without. Good walking shoes (but not new ones you have not broken in) are, I think, the most important item of personal equipment. You never know when you will have to run and sandals or flipflops (which can be bought cheaply in Sri Lanka) are hazardous when you are in a hurry.

Following advice to bring quantities of condoms, tampons, soap, shampoo, toothpaste, toilet paper, spare padlocks, etc, will only fetter you. Buy what you need at village shops as you go; the experience of shopping locally will add to your fun and understanding of local life.

You will not need a sleeping bag, sleeping sheet, camping equipment (it is not advisable to camp), photo albums of your dog and family, your Filofax (note important addresses on a separate sheet of paper to carry in your wallet) or raincoat (buy an umbrella in Sri Lanka for Rs100).

Do not take anything that you value highly and would be devastated to lose. If it is a document, bring a photocopy; if it is anything else, leave it at home. Take photocopies of your passport, air ticket and insurance policy and keep them separately from the originals, in case of loss.

You will need insurance, both for yourself and your belongings. Take visa-size passport photos if you intend applying in Sri Lanka for a visa to enter India, but it saves hassles to get all the onward visas you will need before leaving your home country.

If you plan to drive, take an international driving licence.

If you belong to any organization (Lions, etc) that has branches in Sri Lanka, bring your membership card if you want to make contact and have to prove your identity. A student — or other — ID card could be useful since gate security at some establishments like you to leave an ID card when you enter their premises and you collect it when you leave. Even one you make up with a small photograph and laminate yourself is better than having to part with your passport.

If you have credit cards, bring them since they are accepted in Sri Lanka. However, check first where you plan to use them, even if you see a Mastercard or Visa sign in a window, since some establishments only take the locally issued versions of these cards.

Photographers should bring the film they like; although film can be obtained locally it might not be the kind you want. Films for ordinary print photography are easily obtainable, but are cheaper from specialised shops in Colombo than from a town's general store.

Health

Whether you have the usual cocktail of inoculations recommended for visits to tropical countries is up to you, as nothing is required by law, unless you are coming from a yellow fever area. Since you will be travelling throughout the country and experiencing different locations and being with different people every day, I suggest you have just what the doctor orders. In the UK there are medical clinics run by British Airways which can advise on the current thinking about prophylactics (tel: 071 831 5333 for the nearest location). There is also a travel clinic at the Thomas Cook office in Berkeley Street, London.

Evidence of a yellow fever vaccination (valid ten years) will be demanded en route if you visit Sri Lanka from Africa. The risk of malaria exists out of Colombo although not in the beach resorts. You would be advised to take a course of anti-malaria tablets. Taking these before you go to sleep will reduce the unpleasant effects of the nausea some people experience through taking them in the day. Tablets can be bought locally. Precautions against typhoid and polio are recommended, and an immunization against tetanus is sensible.

There is a risk from cholera, and if you have forgotten or if your six-month validity runs out while you are on the island and you need a booster, inoculations are available locally at a much lower cost than in the west. Should you need an injection of any kind, disposable needles and syringes are available at most pharmacies.

The biggest risk of all nowadays is AIDS, transmitted sexually and by infected blood and needles. The best precaution is sexual abstinence in Sri Lanka because AIDS does exist, although no one knows quite to what extent. This is not hard as, despite scandalous press speculation about child and boy prostitution, offers of sex are not a feature of the country. Foreign women may experience juvenile harassment but rarely more than that. If you do decide to experience romance as well as rail in Sri Lanka, make sure you and your partner are suitably protected. Condoms of various styles are obtainable, even in villages.

Tummy upsets are frequent and the main cause is not cooked food but the water. Try to drink only bottled mineral water, soda water, or water that has been filtered and then rolling boiled for at least 15 minutes and cooled in a container that itself has been washed with boiling water before use. Even if you do all that, you may still suffer. Why? Perhaps the ice in your drink, or the water diluting the fruit cordial, was not boiled. Or perhaps the plate off which you ate was not washed in boiling water. Don't get uptight about it and you will be amazed at how well you feel.

Where the tap water is claimed to be safe to drink, don't try it. It may be safe for someone who has used it all their life, but not for strangers.

If you are on the move throughout your stay, you will be eating food handled by over a dozen pair of hands during a single day. Try not to think about it. Eat sensibly, which means in moderation, staying off raw items like salads and fresh fruit (unless you peel it yourself), and food like cakes and short eats — that has been lying around on a counter all day. (To know what a short eat is, see the section on food, page 47). After the first bout of travelling — and when you have got over the debilitating effect of a long-haul flight, which could take a week — you will be able to stomach most food, and actually enjoy some of the dishes offered.

TRAVELLER'S DIARRHOEA
by Dr Sanjiva Wijesinha

Traveller's diarrhoea is essentially an infection of the intestine caused by a toxin-producing germ called *escherichia coli*; a few cases are caused by other bacteria such as *salmonella, shigella*, rotavirus, etc.

Escherichia coli produces many toxins, of which one is very similar to the cholera toxin. Consequently, the infection gives rise to a classic cholera-like diarrhoea, characterized by profuse water stools. The average length of illness in an otherwise healthy adult is about five to seven days, depending on the particular strain of *escherichia coli*, but this duration may be shortened significantly by antibiotic therapy.

Infection is generally acquired from contaminated food, water and ice. In the tropics, one should be particularly careful of any type of food that has remained uncovered for some time, because this can be infected by flies, which carry the infecting germs on their hairy feet. Poor sanitation and the ubiquitous tropical flies help spread the germs which can contaminate all but the most hygienically prepared and served meals.

Traveller's diarrhoea is usually a self-limiting condition, and with adequate replenishment of the lost body fluids, uneventful recovery normally occurs in a week or so. There are, however, several measures that can be used to shorten the illness and to ease symptoms. Of these, perhaps the most important step is rehydration or replacement of lost liquids and salt. In most situations this can be accomplished by drinking commonly available fluids such as fruit juices and soft drinks which contain water, electrolytes and glucose, the latter aiding absorption of the first two. In the tropics, coconut water — the clear fluid obtained from the kernel of the coconut — is an ideal rehydrating fluid, since it contains sugar and salts in just the right proportions. Other alternatives are apple and orange juice.

Another useful product is prepacked oral rehydration salt. Prepared according to World Health Organization (WHO) specifications, the product is made by many drug companies and commercially available worldwide. For safety's sake, bring a few packets in your hand luggage. The premixed packet contains sodium, potassium, bicarbonate and glucose — and when diluted with uncontaminated water in the correct proportions, provides a solution which is well absorbed by even the most severely affected patients.

Drugs such as loperamide (Imodium) and diphenoxylate (Lomotil) are designed to reduce the number of diarrhoeal episodes and to ease abdominal cramps. They are both extremely effective, and because of the symptomatic relief offered, are advisable where a quick 'cure' is required. In the long run, however, the use of these 'constipating agents' can be counter-productive. Diarrhoea is a protective mechanism, a means by which the body rids itself of whatever agent is irritating the gut. By interfering with this natural process, these drugs may in fact prolong the illness, despite offering short-term relief of syptoms.

Antibiotics have long been recognized as effective in traveller's diarrhoea. The most appropriate drug today seems to be co-trimoxazole (sold under trade names such as Bactrim and Septrim), which is specific against germs such as *escherichia coli* and *shigella*.

It is important in Sri Lanka not to let the sun go to your head and cause you to do silly things. When sunbathing, remember how close you are to the Equator. Even in the chill of the hill country, the sun that seems so pleasant is actually just as fierce as on the beach. Sunbathe in stages or you will get as pink as a lobster instead of a golden tan. Walking barefoot anywhere but on the beach is bound to lead to trouble.

If you do need medical attention, doctors in the resorts are good for typical tourist maladies and will prescribe lots of tablets and charge about £3 for the consultation. For advice on how to find a doctor, ask the people where you are staying.

If you have to be hospitalized, there are several private hospitals and clinics in Colombo. Popular with expatriates is the colonial-built Joseph Frazer Memorial Hospital which has an outpatients department, modern laboratory facilities and doctors available from 0830 to 1830. It is situated at 23 Joseph Frazer Road, Colombo 5; tel: 588386 or 588466.

For dental treatment (although there are village dentists still using drills powered with a foot pedal) state of the art equipment, skill and reassuring attention is available from the UK qualified dental surgeon, Dr A Ratnayake, at 207/8, Dharmapala Mawatha, Colombo 7 (near the town hall); tel: 692562.

For train travel, in case of minor need, you could make up your own first aid kit by visiting any pharmacy: Band aids, cotton wool, bandages, Dettol, aspirin, Septrim, etc.

Creepy crawlies to worry about are the ubiquitous cockroach, which may be unpleasant but not a direct health risk. More dangerous are centipedes — six inch long monsters — whose bite can swell up and be painful for three days. Take care, too, in long wet grass, for leeches. If one latches onto you, it can be removed by soap or salt, which will make the thing wriggle out of its own accord. The hole could fester if you scratch it and don't treat it.

Yes, there are poisonous snakes but you are unlikely to be attacked by one unless you are really off the beaten track, perhaps sleeping on a mat on the floor of a mud hut. Transport to the nearest medical facility as quickly, but as gently, as possible is the answer. Since transport and medical care is never *that* far away — and the snake may not even have been poisonous — chances are good.

So, too, is the chance of recovery from the risk of rabies if bitten or scratched, or licked over a wound, by a rabid animal. If that happens, clean the wound with soap and water and scrub with a brush for 15 minutes to wash away as much saliva as possible. Then head for a doctor and a course of injections. However much you adore animals, the dogs and cats that hang around should not be petted; they could be a source of fleas, if not of rabies.

Minor health problems should always be treated with respect, in case they become major. Most common illnesses are the same as at home — colds, respiratory infections, minor ear, nose and throat infections, gastrointestinal upsets, skin irritations and accidents. Prickly heat is common and will probably stay with you once you've got it until you reach a colder and less humid climate. Hangovers are likely since you may be tempted to drink more than usual because of either the heat, or excessive socializing. Guard against them — and dehydration — with lots of mineral water before you sleep.

Fortunately, although you may be travelling a lot, most of your journeys will be short so if you do want medical attention, it will never be far away. Reduce the stress that aggravates ill health by keeping your luggage as light as possible, your plans flexible in case you have to change them, and your disposition sunny.

Security and Safety

Having your handbag searched when you pop into a Colombo shopping mall (Liberty Plaza, Majestic City) to buy a postcard, soon makes you realize how security-conscious Colombo is. How effective the searches are is another matter, but you get accustomed to carrying nothing with you when you visit the bank, the post office or airline, to escape the hassle.

Terrorism has not been deliberately directed at tourists or foreigners although some have got caught up in it. The anarchy of the 1980s has cooled and the country, except for north and west of Vavuniya and in the Batticaloa district, is safe for tourists. When staying in Trincomalee and Batticaloa, it is wiser not to wander out of your hotel at night. Also avoid getting entangled in political meetings or demonstrations anywhere.

Although the tourist is not a target of terrorists, he — and more especially she — may be the target of feckless fellows out to achieve something. There have been many letters in the local press from female foreigners complaining of sexual harassment from men who walk beside them in the street and 'accidentally' touch them on buses.

Male foreigners and couples as well as solo females are subjected to mild harassment in tourist areas and Colombo. It begins with the question 'where are you going?' as a kind of hello that does not really need an answer. Foreigners, of course, being polite, usually give an answer which the smart chap who has asked the question will seize on to start a conversation. The object is to see what the foreigner wants and to supply it, thereby earning kudos and, probably, a commission.

There are tourist police in the beach resorts and in Kandy who can be approached if the importuner becomes a menace. As long as you keep your wits about you and realize where the conversation is headed, you can out-talk the chap so he will move off and look for someone else.

It is worth bearing in mind that these touts, beach boys, freelance guides, have their own code. If you are staying by a beach you will — without your knowing it — have already been selected by the touts as the client of one of them. He is the one who will approach you while the others wait and see your reaction. If you are recognized as being the client of one of them, no other touts will trouble you.

Most of the young men who serve as unofficial guides to tourists provide a good service, and are reasonably honest. In fact they have a great respect for the strong arm of the law. Look on them as freelance salesmen, collecting commission — which is built into the price anyway — from whatever you spend under their guidance.

They will also escort you by train to other parts of the country, and some are much more charming and knowledgeable about where to eat and stay, and what to see, than the official, overworked guides escorting coachloads of visitors. A good unofficial guide will be your personal security, keeping away human pests and introducing you to Sri Lanka, and becoming a real friend.

Theft is not as rampant as you might expect but, of course, you should not encourage it by leaving your handbag open on the train seat, wallet peeking out of hip pocket, or camera by an open window. Also, it would not be prudent to venture into unknown territory at night with newly met companions.

Do not interpret a Sri Lankan's insatiable curiosity as a threat. On a train you may present the first opportunity the Sri Lankan passengers have had of observing a foreigner at close quarters. Everything about you will be fascinating and those stares are because they are trying to understand what makes you tick, not how to get your watch. When someone asks 'where are you from?' it could be because the person has a relative living in London and perhaps you know him.

There is no need to get paranoid about your personal safety. If you do, your fear will show and somehow what you dread will actually happen. Take simple precautions and relax. On a train do not put your handbag on the overhead luggage rack and then fall asleep. It may attract a miscreant's attention. Put it by your feet and doze in peace.

Pickpockets are a hazard on buses, especially with passengers standing so close to each other. Razor blades and sharp knives have been used to slash holes in bags and even to remove the whole bag from a shoulder. In a hotel room, if you don't have a thief-proof aluminium brief case with a combination lock (and you probably won't have since you are travelling light), deposit your valuables in the hotel's safe (if it's that kind of hotel) or carry them with you all the time. Swimming? Then give your valuables to a known and trusted friend to hold.

Money Matters

What will it cost?

The foreign visitor, especially with pounds, dollars, marks, francs or yen, has an advantage in Sri Lanka because those currencies are strong against the rupee. Inflation, however, pushes up local prices, although it was reported to have dropped to 11.5% in 1993 from 21.5% in 1990.

The cost of a visit to Sri Lanka will vary according to where you stay and where you eat. Actually, if you take time off from rail trips by staying a night or two in five-star hotels (US$75 a night, single, is the fixed minimum rate) and eat in Colombo's top restaurants (allow $25 a head) your holiday could still cost a lot less than a similar standard in other cities in the region, including India.

While the major hotels quote rooms rates in US dollars, they expect payment in officially converted rupees. Minor hotels, and all restaurants, are priced in rupees. With the exchange rate changing from day to day, costs given in foreign exchange in this book are necessarily approximate (they could go down!) while the prices in rupees will probably have risen by the time you get to Sri Lanka.

To help with accommodation costs, I have graded the hotels mentioned in this book as either (1) luxury; (2) standard, or (3) economy. The US dollar being the most easily accepted currency, I have used it for pricing, as follows:

1. Luxury: US$50 and upwards for a single/double
2. Standard: US$20-50
3. Economy: Under $20.

To these prices must be added 10% service charge and usually 10% government tax, although some places absorb this.

A wonderful exception to the price grading is a buffet lunch in any of Colombo's luxury grade five-star hotels, which would come to about $8.00. Great feasts of international class including a rich array of desserts, ideal if you are feeling depressed, homesick, or overdosed on rice and curry.

Meals out of Colombo or the beach resorts will set you back about Rs100 to Rs200 per person, unless you go for something elaborate or special. On the move, snacks and coffee will be less than Rs50. Soft drinks range from Rs10-Rs20, depending where you are; mineral water is about Rs30 for a 1.5 litre bottle. Beer costs from Rs65 (much more in a restaurant) and *arrack*, the local tipple, about Rs200 a bottle.

Travel costs within Sri Lanka are low, even if you hire three-wheelers instead of braving the buses where no trains operate. Few three-wheeler journeys where there are no trains will cost more than Rs1,000, and only long journeys by train will cost up to Rs200.

Treat this list only as a guide to approximate daily expenses at the lowest rate while travelling by train.

Meals:	breakfast, lunch or snack, dinner	Rs 400
Drinks:	tea, soft drinks, mineral water	Rs 100
Reading:	daily newspaper	Rs 7
Night:	guesthouse or resthouse room	Rs 350
Transport:	rail ticket, approx	Rs 100
Extras:	tips, shopping, average a day	Rs 100
		1,057

(Approximately US$22 or UK£14.28 per day)

The minimum amount stipulated by immigration for daily expenditure is US$30, so if you allow that, you should have enough to stay in Sri Lanka at the basic rate with some left over for souvenirs and partying. For special occasions, airport transfers (allow Rs485-Rs750 each way), and contingencies, and a better lifestyle you could have an average expenditure of $50 a day.

Naturally, it depends exactly on how you want to live and how much you want to travel. Even if you stay and eat at the cheapest level, you will probably want to spend money on other things: clothes, admission fees, a buffet lunch, so I feel Rs2,500 a day is allowing enough. That amount, incidentally, is a typical monthly wage.

You will come across the phenomenon of dual pricing. Places of interest such as the zoo, the various botanical gardens, Yala wildlife park and ancient monuments have an admission charge for Sri Lankans and another, much higher, for foreigners. You will probably hate this economic discrimination, especially as you are the victim of it, not the beneficiary. On the other hand, it has been known for resort hotels to give a foreigner a discount but not a local (see *The Island*, January 10, 1994).

The only way is to look at the situation positively and think that the higher price you have to pay is subsidizing the lower charge for locals so they can also enjoy their national heritage. When the double pricing is in private establishments (as in some unscrupuluous resthouses where the staff are trying to make a fast buck) it is a scam, so resist it. To avoid a shock when you come to pay, always negotiate the price (whether for bed and breakfast or a taxi ride) before you accept the deal.

How to Take and Change Funds

The currency of Sri Lanka is the rupee and it comes in coins of Rs1, Rs2 and Rs5 (anything smaller has little use nowadays). There are notes of Rs5, Rs10, Rs20, Rs50 and Rs100 (brown). The new Rs500 note is also brown, so check the figures before parting with it. The largest note, in size as well as value, is the green Rs1,000.

Travellers cheques are best not only for security but because they garner a higher rate of exchange than cash does. Pound sterling, US dollar and German mark travellers cheques are the most common. There are commercial bank exchange counters after leaving immigration and customs in the arrivals hall at the airport.

It is better to change just enough at the airport to get to your hotel and for the first day's expenses. The commercial banks in Colombo do not all have the same rate of exchange, but the difference is slight, although the rate will be higher than changing cheques with a hotel cashier.

The foreign exchange department of the Hatton National Bank, in the same building as the Colombo Marriott Hotel, is open every day of the year, weekdays 0900-1700, Saturdays 0900-1400; Sundays and holidays 0900-1200.

Do not expect to be able to change travellers cheques with ease out of Colombo and the resort areas. For rail trips, change sufficient cash for expenses, plus a reserve of Rs5,000 for an emergency such as a dash by taxi to Colombo. The bank will probably give you only large notes, so change some for smaller denominations. Keep cash and travellers cheques in several places on your person, having small notes for each day's spending in one purse, spare cash in another, and cheques elsewhere. That is why you need lots of zippered pockets. (Money belts are favoured by some but can be itchy in the heat, could slip off in the loo and are an embarrassment when you need sequestered cash in a hurry.)

Credit cards are accepted throughout Sri Lanka and are useful for paying bills in an emergency and also for buying travellers cheques to change into rupees from the card representatives in Colombo. Do ask if your credit card is acceptable before attempting to use it, as some shops display credit card stickers for prestige and don't actually accept them, while others may only accept the local version of international credit cards.

If you need funds to be sent to you from overseas, choose a bank in Colombo that appeals to you, and find out from them what procedure they recommend for doing it quickly, then send that information with necessary telex numbers to the remitter. Transfer from overseas to country-district banks out of Colombo can take ages.

Keep the foreign exchange chits in case you finish up with too many rupees (very unlikely) and want to change them to another currency at the bank at the airport on departure. The chits are needed to prove you have changed foreign funds.

Arrival

On the plane you should be given a combined embarkation/disembarkation card. If not, you will have to find one in the arrivals hall and waste time filling it out while other passengers with cards get to the head of the queue at immigration.

You are required to fill in both sections on the disembarkation card. Put your full name, date of birth, country of birth, sex, nationality, occupation, passport number, place of issue, date of issue, address in country of residence, purpose of visit (the choice is transit, holiday, business, employment, conference, visiting friends/relations, others), port of embarkation, flight number, duration of stay, address in Sri Lanka (if you have not made a hotel reservation, don't leave it blank, choose somewhere from this book), the date and your signature.

Your embarkation card only requires your name, nationality, occupation, sex, passport number, place of issue, date of issue, duration of stay and signature. This section will be placed with your passport to surrender when you leave.

If your flight lands just after a lot of others (from 0530 to 0800 is the peak time for arrivals; Tuesday is the quietest day), you may have a long wait behind other arrivals. Try to join a queue that does not have a lot of Sri Lankan housemaids returning from employment in the Middle East if you want to be processed swiftly. The authorities have a clearance target of a maximum of 45 minutes and if you pass through immigration quickly and only have hand luggage, you can do it in a lot less. One way to jump the queue is to be a VIP, a status accorded you by Air Lanka if you are one of their first or business class passengers.

Visa

Unless you have a particularly exotic passport, entry into Sri Lanka without an advance visa is possible if you are coming as a tourist. At the airport immigration desk, a permit to stay for 30 days is granted, even for a few weeks longer on special request if supported by a confirmed air ticket out of the country and sufficient funds. If the time granted is not enough, you can apply for an extension a few days before the visa expires.

Customs

After immigration, there are duty free shops where liquor and cigarettes can be purchased as well as gold (but better to leave your gold purchase until you leave).

The duty free allowance for tourists, which does not include gold, is 2.25 litres of spirits, two bottles of wine, 200 cigarettes or 50 cigars, 2oz of perfume and .25 litre of toilet water.

The smuggling of drugs can lead to the death penalty and the authorities are very watchful. Unlimited amounts of foreign exchange can be brought into the country. There is a bank in the customs hall for the interchange of foreign currencies, and also a bond storage for left luggage.

If you have only hand luggage there is no need to wait for your bags at one of the carousels but head straight for the green-lit, nothing-to-declare channel. Sometimes there are spot checks there.

Meeting

People meeting you will be in the arrivals foyer to greet you as you emerge, but to achieve this you will have to send them a letter, telex or fax from overseas with details of your flight number, arrival time and date. Your friend takes this to the kiosk outside the airport as proof of having someone to meet, and purchases a ticket (Rs40) that permits entry into the arrivals foyer. The passenger manifests of incoming flights are posted on a noticeboard by the information counter so someone meeting you can check if your name is on the list.

If someone is meeting you they may arrange (for a fee of Rs100) for you to be met at the entrance to the terminal building by a young lady with your name on a board. She will show you through immigration and wait for you after customs to introduce you to the person meeting you.

Arrivals Hall

There are banks in the arrivals hall, on the left after exiting customs, where travellers cheques can be changed. Desks of the representatives of Colombo's major hotels are opposite the customs exit, with tourist board and agency desks and a snack bar on the right.

If you cannot face the journey to Colombo after a long flight, there are some economy rate short-stay rooms on the first floor, overlooking the arrivals hall. Book at the passenger information desk. There is also a place to leave luggage (at Rs60 per bag per 24 hours) and a counter where you can rent a mobile cellular telephone.

At the transport counter arrangements can be made for a taxi into Colombo (34km distant, about an hour's drive) for from Rs700 per car. Prices to all destinations are displayed on a noticeboard by the exit. Or you can book a seat on an Airport Express minivan (tel: 941 687037; fax: 941 699109), but do it at least a day in advance of arrival as pick up is only by request. Cost is Rs485 per person.

There is also a helicopter transfer if pre-booked (see page 61). The fee was $20 per person when the service was introduced in January 1994.

If you are determined not to pay much to reach Colombo, there are some options. There is no dedicated airport bus service but there are plenty of public buses. At the end of the exit mall turn left and walk about 200m to cut around the car park. Cross the access road and gardens to reach the main road. There is a shelter on the opposite side for buses to Colombo. Bus number 187 goes there and the journey will take at least an hour and be quite an experience. It is not a good idea to try it unless you are feeling fit and really have the lightest of luggage.

Another option is a train, but there are only two a day to Colombo, one about 0700 and another about 1800 (their time of departure depends on the train's arrival from Colombo). You will have to walk about 500m to reach the station, passing through the checkpoint barriers on the right after leaving the exit mall. The station was built to serve airport workers, not airline passengers.

Once you start walking away from the airport terminal you will be accosted by all manner of 'helpful' people, offering transport and hotels and doing their best to convince you that they have been sent especially to meet you. If the offer of transport by one of these hustlers does sound appealing, inspect the vehicle — and the driver — first. If you have doubts about either, change your mind.

The nearest resort to the airport is Negombo, 25 minutes by bus. This would be a good place to go to recover from the flight, relax for a night or two and then start your rail tour by taking one of the slow trains (about 100 minutes) into Colombo.

If you fly in on a pre-paid package tour, the transfer from the airport to your hotel will be included. Look for the tour operator representative in the arrivals hall. You may be given a car to yourself or be put on a coach that seems to stop at every hotel but your own for the next three hours. At least it is a way of seeing the coastal resorts at no extra charge.

Staying On

It is possible to extend the usual 30-day visit visa on application in person to the Visit Visa section of the Emigration and Immigration office on Marine Drive (behind the Ceylon Inter-Continental Hotel) in Colombo. Extensions up to 90 days have been known. In all cases you are expected to show a confirmed air ticket out of Sri Lanka and evidence of having exchanged enough funds (based on a rate of US$30 a day) for the entire length of your proposed stay, not just for the days you have already spent in the country. Take along the exchange receipts.

There are forms to fill in and rupees to pay — the fees differ according to your nationality; Brits pay more than Germans or Americans. In theory, you are not supposed to have extensions totalling more than six months in any one year. Some travellers who long to linger in Sri Lanka pop over to India or the Maldives for a few days, then return for another 30 day permit.

Longer, leading to permanent, residence is possible in conjunction with substantial (US$150,000) investment in a Board of Investment approved project of if you are a foreign professional with a skill unavailable in, or of benefit to, Sri Lanka, and show a monthly income of the equivalent of US$1,500. Information is available from the BOI at 14 Sir Baron Jayatilaka Mawatha, Colombo 1; tel: 434403-5; fax: 941 447995.

Foreign husbands of Sri Lankan women need to deposit US$25,000 for a permit to stay. Three-year retirement visas for 250 people a year are also planned.

Departure

It is vital to reconfirm your flight at least 72 hours before departure. If you have a reservation and don't intend to use it, remember to cancel it so that someone on the waiting list can travel instead.

Air Lanka will request you to check in three hours before the scheduled departure time of your flight, other airlines make it two hours. Although it adds to the time you spend travelling, it is worth checking-in early to be ahead of the queues, and to make sure you have a seat.

There are more options for getting to the airport than getting from it. Many travellers take the train from their beach resort to Colombo and then catch a taxi or a three-wheeler to the airport. If you have added a lot of luggage while in Sri Lanka, travelling by bus will not be comfortable, nor is it reliable or convenient since it will be crowded and take a long time.

Trains to the airport leave Colombo Fort station at about 0500 and about 1625; allow at least an hour for the journey. Helicopter transfer (see page 61) is possible at US$20 and there is also an Airport Express minivan (tel: 687037) at Rs485 per person (discount for more than one passenger travelling together). Or you could spend your last night at the (luxury rate) Airport Garden Hotel which provides free transfer to the airport. A favourite option is to travel to Negombo by train for the last night or two, then travel by bus or three-wheeler to the airport (25 minutes).

Another way by rail is to take a train bound for Negombo, Chilaw or Puttalam (14 a day) from Fort station and get out at either Katunayake South (for the Free Trade Zone), 2km from the airport along the main road, or at the main Katunayake station at the end of the runway. Sometimes there are three-wheelers there (Rs100 to the airport); if not it is a five-minute walk to the main road to find a bus or three-wheeler.

Whether you reach the airport by bus, train, coach, taxi or from the helipad, you will have to walk down the long covered mall to the terminal entrance. There are usually plenty of baggage trolleys, some pushed by porters. At the airport entrance there is a security check to see if your ticket is valid; and your luggage is x-rayed.

In the departure concourse, there are shops, a post office and, on the mezzanine, a restaurant where you can wait if checking-in for your flight has not begun.

Friends who have come to see you off can accompany you this far (if you have bought tickets for them at the kiosk for Rs40). If not, they can go to a kind of stadium overlooking the runway to watch flight departures (a good place for plane spotters). Only passengers with flight tickets can pass through the barrier into the checking-in area. Before reaching the desks there is a hand search by security personnel of all your hold baggage.

The check-in process is usually swift. If you have got there early, then you walk to the right to pay the embarkation tax (Rs500). Glass panels separate you from your friends but they can watch you queue for the outward immigration control before you disappear into the main departure lounge.

Upstairs there are duty free shops, including shops selling gold bars, all of which take only foreign currency or credit cards, and a restaurant and cocktail bar.

There are also short-stay rooms and showers, and business and first class lounges. Downstairs are the sterile areas where you wait (after having hand luggage x-rayed and a quick body frisk if you set off the alarm) to board the aircraft.

The airport was designed to handle three million passengers a year but has yet to reach two million, so it will strike you as spacious and even pleasant. The aim is for it to be known as the region's most hospitable airport. Peak times for departures are 2100 to 0200 hours, with Thursday night/Friday morning being the busiest.

Solo or Group Travel

Come alone to Sri Lanka and you will have a great trip; come with someone else and the experience will be influenced by the state of your relationship with that person. It is often by travelling overseas with someone you have known for years that you really get to know that person — but that is not why you go to Sri Lanka. If the relationship with your travelling companion breaks down, it could turn the whole trip sour.

Solo travelling in Sri Lanka is both practical and enjoyable. The usual problem of who keeps an eye on your luggage on a train when you want to go to the toilet is easily solved. Everyone in the carriage will watch your bag when they hear you asking someone sitting near you to keep an eye on it.

Go alone anywhere in the country and people will talk if you want them to, so you will hardly feel lonely. The encounters can be rewarding, the kind you might not experience so deeply if you have a companion wanting to do something else all the time. You might also have a chance to make real Sri Lankan friends whose kindness and graciousness will make what I have written about the calculated approach of some people seem utter nonsense.

On my first trip to Sri Lanka in 1980 I travelled by myself. I stayed on the beach near Trincomalee and unpacked the case of books I had brought with me in case I got bored. I made so many friends that I eventually settled in Sri Lanka — and I still have not read all those books. Had I come with a companion, I would probably have stayed a few weeks and then moved on, unaware of what was waiting to be discovered.

If you do travel with a companion, your individual costs will be lower since you can share a room (double and single rates are usually the same), and taxi fares, as well as experiences and jokes. While being an exclusive group of two may give you a feeling of confidence and is convenient, it could also shelter you from adventures, if your companion is not the out-going type.

If you want to be organised, then visit Sri Lanka with a group, although there are not many companies that specialize in rail tours. It might be better to travel out as part of a package tour, with airport transfer and accommodation arranged, spend a couple of days on the beach and then branch out on your own. You could travel for short trips by train at first, and then try the longer journeys to the hill country.

Tour Companies

Many tour operators to Sri Lanka offer a ride on the Viceroy Special steam-hauled train from the coast to Kandy as an optional extra. The only way to travel on this train is as part of a tour group, since it operates on charter once or twice a week. For information on when the Viceroy is running contact J F Tours & Travels at 189 New Bullers Road, Colombo 4; tel: 587996; fax: 941 580507. J F Tours can arrange charters of the Viceroy Special and other steam trains, as well as any group rail trip.

A UK tour operator which occasionally organizes trips to Sri Lanka to travel by steam-hauled trains is Dorridge Travel, 7 Station Approach, Dorridge, Solihull, West Midlands B93 8JA; tel: 0564 776252; fax: 0564 778907. Groups are led by steam enthusiast Hugh Ballantyne who makes sure the trains stop at the most photogenic locations.

Children

For a child, train travel can be dangerous; Sri Lankan trains tend to lurch a lot and the doors are always open. Sri Lankan passengers, however, are fascinated by foreign children and will quickly alert inattentive parents. Making a trip to Colombo from a beach resort by train with kids could be fun, but to travel extensively by train with a child could be a strain on everyone.

Women Travellers

Judging by letters to the press, women seem to have a hard time in Sri Lanka if they object to being ogled and chatted up. Unfortunately, foreign women are seen by many Lankan men as being free in their favours. Age does not deter suggestions being made; to a Sri Lankan male a foreign woman is a woman whatever her age.

Not everyone minds, of course, so it is really a matter of attitude since very rarely is a man's behaviour menacing, even if it might appear rude. Women train travellers soon adopt some form of defence but should be warned that the cutting remarks that deter western men who get too bold have no effect on the determined Sri Lankan. His type receives all the wrong signals anyway. It helps, of course, if you are modestly dressed and keep an even temper, viewing such incidents as humourous rather than threatening.

Disabled Travellers

Because of the difficulties in boarding trains (steep steps like small ladders giving access from low platforms) and lack of space within carriages, travel by train for the disabled would be difficult. Yet beggars without limbs know how to get on board and blind singers — usually with a child as a guide — patrol the aisles. There are none of the facilities for the disabled traveller which exist in some countries.

CULTURE SHOCK
What to be aware of in Sri Lanka
Taboos

Sri Lankans are very tolerant of breaches in social etiquette by foreigners, so do not let your anxiety to conform and not give offence deter you from enjoying your trip. It is accepted that, as a foreigner, you might not be privileged to know about local habits.

The major culture shock will come when you are invited to eat in a Sri Lankan home and find there is no cutlery. Thus you discover that the technique of eating with your fingers is not as easy as it looks. You use only your right hand, letting your fingers and thumb mix the food together into a convenient sized morsel which you then pop into your mouth using your thumb as a guide. You do not pick up chicken by the bone and gnaw at it as you would at a barbecue. You use your fingers to peel the chicken off the bone; usually meat will be convenient bite size anyway. If you can't manage, you won't cause offence if you ask for a spoon and use that instead.

The second shock comes when you go to the loo and find no paper there (and there is none in train toilets). The secret is always to carry a few sheets of toilet paper with you. However, if you have forgotten, then you must use the traditional method which is to splash yourself clean with water using the utensil provided and your left hand.

The passing of anything, whether money or train tickets, etc, should be done with the right hand.

When visiting Buddhist or Hindu temples, you must remove your footwear. Shorts, whether worn by women or men, are frowned upon for temple visits and you may find yourself wrapped in a sarong.

Many Sri Lankans, whether Buddhist or Hindu, do not eat beef and Muslims do not eat pork, so if you are inviting friends for a meal, choose your restaurant with that in mind. Chinese restaurants are popular since they also have good vegetarian dishes.

Modesty in dress will always be appreciated. A man who feels like 'going native' after a few days and adopts the Sri Lankan male's traditional garb of a sarong will be regarded with amusement if he wears it other than on the beach or in bed.

The sarong is a length of waist-to-ankle cloth with its ends sown together to form a kind of tube. It is donned by pulling over the head and draping around the waist and legs. Secure it by tying it around your waist as you would a beach towel. It is the ideal garment for nightwear as it can act as a covering sheet, and also for using as a shield under which to dress when you are changing in a shared train cabin.

If you have a formal function to attend, a bush shirt and dark trousers, or a safari suit (all of which can be made easily and quickly), are acceptable. For a woman, a blouse and skirt or a cocktail dress is fine. A woman who learns from friends how to wear a sari and dresses in one for social occasions will be much admired.

Perhaps it is the colonial instinct of many visitors from western countries, an urge to educate, liberate and reform, which inspires many foreigners to explain to Sri Lankans how things should be done. Even if the manner in which a local is doing something is neither logical nor efficient, is too slow or unhygienic, and perhaps even sick-making, it is not necessary for you, the visitor, the guest, to try to change or even comment on it. Sri Lanka is not the same as your home country; better to leave it that way, and to learn from it.

A 204 page book has been published with the title *Culture Shock! Sri Lanka* (see *Further Reading*, page 177). Mainly intended for the expatriate who is taking up residence in Sri Lanka, it has much good advice for the adventurous visitor, too. 'Sri Lanka,' the authors warn, 'is not what it initially appears to be'.

Public Holidays

When you are feeling hot, tired and thirsty after a day's travelling by train, it is not only frustrating but almost incomprehensible that you can't have the beer you might be desperate for because it is a full moon day. *Poya Day*, as the day of the full moon is called, is celebrated by Buddhists as a day of worship. Consequently it is a dry day with all liquor shops and even hotel bars closed. True, some places will serve tourists clandestinely with beer in a teapot and cups, or in the back room of a resthouse. Many Sri Lankans, for not all are devout Buddhists, will drink in the privacy of their homes.

As well as *Poya* days there are other national holidays when everything grinds to a halt and it usually takes a couple of days to crank up into action again. Trains intended for commuters do not operate on those days, although there are likely to be several extra trains since holidays are regarded as a time for travelling to visit friends and relatives elsewhere in the country. In this list of holidays, where there are no dates, the holiday is variable and may even change month from year to year.

January 14	Tamil Thai Pongal Day
January	Duruthu Full Moon Poya Day
February 4	National Day
February	Navam Full Moon Poya Day
March 10	Maha Sivaratri Day
March	Id-Ul-Fitr (Ramazan Festival Day)
March	Medin Full Moon Poya Day
March/April	Good Friday
April 13	Day prior to Sinhala and Tamil (National) New Year Day
April 14	National New Year Day
April	Bak Full Moon Poya Day
May 1	May Day
May 22	National Heroes Day
May	Idul Alha (Hadji Festival Day)
May	Vesak Full Moon Poya Day
May	Day following Vesak Full Moon Poya Day
June	Poson Full Moon Poya Day
June 30	Special Bank Holiday
July/August	Esala Full Moon Poya Day
August	Nikini Full Moon Poya Day
August	Milad-Un-Nabi (Holy Prophet's Birthday)
September	Binara Full Moon Poya Day
October	Vap Full Moon Poya Day
November 2	Deepavali Festival Day
November	Il Full Moon Poya Day
December	Unduvap Full Moon Poya Day
December 25	Christmas Day
December 31	Special Bank Holiday

Time

Time in Sri Lanka — as in India — is 5hrs 30 mins ahead of GMT, or 4 hrs 30 mins ahead of British summer time, and continental Europe time. It is 9 hrs 30 mins ahead of Eastern Standard Time in the USA and half an hour ahead of the time in the Maldives. The time is 2 hrs 30 mins behind Singapore and 4 hrs 30 mins behind Australian Eastern Time.

Train times are listed on the 24-hour clock in timetables, but on station noticeboards they are usually on the 12-hour clock.

Sri Lankans are not obsessed with punctuality except where an auspicious time has to be observed for the start of a new undertaking. Meal times are flexible with lunch taken from 1130 to 1400 depending on a person's employment. The evening meal is generally taken late, just before going to bed.

Banking

There are 25 different banks in Sri Lanka with the local People's Bank and the Bank of Ceylon having most branches islandwide. Other local banks are the Commercial Bank of Ceylon, Hatton National, Sampath and Seylan Banks. There is also a National Savings Bank and a State Mortgage and Investment Bank.

International banks, mostly with a single branch in Colombo, but some with branches in the suburbs and Kandy, too, are: ABN Ambro, American Express, ANZ Grindlays, Indosuez, Citibank, Deutsche, Habib, Habib AG Zurich, Indian, Indian Overseas, Mashreq, Middle East, Overseas Trust, Public Bank Berhad, Standard Chartered, State Bank of India, and Hongkong and Shangai Bank. Their opening hours vary from 0900 to 1330 or 1500.

Mail

Pre-stamped aerogrammes (Rs12) for overseas mail can be bought at post offices and are useful to take around with you for when you want to dash off a letter. They are safer and cheaper than airmailing a postcard (Rs14). An airmail letter starts at Rs20 for 10g, more depending on weight and destination. Allow ten to 14 days for mail to reach its destination; a reply could take just as long. For inland mail there are envelopes sold at post offices with Rs1 stamp printed on them. Local mail usually takes one to two days. For incoming mail you could use your hotel or guesthouse base to receive mail as long as there is someone there you can trust to remember to keep it safe for you. The main post office in Colombo (a fine, regal, colonial building outside, a bit of a disappointment inside) will receive mail on a poste restante basis (c/o Poste Restante, GPO, Colombo).

The post office is open 24 hours a day for sending mail and for enquiries, as well as for telephone calls. Poste restante is open 0700-2100; money orders and postal orders can be bought 0900-1500 or 0900-1300 on Saturdays. Telegrams can be sent 0700-2100 and 0800-1400 on Sundays. Registration can be done 0800-1600, weekdays only.

You can have letters franked in front of you and see them popped into the postal bag at the special 24-hour counter on the right of the main stamp sales counters. The philatelic bureau is in the wing on the right and has a fine collection of recent issue and first-day covers for sale, but none of the train issues (see below).

Train Stamps

A 60 cent stamp was issued on December 21 1964 to mark the centenary of the construction of the first railway line in Sri Lanka. It was printed by Harrison & Sons of London in sheets of 100, with alternative rows inscribed in Sinhala and Tamil, and Sinhala and English. The design, in blue, reddish-purple and yellow-green, was of a locomotive and carriages of the first train with a modern train with a diesel locomotive alongside it. In the background were the mountains of the central highlands. It was withdrawn from sale on September 30 1965.

The 125th anniversary of the railways was commemorated with the issue of four stamps on December 29 1989. They were printed in Malaysia in sheets of 50. The 75 cent stamp showed a diesel train on the nine-arch viaduct between Ella and Demodara (1 million printing). The Rs2 stamp showed a colourful scene of a diesel in front of Maradana station passing a colour light signal (1 million). A steam train (it looks like the Viceroy Special) passing a semaphore signal was on the Rs3 stamp (500,000), while the Rs7 stamp showed the first train from Colombo to Ambepussa (5,000).

First-day covers were issued, cancelled with a special handstamp with the slogan: SRI LANKA RAILWAYS 125TH ANNIVERSARY/ FORT RAILWAY STATION/CPO 1989.12.27/FIRST DAY OF ISSUE/COLOMBO.

A stamp was also issued in 1986 to commemorate the inauguration of the Viceroy Special.

Post Boxes

There is a great variety of mail boxes to be seen in Sri Lanka, including imported British cast-iron red circular letter boxes and locally manufactured hexagonal cement ones. The latter have the maker's name and date on the cement base and may be blue (airmail) and green (outstation mail) as well as red.

Post boxes with royal ciphers still exist, including George V, Edward VII and George VI, and the pouting lips kind of boxes of Elizabeth II.

Travelling Post Offices (TPO)

The first travelling post office was introduced on March 1 1892, to satisfy the needs of upcountry tea planters to have the Colombo evening newspapers delivered as soon as possible. It was operated in a 3rd class railway carriage between Colombo and Peradeniya and used until 1909 when a special van was constructed by the railway for use as a TPO. In 1923, it became known as the Kandy Travelling Post Office, becoming, in 1929, the Bandarawela TPO. In 1965 its name changed again to the Badulla TPO. There was also a Galle TPO. The independent travelling post office to Kandy came into existence in 1972.

Mail trains still run (with provision for late fee letters to be posted) to Galle and Badulla.

Rail Postcards

Many picture postcards showing railway scenes, trains and stations were published at the beginning of the century and make interesting collector's items. Because these postcards were sent abroad by visitors to Ceylon, it is rare to find them in Sri Lanka today. Better hunting grounds are the philatelic dealers and antique shops of Britain.

Over two dozen cards are known but there are probably many more, with views such as the Kadugannawa incline and 'the railway showing Horse Shoe Bend going through Scrubbs Estate on Nanu Oya Pass'.

Faxing

While some post offices have fax machines, the best way to send a fax is through private communications bureaux. These exist in nearly every town, sometimes in a dedicated communications centre, elsewhere in the back of a grocery store. A major bureau in Colombo which accepts credit cards and is open 24 hours a day (for photocopying, telephoning and telexing as well as faxing) is COLAG Communications, in the basement of the building with the Air Lanka office, at 55 Janadhipathi Mawatha, Colombo 1 (opposite the Intercon); tel: 446534; fax: 941 446 535.

Telephone

The international code for Sri Lanka is 94 followed by the area code without zero (ie: Colombo is 01 if phoning from other places, referred to locally as 'outstation'). But you need 941 in front of the actual number if phoning from overseas, which is why I have quoted that when giving Colombo fax numbers in this book. However, numbers quoted in this book for Colombo telephones do not include the prefix of 01 since you do not need to dial that when calling within the Colombo area.

All outstation numbers given here have the exchange prefix included since that is what you must dial if calling from Colombo. You drop the prefix if dialling from the same area. Phone numbers which have a 071, 072 or 073 prefix are cellular telephones and you always need to dial the full prefix and number, unless dialling from overseas in which case the zero is dropped.

Mobile phones are available for rent for short periods through the airport counter (Celltel, tel: 541541) or hotel business centres, and through Mobitel (tel: 071 55777). Rates on a monthly package start at Rs250 per day plus call charges. However, as yet mobile cellular phones do not provide islandwide coverage, although the main areas are covered.

The access number for overseas calls is 00. Overseas telephone calls can be made through a communiations bureau; rates are lower 2200-0600 and at weekends. Recently introduced are payphones using Lanka Payphone cards which are sold at outlets near their yellow telephone booths, ranging in price from Rs100 to Rs800. Direct dialling, either anywhere in Sri Lanka or overseas, is possible on these telephones, which avoids the usual mark up charged by hotels, but is rather public and noisy.

Drinking Water

There are several varieties of locally produced mineral water available from about Rs30 a 1.5 litre bottle. For easy carrying so the bottle does not split it is better to decant the contents into your own, unbreakable water bottle. Good soda water (at Rs15 a 1.5 litre bottle) is also available.

If neither mineral or soda water is available, you could try the soft drinks (Sri Lanka has both Coca-Cola and Pepsi Cola) or the excellent ginger beer (Elephant brand), and fresh coconut water.

Alcohol

There are two breweries and you will know instantly by tasting which beer is from which. The Three Coins label of lager, pils and Gold Brew, produced by the McCallum Brewery lacks the bite of the Lion brand of beers brewed in Nuwara Eliya. The Lion range consists of Lion lager, Lion pilsner, Royal pilsner, in ascending order of strength, and the brewery also produces Carlsberg, under licence.

Draught Lion lager is available in some outlets in Colombo including the Echelon Pub at the Colombo Hilton and at the German Restaurant opposite the Galle Face hotel. The real ale buff will be ecstatic at the Lion brewery beer shop in Nuwara Eliya (see page 125) where draught beer is cooled by nature. Beer costs from about Rs65 a bottle and rises to as much as three times that according to where you buy and quaff it.

Sri Lanka's answer to Scotland's whisky or France's cognac is called Arrack. There are many brands available, ranging in price for a 750ml bottle from Rs100 to over Rs200. The purest is coconut arrack made with distilled toddy (the sap extracted from the bud of a coconut palm). Since there is not enough toddy, most brands of arrack only have a percentage of the toddy distillate blended with neutral spirits.

Connoisseurs drink arrack neat or on the rocks, while tourists prefer to disguise the smell and the taste with a cola or Sprite or 7UP.

Toddy (*ra*) is worth seeking out, an easy task from March to December on the west coast from Panadura to Hikkaduwa where coconut palms grow around the coastal railway line. A tree's nuts are sacrificed to yield the sap which is called toddy, tapped from a tree's flower spathe every morning and evening by agile men in blue loincloths. They move from the top of one tree to another by coir (coconut fibre) ropes slung between the trees, lowering gourds of toddy to the ground where it is collected in wooden barrels to be taken by bullock cart to the nearest distillery.

Although there are toddy taverns open in some villages for a couple of hours in the evening, where a bowl of the milky looking stuff costs Rs12, by that time the toddy is pretty strong. The best way to sample it is fresh from the tree, when it is sweet, not very alcoholic and tastes like nectar.

Although there are dry days — and even dry towns, such as Kalutara and the sacred area at Anuradhapura — there are no restrictions on the importation, and sale by licensed premises, of foreign liquor. Your favourite Scotch or gin might cost a little lower than in your home country by the bottle, and is sold in 25ml measures in bars. To buy from retail shops in towns and villages you have to speak to the custodian through a mesh of chicken wire, but in Colombo supermarkets all brands of imported liquor are available on the shelves (which are covered over on *poya days*).

Smoking

Smoking on trains and buses is officially only allowed if no other passenger objects. If there are objections then you either put out your cigarette or make your way out of the train compartment and smoke by the door.

In a letter to the *Daily News*, February 2 1994, W S Ellapperuma wrote: 'Early one morning the bus was packed with standing passengers. One of them lit a cigarette. As it was a nuisance to the passengers, I told him that smoking in the bus is prohibited. Very harshly he retorted that I had no authority to correct him and lavishly distributed the remainder of his packet to other passengers, the driver and the conductor included. They all began to smoke while I was at the butt-end of their jokes.'

Sri Lankan cigarettes are sold in packets of 12 or 20 costing Rs36 and Rs60 respectively. Local cigars are also available and have a good reputation.

Food

Within a few paces of each other in Colombo are places where you can eat a packet of rice and curry for Rs25, enjoy a Chinese meal or a local buffet or tuck into a steak or half a chicken for Rs150, gorge yourself silly at a five-star hotel's lunch buffet for about Rs400, or dine à la carte on gourmet fare for Rs1,000. The range is amazing and low in cost compared with similar places in other countries.

There are dozens of Chinese restaurants, including some with real Chinese chefs, and Thai, Korean and Japanese places, too. There are fast food joints (Pizza Hut), seafood restaurants and European-style bar restaurants (Alt Heidelberg), even a Mexican restaurant (Santa Fe) and fine dining establishments (Don Stanleys, Chesa Swiss). The restaurants of the luxury hotels attract local custom and have their speciality outlets, like the Navaratna for Indian food (Taj Samudra) and Il Ponte (Italian) at the Hilton.

The staple diet, of course, is rice and curry. This is not a misnomer since rice is the centrepiece, and main point of the meal, with a number of different curries served in dishes to go with it. The westerner might prefer to eat curry and rice but for the Sri Lankan heaps of rice is essential. Not all the curries are spicy hot since the word curry refers to the accompaniment rather than to something necessarily fiendishly hot. Devilled is the word in Sri Lanka for that, as in devilled fish, which is fish smothered in chillies and flame-red chilli sauce.

Curries are actually best savoured when they are not hot, in temperature, which is why they are ideal for buffet service or when the dishes are allowed to remain on the table to cool before you are called to eat.

The best rice and curry meals are those that are home-cooked, preferably in a rural kitchen in clay pots over a wood fire. The second best are those served in country resthouses (inns) for local guests. Of course, some curries are hot and if they are not hot enough, fried and crushed raw chillies will be provided to add more fire. If they should be too hot, try a piece of pineapple to counteract the fieriness. You will have a wonderful time identifying the ingredients of curries and it will amaze you not only what different kinds of plants, tubers, and leaves can be eaten, but how good it all tastes.

Another attraction of Sri Lankan cuisine is the snacks, some of which are called short eats — savoury patties, deep fried hard boiled eggs with a lentil mix, fish balls, battered rolls stuffed with vegetables... Add to this a kind of pancake called a *hopper* (or egg *hopper* if an egg is fried in it) and string *hoppers*, like a nest of vermicelli, and all kinds of *roti* (pancake-style bread) served with curries, and you have the ideal food for travelling since it can all be popped in a bag for you to takeaway to eat on the train.

On the sweet side there is a kind of creme caramel called *wattalapam* and something which will make yoghurt for ever seem insipid: buffalo curd, a thick and slightly sour creamlike substance made in — and best eaten from — a clay pot. Kitul treacle or jaggery, either from the kitul or coconut palm, a kind of hard fudge produced when toddy is boiled to crystallization, is the ideal sweetener for curd.

Food on trains and in railway restaurants (hardly this!) will only be of the short eat variety. Actually, in this book I have had to resort to describing most eating places as snack bars, especially the food outlets at railway stations which are far from being restaurants. In every village and town you will find eating houses describing themselves as hotels but they do not have any rooms for overnighting guests and are, in fact, local style snack bars.

Fruits

Sri Lankan fruits are delicious, as well as unusual, with some you may never have seen before. You can buy them from wayside stalls, from vendors on trains or platforms, in the markets in the Colombo suburbs, and in the weekly fairs held in villages. These are some seasonal fruits worth trying:

April-June	Avocado
April-June	Jak (also September-October)
April-June	Mango (also November-December)
May-July	Durian
June-August	Mangosteen
June-January	Pineapple
July-August	Rambattan
Year round	Papaya

Language

Sinhala (not Sinhalese, which is the race), Tamil and English are all official languages. Station names appear in all three languages and tickets and other documents are printed in three languages, too. Since the Sinhalese form the majority of the population, that is the language you will hear most often. Do not worry about understanding it (sometimes it is better not to know what people are saying about you) since you will find English speakers everywhere.

There are phrase books, but all have incomprehensible pronunciation formulas to learn, which makes saying even the simplest phrase difficult, especially as one word can mean two different things in Sinhala; *lunu*, for example, is either salt or onion, depending how you say it. Also, whenever you try to speak Sinhala you will find Sri Lankans who speak a little English will be keen to try it out on you, rather than listen to your atrocious pronunciation.

Some useful words are in Chapter 10, page 179.

Media

There are two daily newspapers in English, the *Daily News* (Rs7) and the *Island* (Rs7), which are available islandwide, and one evening paper, *The Observer* (Rs4), sold in Colombo. On Sunday there are the *Sunday Observer* (Rs8), 'Sri Lanka's English newspaper with the largest circulation', the *Island Sunday Edition* (Rs9), 'the English newspaper with the largest circulation in Sri Lanka', the *Sunday Times* (Rs9), and the new *Sunday Leader* (Rs9). All carry international news from the various press agencies and their own versions and interpretations of local news.

An invaluable magazine available free to visitors (pick up a copy at the airport or at your hotel) is *Explore Sri Lanka*, published monthly. Copies are also available from the publisher at 24 Temple Lane, Bambalapitiya, Colombo 4; tel: 503109, fax: 941 503109. It has original articles every month, a restaurant listing, a table of flight times, a briefing for visitors and a street map of Colombo.

There are English news bulletins on the television stations and the several radio stations. BBC World Service television and CNN are also available.

The major hotels have bookshops (see page 170) with the latest paperbacks and international news magazines but no newspapers from England. The *International Herald Tribune* and the *Asian Wall Street Journal* are available the day after publication.

For secondhand books, either to buy or to borrow for a fee against a deposit, visit the bookstalls by the roundabout, a five-minute walk along the main road that is ahead of you when you emerge from Maradana station (cross the road by the overhead bridge — the traffic is horrendous).

Chapter Three

Getting Around

Buses

The dedicated bus traveller in Sri Lanka has plenty of choice, although at times it can be confusing. Basically, there are two types of bus operation. The buses which look like buses — with an entry at one end and an exit at the other and rigid seats and a high roof with room to stand without crouching — used to be under government ownership. Now they have been 'people-ized' and are run by companies in which the government has a share. They are still sometimes referred to as CTB (Ceylon Transport Board) buses, and are generally a grubby aluminium and red or yellow in appearance.

The other kind are the private buses, mostly of the coach type, built in Japan, with padded seats including some which flop down in the aisle, and rarely enough leg or head room. Fares on these cost a little more than on the people-ized variety. On all buses be sure to collect a ticket when you pay and insist that the conductor gives you one, which he might not do. There is a fine for ticketless travel, even if you have paid. Tickets are sometimes printed, and sometimes handwritten by the conductor.

Buses of both kinds serve towns and villages throughout the island. On some days, private buses that normally run on some routes may be missing, either because of a breakdown and no substitute to do the run, or because the owner has accepted a more lucrative charter than relying on picking up passengers to make his day pay.

There are two separate bus stations in major towns for the former CTB buses and the private ones. It is better to board a bus at its starting point than on the way if you want a seat on a long journey. You will sometimes come across the extraordinary sight of a private bus with half a dozen passengers hanging on its side and the whole bus canting to its left.

Information on the departure times of buses is difficult to obtain, and often unreliable, since departure depends on a bus arriving in the first place. Then it might wait until it is full before leaving, or leave immediately if the driver knows there are plenty of passengers to pick up on the way.

There are some long distance buses, though, that keep approximately to a schedule, and even some that have reserved seats and air-conditioning. These are obviously preferable since they are more comfortable and there is the possibility of seeing something of the countryside instead of the back of someone's head. For a short journey in rural areas, a local people-ized bus can be great fun, but not in a town at rush hour.

On the road between Mount Lavinia and Colombo, you might be lucky enough to see, and even ride on, a former London Routemaster double decker bus. Although several were donated to Sri Lanka, only a few remain on the roads.

To catch a bus other than in Colombo, you will have to ask locally about the services available. Sometimes buses meet trains where there are bound to be a lot of passengers, such as at Hatton for Adam's Peak in season. The old system of integrated train/bus transportation no longer exists. The bus stations in any town or village will be easy to find since bus travel is a way of life.

You will have to ask the conductor for accurate information on where the bus is going, as even other passengers might not know its final destination. In some cases buses with the same destination take different routes and buses with the same number go to different places.

In Colombo, there are two bus stations and four established areas from where private or people-ized buses begin their journeys. Private buses consist of (1) general buses that run on suburban and long distance routes, picking up and putting down passengers at designated spots, and (2) Intercity air-conditioned buses carrying only sitting passengers with tickets to its destination, but which will stop on request to put down (not pick up) passengers. There are also a few *Laksiri* buses plying in the same manner, but these are not air-conditioned.

People-ized buses are either (1) the general bus, stopping and picking up passengers wherever required, and (2) the *Laksiri* type for which a ticket to the bus's final destination is necessary, although it will stop and drop passengers as requested. These carry seated passengers only. In some buses seat reservations can be made either on the day of travel or in advance. Except in the rush hours when they serve the Free Trade Zone at the airport, bus services to the airport are patchy.

There are no published timetables for buses. The following times have been discovered by going to the bus stations and asking, so the times should be regarded as approximate: buses may start from different points or may not operate. Fares have not been given, especially as there are rumours of an increase.

Colombo Bus Stations

All the Colombo bus stations are between five and ten minutes walk of Colombo Fort railway station.

The CBS (Central Bus Station), off Olcott Mawatha, on the opposite side of the road and to the right of the train station as you leave it, is for people-ized buses. It was formerly the CTB bus station.

The Bastian Road Bus Station, also to the right of Fort railway station, is for private buses.

The People's Park Bus Station is behind the CBS and was formerly known as Saunders Place bus station. It is for private buses.

The Olcott Mawatha bus stops, where private and people-ized buses park on the side of the road opposite the railway station.

Olcott Mawatha bus stops, where people-ized buses park on the railway station side of the road.

CTO (Central Telegraph Office) bus stops, where private buses park, across the road from the Fort railway station.

Central Bus Station (tel: 328081, 320705)
people-ized bus services only

Destination	Bus Number	Times	Remarks
Akkaraipattu	98	1730	via Ratnapura & Monaragala
Alutgama	400	0730-2110	every 30 minutes depending on availability
Ampara	98	0530 1900	via Ratnapura & Monaragala
Anuradhapura	15	1315 1530	via Dambulla
Anuradhapura	4	0900	via Puttalam
Anuradhapura	57	0950 1430 2400	via Kurunegala & Galgamuwa
Avissawella	677	0840-2045	every hour, via Hanwella
Badulla	99	0130 0600 0730 0800* 0900 0930 1100 1230 1930 2200 2300*	via Ratnapura, Balangoda, Haputale & Bandarawela
		(*Laksiri buses, seating only. Seats can be reserved up to four weeks in advance at Laksiri office in CBS building.)	
Balangoda	99	0830 1030 1200 1300 1415 1600 1800	
Batticaloa	48	0530 2030	
Bibile	38	0730	
Dayagama	13	1400	via Hatton, Talawakele
Deraniyagala	699	0800-1800	hourly via Hanwella & Avissawella

Destination	Bus Number	Times				Remarks
Embilipitiya	3	0500	0630	0800	0930	via Ratnapura & Pelmadulla
		1100	1230	1400	1515	
		1630				
Galenbindunuwewa	15	0545	1215			via Anuradhapura
Galle	2	0030-0500				hourly
		0500-1800				every 15 minutes
		1800-2030				hourly
Gampaha	200	0540-2000				every 30 minutes
		2000-2200				hourly
Gampola	19	1000	1130			
Hambantota	32	1000				
Hanwella	143	0500-2230				every 30 minutes
Hatton	18	0230*	0500	0640	0800	
		0900	1220	1500	1600*	
		1640	1730			
		(*Laksiri buses, seating only, same day seat reservations only at CBS enquiry office.)				
Horowupotana	15	0730	2200			via Dambulla & Anuradhapura
Kahatagasdigiliya	15	1230	1800			via Dambulla, Kekirawa & Anuradhapura
Kalmuna	98	1630				via Ratnapura, Embilipitiya & Ampara
Kalutara	400	0545-2110				every 30 minutes
Kandy	1	0130-043				hourly
		0430-2045				every 15 minutes
		2045-2400				hourly
Kataragama	32	0630	0800	0900	1320	
		1630				via Galle
Kuliyapitiya	92	0745	0900	1000	1100	via Negombo & Kochikade
		1200	1300	1400	1500	
		1600	1700	1800		
Kurunegala	5	0530	0645	0715	1030	via Ja-Ela & Minuwangoda
		1245	1415	1615		
Kurunegala	6	0440-1700				every 30 minutes
		1700-2000				hourly
Lihiniyagala	48	0615	0715			via Dambulla, Habarana & Polonnaruwa
Maskeliya	23	0740	0830	1100	1330	
		1445				
Matale	8					via Kandy
Matara	32	1045				
Matugama	430	0630	0720	0745	0810	via Kalutara & Nagoda
		0845	0930	0950	1045	
		1555	1610	1645	1715	
		1830				

Destination	Bus Number	Times				Remarks
Medirigiriya	48	1130				via Dambulla, Habarana & Mineriya
Monaragala	98	0700				
Nawalapitiya	78	1000	1530			
Negombo	240	0415-2230				every 10 minutes
Nittambuwa	180	0600-2030				every 30 minutes
Nuwara Eliya	79	0630	1400			
Paymadu	4	0500				via Puttulam & Anuradhapura
Polonnaruwa	48	0245	0900	1015	1200	
		1330	1445			
Rakwana	67	1000	1245	1445		via Ratnapura & Pelmadulla
Ratnapura	3	0440-1815				every 30 minutes
Sigiriya	48	1045				via Dambulla
Sripura	15	0630	0830			
Talawakele	13	1030	1125			
Tangalle	32	0730	0930	1130	1530	
Trincomalee	49	0515	0645	0800	0930	
		1030				
Vavuniya	4	0730				via Puttalam & Anuradhapura
Walapanne	21	1050	1535			via Kandy
Weliweriya	228	0530-2030				via Biyigama every 30 or 45 minutes
Welimada	99	0400				
Welimada	13	0930				via Avissawella, Hatton, Talawakele & Nuwara Eliya
Welimada	79	0800				via Peredeniya, Gampola & Nuwara Eliya

Bastian Road Bus Station
private bus services only
(Private Omnibus Operators Association, tel: 421731)

Destination	Bus Number	Times	Remarks
Alutgama	400	0600-1700	every 15/20 minutes
(Intercity)	400	0730-1700	every 30 minutes
Ambalangoda	2	0545-1900	every 15 minutes
Ampara	22	0500	via Kandy & Mahiyangana (3 buses)
Anuradhapura	4	0430-1900	every 30 minutes via Puttalam
Anuradhapura (Intercity)	15	0530-2100	every 30 minutes via Dambulla & Maradankadawala

Destination	Bus Number	Times	Remarks
Anuradhapura	15	0445 0610 0700 0815	via Dambulla & Talawa
Anuradhapura	57	1215	via Warakapola & Ambampola
Avissawella	122	0540-2040	every 10 minutes
Badulla	99	0345-1800	every 40 minutes
		1800-2400	every hour
(Intercity)	99	0900 1000 1100 1200	
		1300 1400 2100	
Badureliya	430	0530-1900	every 20 minutes
Balangoda	99	0915 1215-1600	hourly
Bibile	22	1530	
Eppawala	57	1345	via Kurunegala & Tambuttegama
Galle	2	0500-2000	every 15 minutes
(Intercity)	2	0430-2000	every 10 minutes
Gampola	19	0500-1800	every 30 minutes via Peradeniya
(Intercity)	19	0930	
Godagama	190	0415-1930	every 15 minutes
Hanwella	143	0530-2000	every 10 minutes
Hendala	260	0605-2100	every 10 minutes
Homagama	138	0545-2230	every 5 minutes via Kottawa
Horana	120	0530-2000	every 10 minutes
Kaduwela	143	0530-2000	every 10 minutes
Kagama	15	1230	via Dambulla & Kekirawa
Kandy (Intercity)	1	0430	every 15 minutes
Kirindiwela	231	0700-1900	every 30 minutes
Kuliyapitiya	92	0500-1800	every 30 minutes
Kurunegala	6	0530-0900	every 15 minutes
		0900-1930	every 10 minutes
(Intercity)	6	0730-1730	every 30 minutes via Warakapola
Kurunegala	5	0530-1800	every 10 minutes via Minuwangoda
Maharagama	138	0530-2230	every 5 minutes
Matale	8	0500-1700	every 30 minutes
(Intercity)	8	0830	every 2 hours
Matara	2	0130 0230 0300 0330	every 15 minutes to 0130
(Intercity)	2	0300 0530	every 30 minutes all day
Mapalagama	435/1	1630	
Matugama	430	0430-1900	every 15 minutes
Minuwangoda	265	0700-1930	every 15 minutes
Moratuwa	100	0600-2000	every 5 minutes
Morawaka	396	1100 1200	via Matugama
Nawalapitiya	19	0830 1200 1330	
Nittambuwa	180	0515-2000	every 10 minutes

Destination	Bus Number	Times	Remarks
Nuwara Eliya	79	0500-2000	every 45 minutes
(Intercity)	79	0730	
Paduka	125	0700	every 30 minutes
Panadura	100	0630-2100	every 5 minutes
Passara	99	2000*	via Badulla
		(*Laksiri bus, seating only, same day seat reservations possible.)	
Pelawatta	435/1	1130 1430 1510	via Matugama
Polonnaruwa	48	0430-1800	every 30 minutes
		also 2100	via Dambulla, Habarana & Minneriya
(Intercity)	48	0530 0630 0730 then hourly until 1300	
Pundaluoya	19	1130	
Puttalam	4	0500-1800	every 30 minutes via Chilaw
(Intercity)	4	1200-1600	(depends on availability)
Rakwana	67	1230	via Ratnapura
Rakwana	67	1315	via Kaduwela
Ratnapura	122	0430-1800	every 15 minutes
Tangalle	32	0645 0745 to 1500	(depends on availability)
(Intercity)	32	0830 0900	
Tawalama	396	1300	via Matugama
Trincomalee	48	0500-1000	every 30 minutes
(Intercity)	48	0500-1000	(according to demand)
Warakpola	1	0600-1230 1230 1400 1600 1700	(depends on availability)
Warakpola	1/2	0600-1800	every 20 minutes
Wattegama	9	0530 1130	
Welimada	79	0845 0930 1200 1430 1700 1900	via Nuwara Eliya
(Intercity)	79	1600	

Peoples Park (formerly Saunders Place)
private bus services only

Destination	Bus Number	Times	Remarks
Ampara	98	0615 1400 1500 1600 1800	via Ratnapura, Embilipitiya & Monaragala
(Intercity)	98	1615	
Balangoda	99	0930 1130 1215 1300 1415 1500 1545	
Chilaw	4	0415-0600	every 15 minutes
		0600-1930	every 10 minutes
(Intercity)	4	0600-1600	every 30 minutes

Destination	Bus Number	Times				Remarks
Embilipitiya	3	0930	1030	1145	1400	
(Intercity)	3	1300				
Gampaha	200	0600-2000				every 10 minutes
Hatton	18	0530	0630	0700	1400	via Avissawella & Ginigatena
(Intercity)	18	0900	1000			
Kegalle	1	0530-2015				every 15 minutes
Monaragala	98	0715-1630				hourly
(Intercity)	98	0830	1800			
Negombo	240	0430-2030				every 10 minutes

Olcott Mawatha Bus Stands
private and people-ized bus services

Destination	Bus Number	Times	Remarks
Bolagalla	199	0700-2100	every 30 minutes
Bopitiya	275	0600-2130	every 30 minutes
Delgoda	234	0530-2230	every 10 minutes
Kelaniya	235	0600-1800	every 10 minutes
		1800-2100	(when available)
Kiribathgoda	230	0530-2000	every 15 minutes via Kelaniya
Mahara	261	0530-0600	every 15 minutes
		0600-2230	every 5 minutes
Pugoda	224	0530-2130	every 30 minutes
Ragama	262	0600-2030	every 10 minutes
Weliweriya	228	0530-2130	every 30 minutes

Olcott Mawatha Bus Stands
people-ized bus services

Destination	Bus Number	Times	Remarks
Bulatsinhala	285	1645	
Dekhenpura	120	1700	
Horana	120	0445	
		0600-1000	every 10 minutes
		1000-1600	every 20 minutes
		1600-1730	every 5 minutes
		2400	

Destination	Bus Number	Times	Remarks
Ingiriya	125	0520-2300	every 20 minutes
Ingiriya	450	1710	
Maharagama	138	0520-2200	every 10-15 minutes
Moratuwa	101	0430-2245	every 15 minutes
Moratuwa	100	0330-0030	every 15 minutes
Neboda	458	1615	
Panadura	133	0430-0030	every 20 minutes
Pitakotte	115	0500-2200	every 15 minutes

Central Telegraph Office Bus Stands
private bus services only

Destination	Bus Number	Times	Remarks
Airport	187		
Hendala	187		Frequent service but no
Ja Ela	187		regular times; all routes
Kadawata	230		
Narahenpitiya	103		

Lake House Bus Stand
special private bus service only

Destination	Bus Number	Times	Remarks
Kataragama		0900	Reservations up to 10 days in advance at Lake House, tel: 421181, ext. 259

Three-Wheelers

Called a ground-helicopter in Hikkaduwa, this is what is known as a *tuk-tuk* in Thailand or an *auto*, short for auto-rickshaw, in India, but which Sri Lankans prosaically call a three-wheeler. With three wheels and a noisy engine they are encountered everywhere (except sometimes when you really want one), replacing the Morris Minors that used to do the job of casual taxis.

They can be hailed whenever you see an empty one. It is wiser, though, to look for one that is parked so you can agree on the price before boarding as they don't have meters. The minimum fare is supposed to be Rs20. Always bargain, even if you don't know the exact fare; the driver will quote more than it really is. At least no tip is expected.

While some drivers own their own vehicles, others hire them from a boss to whom they must pay a fixed rental each day. In Colombo most of the drivers will speak a least a little English and many of them are very knowledgeable about the country and make excellent guides. If you have a lot of places to visit in Colombo it is often worthwhile to hire a three-wheeler for the whole morning. And when you do find a good driver whose fare is reasonable, encourage him by using him again when you get a chance.

Three-wheeler drivers in Colombo not only serve the city but will accept hires out of town, such as to the airport (expect to pay half the amount charged by hotel taxi). It is not always a comfortable ride but it is a breezy one.

The three-wheeler drivers who lurk outside Fort railway station invariably charge more than they should. You could ask a few how much to your destination to get an idea, and then walk to the end of the line and bargain with the drivers there. There is no organized queuing system at the station so you can take any vehicle you like.

In country districts — away from the tourist resorts — the three-wheeler drivers seem more laidback, prepared to quote a reasonable fare even for long journeys like Matara to Tissamaharama or Sigiriya to Dambulla. They are the best alternative to bus travel (when there are no trains) and for one or two people with luggage are ideal since you can stop wherever you want on the way.

The driver will usually start a long journey by pulling into a petrol station and asking you to give him an advance on the fare to pay for fuel. Remember to deduct it when you pay the final amount.

Remarkably few of these vehicles are involved in major accidents, possibly because they are easily manoeuvrable and an alert driver can avoid an accident in the way a car could not. Some versions have doors, which seems an unnecessary refinement. Some owner-driven three-wheelers boast a music system while others have a kind of altar instead of dashboard. They have sidings which can be rolled down from the canopy when it rains.

Taxi!

Whenever I am with a Sri Lankan colleague, I let him hail the three-wheeler and negotiate the price while I wait out of sight.

When he has bargained it to an acceptable figure, I stroll over as though we've just met. 'Hop in,' he says, 'I'll give you a lift.'

That way I've learned which is a Rs30 ride (for which I'd be charged Rs50 if I did the negotiating).

One three-wheeler driver I use regularly has become such a good friend, he leaves me to pay what I feel like. It's a clever ploy because I rarely undercharge myself.

He told me that he was recently hired to take three Japanese passengers to Kandy. It seemed a drastic way to cut down on holiday expenses.

'Oh no,' he said. 'They paid me four hundred rupees more than the hotel taxi would have charged. They liked the ride so much.'

Once, when I was in a hurry, I hired a three-wheeler at Fort station. The fare was outrageous but I agreed because the driver knew the area I wanted to visit, and I didn't. I knew I'd been overcharged, but what to do?

A couple of weeks later, by chance, I got in the same three-wheeler at the station for a journey I knew should cost no more than Rs40. When we reached the destination I proffered the exact fare. The driver refused.

'That's your free ride,' he said with a grin. 'Good customer, no?'

Fair driver, yes!

from *Explore Sri Lanka*

Taxis

There are four kinds of taxi: old cars, hotel vehicles, resort vans and cars and radio cabs.

The old cars can be a delight, real bangers over 30 years old, almost classic cars. Morris Minors are favourite vehicles, although these are being replaced by three-wheelers, even in country towns. None of them have working meters or fixed prices; you negotiate before getting in. You will find them in the busiest part of town, not always at the station, so you will have to walk to them (another reason to carry only light luggage).

Hotel vehicles are those in the livery of major hotels, either owned by the hotel or a travel agency or under contract to the hotel. The Colombo

Hilton taxis are painted fire-engine red, a distinctive status symbol. Hotel cars have fixed prices (the cost can be added to your hotel bill), are air-conditioned and are usually driven by men who are knowledgeable as guides, too. They are available for tours as well as for short or half-day hires around Colombo. While on tour, the driver arranges his own accommodation and meals (actually usually provided free by where you eat or stay) and a subsistence allowance is charged to your bill.

Resort vans and cars operate on tours under the same principle. These vehicles are not run by the resort hotels outside which they park, and their prices are not fixed; they will charge as much as they can get. Vans are favoured over cars by drivers in the resort areas since they can then operate under charter to tour operators. Many of these vehicles are diesel (cheaper than petrol) and quite luxurious, with air-conditioning and reclining seats. The drivers are helpful but likely to try to persuade you to go to places where they know they will get a commission.

Radio cabs belong to one of three firms: Quick Cabs (tel: 502888), GNTC (tel: 688688) and Ace Cabs (tel: 501502). Although based in Colombo they will pick up passengers out of Colombo if ordered in advance. The cars are metered, charging Rs24 per kilometre, with a flagfall charge of Rs28. Long trips out of Colombo which involve a return hire are calculated per kilometre, less a discount of as much as 45%. Quick Cab drivers wear ties, are not supposed to smoke in the car, and the cars are air-conditioned. Both companies accept payment by credit card. In Colombo, because of heavy traffic and peak demand, do not expect a radio cab as soon as you ask for it; better to give at least 30 minutes notice.

Self Drive

It is possible to hire a car to drive yourself, but not wise. The better driver you are, the more appalled you will be by the standard of driving, especially in rural areas where, even though the roads are less frenetic, drivers, cyclists and people launch themselves into the road without a glance either way, relying on fate to get them through, while you shoot through the windscreen because you've had to slam on the brakes. Seatbelts should always be worn. Driving yourself is going to add stress and spoil your enjoyment; better (and actually cheaper) to hire a vehicle with a driver.

The Avis Rent-A-Car licensee is Mackinnons Travels Ltd (4 Leyden Bastian Road, PO Box 945, Colombo 1; tel: 449632; fax: 941 447603).

Rates start at US$16 a day and rise to $625 for a month, unlimited kilometrage, air-conditioned car, including insurance, oil and maintenance. Drivers must have a national and an international licence which are used to obtain a temporary local driving permit. Minimum age is 23, and you have to leave your air ticket as security. Driving in Sri Lanka is on the left. The vehicles are prohibited from use in wildlife sanctuaries.

Motorbikes

Motorbikes can be hired, usually on an informal basis, in towns around the resort areas. Hikkaduwa is a popular place for bike hire. If you do rent one, be sure to check it thoroughly, perhaps with a test drive. As well as the fee (about Rs650 a day) you will be asked to leave your passport as security.

You will often see whole families on motorbikes with the father driving while a youngster sits on his lap, and the wife rides pillion with a couple of kids between the two of them. Crash helmets are compulsory for both driver and pillion rider.

Bicycles

Bicycles can be hired in the resort areas and are great for discovering what lies down the country lanes away from the beach, or for pedalling around Anuradhapura. Unfortunately, they are usually real bone shakers and, if they do have brakes, then something else will be wrong. Visitors who have brought their own bikes to Sri Lanka seem to fare pretty well, although taking a bike on a train in the guard's van involves a lot of bureaucracy.

By Air

Helicopter

There is a semi-scheduled helicopter service from and to the airport, introduced at the beginning of 1994, price US$20 one way. It is available by prior booking for a minimum of 15 passengers. There is a ticket counter in the arrivals hall (after customs clearance) at the airport. The helicopters use the helipad at the Airport Garden Hotel, five minutes drive by transfer coach from the airport. The lobby of the Lanka Oberoi Hotel is the Colombo check-in point. (Lankair, 104 Nawala Road, Colombo 5; tel: 589960; fax: 941 589968.)

A Bell Long Ranger 206 helicopter, five-seater luxury version, is available for charter at US$500 per flying hour, plus 5% tax. As both its doors can be removed it is suitable for professional photography. It is based at the domestic airfield at Ratmalana, south of Colombo. (John Keels Aviation, 4 Leyden Bastian Road, Colombo 1; tel: 448065, airport 633301; fax: 941 447603.)

Scheduled helicopter tours are operated on different days of the week from the west coast resorts to Kandy and the Uduwalawe wildlife park, starting at $175 per person. The aircraft are luxury Russian 24 seaters which are also available for airport transfers and private charters. (Ace Airways, Cargills Building, 30 Sir Baron Jayatilaka Mawatha, Colombo 1; tel: 447239; fax: 941 436382.)

Sky Cabs

A 45-minute scenic flight over beaches, paddy fields, plantations, villages and temples for a maximum of three passengers in a single-engine fixed wing aircraft (Cessna 177) or twin-engine Piper Aztec, costs $49 per person. Other flights operated by Sky Cabs from their base at the airport at Ratmalana are an hour flight to and around Adam's Peak ($80 per person), to Yala wildlife park with a half-day safari, at $195 per person, and to Galle with city tour and time on Unawatuna beach for $120 per person. There are also packages to Sigiriya and Trincomalee. (Sky Cabs Ltd, PO Box 683, Colombo; tel: 633332; fax: 941 430203.)

By Sea

A novel way of travelling around Sri Lanka is to cruise by cargo passenger ship from Colombo to Trincomalee and back, or go by sea one way and the other by train. The *Mercs Habarana* is a cargo vessel with two suites, one double cabin and two single cabins (priced from Rs2,500 per person per day), which takes six days for the round voyage, three days for the half-voyage. Accommodation, linen, three meals a day, coffee/tea, arranging of port permits, insurance up to Rs250,000 and transport to/from the vessel in Colombo, is included in the cost. The ship can be used as a hotel during its two days in Trincomalee. (Mercantile Shipping Company Ltd, 108 Aluthmawatha Road, Colombo 15; tel: 331793; fax: 941 331799.)

Vintage Vehicles

Motorcars over 40 years old are still driven on Sri Lanka's roads, especially in rural districts where they are often found outside country railway stations as taxis. Morris Minors are quite common but classic cars such as Austins and Rileys are more likely to be owned by enthusiasts, while cars in the vintage group come out only for rallies.

British planters and wealthy Ceylonese brought the first motorcars to the island. There were several Daimlers and Rolls-Royces as well as cars with names that conjure up the 1920s, such as Napier and Graham Paige (now seen in rallies). The oldest motor vehicles in running condition are an Albion Murray lorry with solid tyres dating from 1908, and a small open two-seater Paltney car registered in 1913. A Robey steam lorry from the 1920s and an open-sided Chevrolet bus of 1935 vintage also take part in rallies.

The value of vintage and classic cars is appreciated by Sri Lankan enthusiasts who hunt in tea plantations and jungles of the interior for vehicles to restore. Their export is forbidden by law so it is possible to see priceless 1920s Mercedes-Benz, Daimlers and Austin Sevens, as well as BSA motorbikes, on the road, not in museums.

A vintage motorcar is one with a registration number preceded by a letter of the alphabet from A to Z. The letter indicates where the car was registered, not the year. Colombo was assigned the letter C, while X and Y indicate all-island registration. The system was changed in the 1930s.

Classic cars are those registered between then and 1950. A pair of letters, such as CE, CY or EN, derived from Sri Lanka's colonial name of Ceylon, was used in front of numbers for registration. A Vintage Car Owners' Club and a Classic Car Owners' Club are both very active (see page 175).

Chapter Four

Good Training

Ticketing

Buying a ticket to ride in Sri Lanka is simple: you turn up at the station at least ten minutes before the train is scheduled to depart (or earlier if you are boarding at its originating station), go to the counter for 2nd or 3rd class travel (there may be a short queue), pay your money and collect your ticket.

Anyone who visits Sri Lanka after travelling by train in India with its compulsory reservation system will appreciate this simplicity since there is no need to spend hours, days before your journey, queuing for reservations.

Advance Reservations

Reservations up to ten days in advance can only be made on a few trains and then only for sleeper accommodation or for a seat in an observation saloon, or on the Intercity Express. Sleeping accommodation (sleeperettes, not berths) is actually available on day trains which have been rescheduled.

Train Number	Name	Routing	Reserved Accommodation
05	Podi Menike	Fort-Badulla	Observation saloon
06	Podi Menike	Badulla-Fort	Observation saloon
09	Intercity	Fort-Kandy ⎱	Observation saloon and
10	Intercity	Kandy-Fort ⎰	all seats (2nd class)
15	Udarata Menike	Fort-Badulla	Observation saloon
16	Udarata Menike	Badulla-Fort	Observation saloon
29	Intercity	Fort-Kandy ⎱	Observation saloon and
30	Intercity	Kandy-Fort ⎰	all seats (2nd class)
45	Night Mail	Fort-Badulla	1st class berths 2nd & 3rd sleeperettes
46	Night Mail	Badulla-Fort	1st class berths 2nd & 3rd sleeperettes
77	Yal Devi	Fort-Vavuniya	2nd & 3rd sleeperettes
78	Yal Devi	Vavuniya-Fort	2nd & 3rd sleeperettes
79	Udaya Devi	Fort-Batticaloa	2nd & 3rd sleeperettes
80	Udaya Devi	Batticaloa-Fort	2nd & 3rd sleeperettes
81	Express	Fort-Trincomalee	2nd & 3rd sleeperettes

Train Number	Name	Routing	Reserved Accommodation
82	Express	Trincomalee-Fort	2nd & 3rd sleeperettes
89	Night Mail	Fort-Vavuniya	1st class berths
			2nd & 3rd sleeperettes
90	Night Mail	Vavuniya-Fort	1st class berths
			2nd & 3rd sleeperettes
58	Ruhunu Kumari	Maradana-Matara	2nd class saloon
59	Ruhunu Kumari	Matara-Maradana	2nd class saloon

NOTE: Fort and Maradana are the main stations in Colombo.

The berth reservations offices (this is not where you reserve for Kandy, but only for long-distance trains) is at Colombo Fort station. Not a computer in sight, only ledgers for passengers' names, a copy of each page being given to the train guard at the time of travel. Availability of seats/berths is chalked up on a blackboard on a wall of the office. At peak times of travel, reservations could be hard to get and you may have to start queuing outside before 0830 (opening time) on the first day of the ten-day advance booking period. For instance, if you want to travel on the 23rd, the first chance of making a reservation is on the 12th (day of travel plus ten days in advance). There is no waiting list procedure.

The office is in the front of the station, with access from the forecourt, to the left as you face the station.

Berth Reservation Office

Counter A: Northern Line
Counter B: Main Line
Counter C: Trincomalee/Batticaloa
Counter D: Northern 3rd class sleeperettes

Opening hours are 0830-1530 daily with lunch at 1230-1300; Sundays and holidays 0830-1200.

I began queuing at 0810 one morning; fortunately the station has an awning which provides shade. There were 12 people in front of me and I was convinced they all wanted berths on the train I was hoping to travel on, so I wondered what to do. At 0825, a clerk came and divided the queue to those going to Badulla on the left side of the door and those for Batticaloa on the right.

At 0830 the door opened and Badulla passengers were directed to counter B; Batticaloa people to counter C. I was second in the line and had prepared for my request by writing down on a scrap of paper the date of travel, the train time and its number, and the number and class of berths required with the passengers' names. I gave this to the clerk who consulted his ledgers and began to enter all the names, then changed it to my name and 'party of four'. My return reservation request was also accepted, even though it was 12 days before the date of travel.

The details were passed by the ledger clerk to the ticketing clerk who gave me a cardboard train ticket and a berth ticket for each passenger for the journey from Colombo, and a cardboard seat ticket for each passenger, and a pink chit for four passengers reservation for the return journey, all with berth or seat numbers marked.

The process did not take long because I knew the train details and had everything written down so the clerk could understand. However, there are no reservation request forms as in India, so take along your own chit.

Reservations to Colombo can be made from the station served by the train on which you want to travel; the same advance period applies. If the station does not have a quota of berths or seats, or if it is exhausted, a message can be sent to Colombo. Or you can turn up at the station when you want to travel and see if there is accommodation not taken up that you can have. Sometimes stationmasters can be very helpful in such circumstances.

In theory, reservations can be made from outstations not served by the train on which you want to travel, but since this is subject to space availability — and reserved accommodation is very limited — it is unlikely to be successful. Queuing in Colombo or at your originating station on the first day of the advance period is the surest method.

Reservations are necessary to travel in some kind of comfort on night mails but for daytime trains (except Intercity) there are seats that are not reservable so early arrival at the originating station could make sure you bag one.

Intercity

Seats on Intercity trains from Colombo to Kandy can be reserved at the ticket counter (number 17) which has its sales window open on to the forecourt. Reservations may be made up to ten days in advance and on a 'space available' basis on the day of travel. Reservations for the return journey up to 14 days from arrival date can also be made there. Round-trip tickets purchased in this manner show a saving of 50% over two separate one-way tickets. Reservation tickets and train tickets are issued by the same clerk at the same counter.

Reservations cannot be made by telephone. Tickets are marked with train number, coach number, seat number and date of travel.

The train is all 2nd class apart from an observation saloon at the end of the train, which is 1st class. It is possible to upgrade a 2nd class ticket to sit in the observation saloon.

The reservation counter at Colombo Fort station is open 0600-1700, closed 1430-1535.

Sometimes, if there are no reservations available in Colombo for the return journey from Kandy to Colombo, it is possible to make the return reservation when you get to Kandy, but this is charged as two one-way fares, instead of the return fare. The return fare is applicable only if the return journey is within ten days of making the outward journey.

Other Trains

Second class seats can be reserved on the *Ruhunu Kumari* express from Colombo to Matara and back. At Fort station (counter number 14) you can make a reservation and buy a ticket from 0900 on the day of travel for the train which departs at 1545. You will be given a separate cardboard ticket showing the seat number and date of travel. If you board the train en route and there is a seat available, payment of the reservation fee of Rs15 to the guard will enable you to travel in the special 2nd class carriage. He will give you a pink reservation chit as receipt.

Reservation fees — charged in addition to the ticket price — are:

1st class sleeping berth	Rs50
Seat in air-conditioned coach	Rs50
Seat in observation saloon	Rs35
2nd class sleeping berth	Rs30
2nd class sleeperette	Rs15
2nd class reserved seat	Rs15
3rd class sleeperette	Rs12
3rd class reserved seat	Rs12

Special Reservations

For a large group, a reserved compartment can be booked through the commercial superintendent. The cost is Rs10 per 2nd class seat and Rs8 per 3rd class seat.

Platform Ticket

To be on any railway station you are supposed to have a platform ticket, particularly important when you try to leave the station. While this is necessary at major stations like Colombo Fort and Maradana and Galle, it is not possible to enforce this rule where people can wander on and off a platform from the railway track. Platform tickets (Rs1.50) are sold at ordinary ticket counters.

Collectors of platform tickets should try to buy them at rural stations.

In March 1994 I saw someone issued a platform ticket at Homagama station (on the Kelani Valley Line) that must have been printed nearly 50 years before. It was entirely in English and gave the original price as 5 cents. The current platform tickets are in three languages and do not give the name of the issuing station in English, as the old ones do.

Ticketless Travel

In my innocence I once offered a seat to a friend I met on the train so he could travel with me in 2nd class. He only had a 3rd class ticket and I expected to be able to pay the difference to upgrade his ticket. When the railway police ticket checkers came along, I explained what I wanted to do. To my horror, my friend was issued with a summons for travelling in 2nd class on a 3rd class ticket and, at our destination, I had to pay a fine of Rs400 on his behalf to the stationmaster.

Learn from my expensive generosity. In theory, it is possible to pay excess fares on the train but only to the guard of the train (not to the railway police who are the travelling ticket checkers). If you want to upgrade your ticket, or anyone else's, seek out the guard (he never leaves his van to check tickets unless there is a reserved passenger compartment as part of his coach). He will issue a pink excess fare book ticket for the difference.

The railway police who do the ticket checking receive a commission, so they are naturally keen to do their duty. On the other hand this does give them a certain power of discretion and they may waive the fine of someone obviously too poor who has made a genuine mistake by sitting in the wrong coach.

Fines for ticketless, or wrong ticket, travelling, are:
Ticketless in 1st class — Rs400 plus double journey fare
Ticketless in 2nd class — Rs300 plus double journey fare
Ticketless in 3rd class — Rs200 plus double journey fare.
Fine for pulling communication brake chain: Rs20.

Ticket Nipping

From regulations:
'For ticket examining and collecting purposes, stations are provided with ticket nippers of two kinds, viz: (1) a nipper to cut off a triangular piece out of a ticket, indicating that it had been examined, (2) a cancellation nipper punching two small holes.

When nipping tickets the ticket must be held with the left hand with the back of the ticket turned up, and the nipper must be held with the right hand, and pressed firmly cutting a V-shaped bit off the edge.'

Ticket Inspection

At the major stations, you should show your ticket before going on to the platform. On board the train it will be checked either by the railway police looking for ticketless travellers, or by the berth or reservation car attendant, or by the guard if it is a saloon attached to the guard's van. You should surrender your ticket when leaving the platform. Sometimes, if you try to exit from the end of the platform to take a short cut across the railway line, there will be a ticket collector there, too, hiding behind a bush.

Cancellation

If you miss the train for which you have bought a ticket and want to get a refund, this can usually be done at the station where the ticket was purchased, but the ticket must be surrendered to the stationmaster within 60 minutes after the departure of the train. A commission of 25% will be charged as the cancellation fee. Refunds on tickets with a value of less than Rs10 will not be made.

Refunds on tickets with reservation for sleeping berths, sleeperettes, etc, are as follows:

— If the cancellation is less than six hours before the time of departure of train, no refunds will be made

— if the cancellation is over six hours but less than 48 hours, the refund will be made only on the travel ticket, less 25% commission

— if the cancellation is over 48 hours, the value of both travel ticket and reservation ticket less 25% commission will be made.

Refunds on partly used tickets will be made by the commercial superintendent. You will need a certificate of non-use, obtainable from the stationmaster where you terminated the journey and surrendered the ticket.

Lost Tickets

No refunds or duplicate tickets will be issued for lost tickets, so make sure your advance reservation tickets are kept in a safe place.

Breaking the Journey

If you want to break the journey, say from Galle to Anuradhapura with a break in Colombo, this is possible as long as the total distance from origin to destination is over 80km. One stop off on the way is permitted for a maximum of 24 hours. However, if you have a reservation to your original destination, that will be forfeited and you would have to make another reservation and pay for it again. You should get your travel ticket endorsed by the stationmaster where you break the journey, so that you are allowed to use it again. The saving in getting a through ticket instead of two journey tickets is no more than a rupee or two, and might not be worth the trouble.

Fares

By international standards the fares charged for travelling by train in Sri Lanka are low indeed, but not for residents. Fares on suburban routes are based on 21 cents a kilometre (3rd class); on long-distance routes it is 17 cents a kilometre. Fares for 2nd class travel are calculated at 47 cents per kilometre; for 1st class at 82 cents per kilometre.

The minimum charge for a journey in 3rd class is Rs2, for 2nd class Rs3, and in 1st class, Rs4.

Fares to major destinations from Colombo Fort station are (in rupees):

To:	1st class	2nd class	3rd class
Anuradhapura	168.25	96.50	35.00
Avissawella	51.00	29.25	13.25
Badulla	240.50	137.75	50.00
Bandarawela	213.25	122.25	44.25
Batticaloa	287.00	164.50	59.50
Bentota	50.25	28.75	10.50
Galle	93.50	53.75	19.50
Hatton	143.50	82.25	25.75
Hikkaduwa	78.75	45.25	16.50
Kalutara	34.50	19.75	8.50
Kandy	99.25	57.00	20.75
Katunayake Airport	28.00	16.00	7.25
Kurunegala	78.75	45.25	16.50
Matale	122.25	70.25	25.50
Matara	128.75	74.00	26.75
Nanu Oya	170.75	98.00	35.50
Negombo	32.00	18.50	8.25
Polgahawela	60.75	35.00	12.75
Polonnaruwa	213.25	122.25	44.25
Trincomalee	243.75	139.75	50.50
Vavuniya	209.25	120.00	43.50

The extras charged on top of the journey fares for seat or berth reservations are given on page 68. Return fares, where they are available, such as for journeys where reserved accommodation is booked, are double the single fares. The fare on the Intercity Express between Colombo and Kandy is: Rs60 one way, and Rs90 for a return journey undertaken within ten days of the outward journey.

Children under three years of age travel free: children aged between three and 12 pay half fare.

Network Travel Card

In the pipeline for a long time is something likely to be called a Tourist Green Card Ticket, if it is ever produced. It would be valid for 14 days for unlimited travel in 2nd class anywhere in Sri Lanka, sold only to foreign passport holders. Seat and berth reservation charges would be extra.

Luggage

All trains have overhead racks where luggage can be stored. There is usually space under the seat for luggage storage, too, possibly safer if you are worried about your bag being lifted from the overhead rack while you are dozing.

Officially, luggage must not obstruct corridors or doorways. There is a free baggage allowance per adult (half the amount for children with half tickets; no allowance for children below three years of age):

1st class   35kg
2nd class   30kg
3rd class   20kg

Backpacks are anti-social as items of luggage if wielded carelessly in a crowded train carriage. Their size limits their value if they cannot be stored in the space available in the luggage rack or under the seat. It also makes them inconvenient when you are trying to board — or move along the vestibule of — a crowded train. The best luggage for rail travel is a small suitcase with firm sides that can lie flat on a rack, or a holdall that can be carried with a shoulder strap.

Instead of carrying all the luggage you have with you on every journey, it would be worthwhile finding a base to leave the mother bag during your rail journeys and take only a baby bag with you. This is one of the advantages of basing yourself at a major hotel in Colombo since they have left luggage rooms. There is a left luggage office at Colombo Fort station, but it seems to be used as a thoroughfare from platform to forecourt so may not be all that secure for a long period.

Train Types

Intercity Express

The Intercity Express linking Colombo and Kandy is the railways' prestige scheduled service. The carriages, built in Romania, have a maroon and orange livery with bright, cream interior decor and seats upholstered in red rexine. The seats are fixed and somewhat hard but the journey is fast and at times passengers have to cling to the metal brackets to avoid being jolted out. All seats are reservable, 2nd class, and, in theory, there should not be any interlopers on board.

The carriages are marked with a letter of the alphabet and seats have their numbers on the wall panel above them. Each carriage has 56 seats in two sections, with two toilets in the centre of the carriage dividing the sections. The seat number is shown on the journey ticket, together with the carriage number.

Seats are in pairs with the numbering starting with the left side pair, 1-14, then continuing with the right side pair, 15-28; in the second section, the left side pairs are numbered 29-42, the right side pairs 43-56. This means that window seats are the odd numbers 1-41, and even numbers 16-56. For views, the best seats for the ride to Kandy are on the right, facing the engine; on the left facing the engine on the way back. However, there is no way of knowing which way the seats will be facing so insisting on, say, seat number 28 for the trip to Kandy only gives a 50/50 chance of being on the right side. The pair of seats at the end of each carriage face each other, which means you will be playing kneesy with the passengers sitting opposite you.

The toilets are western style and are watered and disinfected enthusiastically before the start of the first journey of the day. The carriages have fans, not air conditioning, and windows which slide upwards for uninterrupted views of the lush scenery.

Each train has an observation saloon, with 24 seats, at its rear, with a premium of Rs35 payable over the usual fare. Seat numbering changes according to the model. While some passengers prefer the end seat facing the huge window giving a panoramic view of all that the train passes, these can be hot and shadeless if the sun is shining.

When these trains were introduced there was great excitement about the loudspeaker system which allowed taped music to be played throughout the two-and-a-half-hour journey. It was excruciating. Mercifully, the practice seems to have been abandoned, or perhaps the tape recorders no longer work.

There is a buffet car on the train with soft drinks and short eats. When business is slack, a steward passes along the vestibule serving at seats and popping each item into a plastic bag with tongs before handing it over. There are no drop down tables attached to the seats.

The Intercity express usually leaves from platform 2 at Fort station. If you get there early you will see it being parked halfway up the platform to enable the shunting engine that brings it in to change tracks at the platform's buffer end.

The current timetable for the Intercity service:

Train	D: Fort	A: Kandy	Train	D: Kandy	A: Fort
9	0655 ⟶	0930	30	0630 ⟶	0900
29	1535 ⟶	1805	10	1500 ⟶	1730

The train makes only one scheduled stop in both directions, at Peradeniya. If other trains are running late and blocking the single-line track ahead of it, it sometimes makes unscheduled stops to wait for the line to clear.

Express Passenger

The trains which serve the main lines as expresses are a combination of old and new carriages, usually Romanian-made. They all have vestibules linking the carriages and seats which are fixed, although some recline slightly and some have arm rests which can be raised to squeeze in a third passenger in a 2nd class pair.

All scheduled trains (except Intercity) have unreserved 3rd class seats. In old carriages the seats are wooden benches for two on one side and for three on the other. These are actually preferable to the new 3rd class carriages which have rexine covered bench seats which get sticky in the heat.

Seats in 2nd class are upholstered in a grubby brown or red rexine with the Sri Lanka Railways insignia embossed on them. They are in pairs with the end pair facing each other (more knee touching). One such pair is usually designated by a sign above it as reserved for clergy. Avoid those seats because if a monk gets on he is entitled to sit there.

Main passenger expresses have a buffet car but no seatside service. The buffet car separates 2nd and 3rd class and, if the train is full, will be packed with passengers. On some trains running during the day, reservation is possible both in 2nd and 3rd class sleeperettes, which are seats that recline slightly.

Slow Passenger

Slow passenger trains are of two types, both stopping at every station, including ones you will not know are there. One has the same kind of carriages as express trains, but might be older, and will be 3rd class only. The other ones are the 'local' trains which usually serve part of a line, such as Alutgama to Galle or Nawalapitiya to Kandy, instead of the whole line. These are the old 'power set' coaches, trains that can be driven from either end and have the power car as part of a passenger carriage, instead of a separate locomotive.

The carriages have wooden interiors and floors with pairs of conservatory-style wooden doors that open inwards. Seats are park-bench design, with wooden slats, and run the length of the carriage instead of widthwise. The windows are small, in wooden casements, and can be opened by sliding them upwards. The carriages are spacious, built for standing passengers, and have wooden rails down the centre for passengers to cling to when the train picks up speed, which it often does as, despite their age, power sets are nippy.

Travelling on a local, possibly standing in the open doorway, is much more fun than a slow passenger train, or even a fast one since you have a chance to see the scenery and observe the rural way of life at close quarters. At peak hours, however, such as when schoolchildren and office workers are travelling, they can get very crowded. There is no vestibule and only some have toilets.

Power Sets

This term refers to the spanking new, orange and grey liveried trains first introduced in 1991, built in Japan and Korea. The power car is part of the train, hence the term power set, and the trains can be driven from either end. The carriages have sliding doors, and windows which can be raised and kept open. They also have fans.

The interior is very bright, a contrast to the old power sets, with light grey panelling and orange fibreglass seats which run lengthwise. The fittings are in metal with straps for standing passengers to hold. While they do not have the charm of the older local trains, they make all-station travelling much brighter, like being a commuter on a tropical version of London's Metropolitan line.

There is no link between carriages and no toilet. In rush hours they are packed since they run on the busiest suburban lines. As in Bombay's suburban railway, young passengers dangle recklessly from the outside of the trains and some even perch on the roof.

Hitachi

The all air-conditioned train used on special occasions is called the Hitachi in Sri Lanka, after its maker's name. In operation since 1970, it has retained its spruce appearance through not being used much, except on charter. Compared with all other trains in Sri Lanka it is very luxurious, with air conditioning, comfortable reclining seats which can be turned to face either way, or to the window, sliding doors between the vestibuled carriages, and passenger entrance doors that remain closed during the journey.

Occasionally it is chartered by the Colombo Hilton Hotel, becoming the 'Colombo Hilton On Wheels', with catering and entertainment on board as lavish as anything provided in the hotel itself.

Colombo to Jaffna is a trip that you will find,
By air-conditioned Hitachi, distance you won't mind,
To refresh you there is always Palmyrah Toddy,
Vitamin packed, it's cool and sweet and good for your body.
Air-conditioned Hitachi's luxurious tourist train,

Blazing sun or biting wind or even monsoon rain,
She will take you there and back in comfort of your choice,
You won't even notice that there's hardly any noise.

from the May 1981 timetable

Viceroy Special

The Viceroy Special makes regular trips from Alutgama and Colombo to Kandy and back as part of a package deal marketed by the travel agents who charter the train. The package usually includes a visit to the elephant orphanage at Pinnawela (reached by tour bus from Rambukkana station) and a tour of Kandy, as well as meals on the train and hotel accommodation with meals. It is not possible to buy a ticket just to travel on the Viceroy Special, but it is always worth contacting J F Tours & Travels (tel: 587996; fax: 941 580507) in case they can suggest something. They can also give the times the train will be at certain stations if you want to photograph it.

In an attempt to resuscitate the tourist industry after the disturbances of 1983, the Ceylon Tourist Board invited several travel agents to visit Sri Lanka. One of them was a rail enthusiast from Britain, Cliff Jones, who, when he saw some steam engines lying idle in the rail yards, realized this was a novel attraction for visitors. Jones did research and promoted the project in the UK and with the Sri Lankan government, while local tour operator Hemasiri Fernando, through his company J F Tours and Travels and in cooperation with the then general manager of the railways, Mr G P S Weerasooriya, set to work to revive steam in Sri Lanka.

The result was the inaugural run on February 2 1986 of the train named Viceroy Special. Since then a journey on the Viceroy has become a must for tourists who like travelling on a steam train, and also for those who want an organized visit to Kandy by rail.

The Viceroy Special consists of four coaches, all painted in the bright red livery of the former Ceylon Government Railways, and outlined in gold with the CGR crest displayed on body panels. The first coach is the power car and crew quarters. The second is an air-conditioned coach with reclining seats in pairs for 24 passengers and two western-style toilets with wooden seats (restored fittings). There is a dining car (no air-conditioning) where smokers congregate and which has a bar (the only one on a train in Sri Lanka), galley and dining tables, although meals are served to passengers on tables at their seats. The last carriage is another air-conditioned coach for 24 passengers. Both coaches have observation windows and have been restored from wooden carriages with many of the original fittings, such as old-fashioned fans.

Four steam engines, all British built, have been brought out of retirement to pull the Viceroy Special. The main one, Sir Thomas Maitland, number 251, was built in 1928, the oldest, number 213, in 1922, number 240 in 1927 and the most recent, number 340, in 1945.

Special Trains

Mail Trains

The transport of letters to all stations between Colombo and Galle, Kandy and Badulla is done by travelling post offices attached to trains, with mail actually being sorted on board. It is delivered in bags to postmen waiting at the stations (see page 42).

Educational Trains

In 1991, a 75-year old railway carriage was refurbished as a classroom, complete with tables, chairs, lights, blackboard and television. The idea was that the carriage should be taken to rural areas to promote the learning of English. Sponsors of the classroom on wheels were John Holland International, manufacturers of concrete railway sleepers, and the Rotary Club of Colombo West, in conjunction with the railways.

On December 17 1993, at Gampaha railway station, another mobile classroom was launched. The Mobile Science and Technology Exhibition was set up in a train with the intention of popularizing science and technology for children and adults. It was planned that the train would tour continuously for three years, holding an exhibition in each venue for six days. It was organized by the Ministry of Science and Technology, the Sri Lanka Association for the Advancement of Science, Sri Lanka Railways and the Bank of Ceylon.

Class Distinction

1st Class

There are three types of 1st class accommodation, which is only found on long-distance trains: observation saloons, air-conditioned coaches and sleeping berths.

Observation saloons have seats in pairs and all are reservable in advance for an extra Rs35 over the 1st class fare. The fee is payable even if you don't reserve in advance but occupy one on the journey. The guard will collect the extra and issue an excess fare book ticket.

Observation cars are located at the rear of a train although on some sectors they might be behind the engine until the engine is put back at the front of the train. They all have wide windows that open, fans, reclining seats in pairs, and drop-down tables. The saloon has a toilet between it and the guard's van, and to get to the rest of the train you must pass through the guard's van.

Total capacity is either 20 or 24. The seat numbering system is not consistent so it is impossible to know which are the window or rear seats for the best views. Even the booking clerk won't know. In railway speak, these carriages are known as OFVs — Observation First (class) Vans.

In theory no vendors or interlopers are allowed in 1st class but since passengers are usually in a holiday mood there could be a party — rather than a peaceful — atmosphere. Once I found an old lady had comfortably installed herself on the floor in the lobby outside the sole toilet, making entry into it difficult. When I complained to the guard, he was unimpressed. 'She's not in your seat, is she?'

An air-conditioned carriage is sometimes attached to major trains, and there is a supplement of Rs50 to pay over the 1st class fare for the privilege of sitting in it. The carriage has reclining seats in pairs and is comfortable enough although it is gloomy and the atmosphere induces drowsiness, especially as the windows (usually grimy) are necessarily kept closed.

There are two types of 1st class sleeping carriage in use, either Indian or the newer Romanian makes. When you first enter one, you think how wonderful it is (especially compared with India's 1st class cabins). There are only two-berth coupés (six of them) and each has access to a toilet.

The bunks, upper and lower, will be made up with sheet and pillow, with a blanket and second sheet tucked under the pillow in case of need.

Disenchantment begins when the person who is to share the tiny cabin with you tries to get in and you realize, because of the toilet, that the coupé is quite small, with only about 60cm space between bunks and the toilet wall. The toilet is not actually exclusive since it also serves the adjoining coupé. It thus has two access doors (one from each coupé) and an ingenious gadget that locks both doors simultaneously from within. It is western in style, and toilet paper is provided.

In the Indian-made coupés the cabin itself has a mirror but no light above it, only the main one behind, and a water jug and glass on the ledge. A sign reads: NOT TO FILL WASHBASIN FULL, which would be difficult since there is never a plug.

The bunks fold back to the wall, or would do if the fittings worked. Since these carriages are used only for overnight travel, no one folds them back. This means having to sit hunched up and to take great care not to bang your head on the upper bunk when moving about.

There is a lack of places to put things. A fold-up shelf has been added to the exterior toilet wall but there are no pockets for belongings and only one hook, high up on the wall. There is no night light, just two strip lights, although there are reading lights which rarely work. There are two ashtrays and flop-down supports to get into the upper bunk. The light switches and controls for the two viciously whirring fans are above the lower bunk.

The newer (1989) 1st class coaches come from Romania and are impressive to look at, with natural-colour wood louvres and arborite panelling, and buff corduroy upholstery. The upper berth, suspended by removable chains from the ceiling, folds down to form the backrest for the lower berth which can be used as a comfortable settee during day time travel, facing the toilet door.

There is a wide picture window which can be raised completely, giving a wonderful panorama of the passing scene. The window is protected by an outer metal screen but do not, as I did, leave the window open at night and the screen closed because rain manages to penetrate the ventilation slits.

There is one ashtray in the cabin, below the window. At upper berth height there is one small fan with its control switch and also the light switch for the toilet, above the toilet door. The corner of the cabin contains a washbasin concealed under a raisable top, with a rubbish bin under it. Above it is a cupboard which has a mirror inside. There are some shelves in this unit, and space for luggage under it. Because there are no hoops for glasses or a water jug, as in Indian models, none are provided.

The cabin light control is above the sliding door. There are two wooden louvre screens which can be lowered to give an opening on to the carriage's corridor. The bunks each have a light at the corridor end of the cabin (not at the window side as in the Indian models), which means the bunks are made up with the pillows by the corridor side instead of at the window side, which is where the fan is. There is a small pouch for papers by each bunk and some clothes hooks. There is a floor carpet and a ladder, padlocked to the wall, to reach the upper bunk. A useful fitting is a stool which revolves.

The toilet has two doors, one from each of the two cabins sharing it, but there is no lock on the cabin side of the door which means that someone could enter your cabin through the toilet from the neighbouring cabin. Inside the toilet, the bolt on one door, thanks to a system of levers, locks the other access door at the same time. The fittings are aluminium with those annoying taps which require you to push and wait, and wait, for water to flow.

There are two doors at the end of each coach and these are kept locked at night by the attendant. The corridor windows in the Romanian-built coaches raise upwards to open. Some of them are fixed with only a small fanlight opening. Curiously, the attendant's pull-down seat is in the corridor, not at the end of it, so when he is using it, movement along the corridor is restricted.

While the 1st and 2nd class sleeper coaches are linked by a vestibule, with the door between them closed at night, there is no vestibule link with the rest of the train, hence it is impossible to get to the buffet car.

2nd Class

For overnight travel, the 2nd class sleeping berths are good value. However their use was discontinued early in 1994 and it is not known if they will be returned to service.

Both Indian and Romanian coaches have 14 two-berth coupés with a toilet at each end of the carriage. Because they do not have a toilet between them, the coupés seem to have more space then the 1st class ones. The other difference is that nothing extra is provided: no bedding or pillow. Passengers usually sleep in their travelling clothes anyway.

Actually, sleep in either 1st or 2nd class is not easy because of the continual stopping and starting (there are 31 scheduled stops during the 12-hour journey by night mail from Colombo to Badulla), plus shunting on loops while waiting for the single line to clear.

It is even less comfortable in the 2nd class sleeperettes (Rs15 extra), which are reclining seats in pairs in carriages where the light shines all night and people pass up and down the vestibule, if there is any space to pass.

On the *Ruhunu Kumari* running between Colombo and Matara, seats can be reserved (Rs15) in the 2nd class section in the guard's van, either in advance of travel or on a space-available basis on board. There are no observation windows but the advantages are in having a seat in an otherwise crowded train, and no interlopers.

Ordinary 2nd class accommodation depends on the train. Carriages on the main trains are made in Romania. They are lighter than those made in India and roll a lot, making walking down the aisle with a cup of tea impossible. In 2nd class, the seating layout is 2 by 2, with 28 seats in each compartment. The seats all face the same direction except for two pairs of seats at one end of the compartment which face all the others. These usually have a stencilled notice in Sinhala, Tamil and English saying they are reserved for clergy.

Seats are comfortable with arm rests (which can be raised) and plenty of leg room. They can be reserved during a passenger's absence by placing something on the seat; even a handkerchief is sufficient to denote that it is occupied.

There are two 2nd class compartments to a carriage with two toilets in between them. The toilets give a choice of western or eastern positions. They are usually corroded and very basic. They have washbasins with water activated by a foot pump, or by pushing a button for a long time.

Windows in the compartments are the casement type, which have to be pushed up and secured with catches at the sides to remain open. At the first sign of rain, passengers close the windows and the compartment rapidly becomes very stuffy. There are two ceiling fans and strip lights which are always on. Controls for the fans are in the compartment.

The seats are upholstered in fawn rexine with a motif that I thought represented the letters CGR for Ceylon Government Railway. I wasn't far wrong. They are the Sinhala characters LA DU DE for *Lanka Dumriya Departamenthua*, which means Ceylon Government Railway.

There are no smoking signs in some carriages but they are cheerfully ignored, unless other passengers complain.

3rd Class

Sleeperettes in 3rd class (Rs12 extra) are similar to those in 2nd class (which is not actually a recommendation) and are inevitably more crowded.

Ordinary 3rd class accommodation ranges from the light, Romanian coaches with fans, a pleasant decor and solid upholstered seats to the wooden bench accommodation of a 'local'. Some trains have retired 2nd class carriages servings as 3rd class.

While seating in 3rd class is adequate, and fellow passengers will certainly add to the fun, the major trains are so crowded you may not even get a seat. Knowing this, many passengers buy 3rd class tickets and then stand in 2nd class, adding to the crush there.

Seating in 3rd class on express or slow trains is usually bench style in 2 × 3 layout, although as many people as possible squeeze on to the benches. Many commuter trains have only 3rd class and regulars bag the same seat every day and keep seats for their friends. Some passengers who meet and travel on the same train form their own social groups and, at holiday times, make special rail trips to the beach or hill country together.

Train Staff

A guard in uniform is usually the smartest dressed man on the train. He wears white trousers and a white shirt (and how he keeps them clean is a mystery) with a black tie, black shoes and a black tunic with chrome buttons and a black cap. He will carry a whistle and green and red flags.

Berth and reserved seat attendants are dressed in khaki suit, safari style. Their job is to check reservations and assign accommodation on a space-available basis for those without reservations; they are to be found only on long distance trains.

Ticket checkers are railway police, also in khaki uniforms with caps. They always patrol in groups, boarding a train when least expected.

Security

At Colombo, Galle, Kandy and some other stations, there used to be baggage searches by railway security before passengers were allowed on to the platforms. Foreigners were usually waved through without being checked. Since other stations had no check at all, and trains can be boarded anywhere they happen to stop, these checks were an inconvenience rather than effective security. Armed security guards travel on some trains. They are usually charming young men who jump off at each station to patrol before jumping on again, and resuming conversations with tourists.

Locals leave their bags unattended on their seats for ages, even at station stops, when everyone is leaping on and off, and no one touches them. Whether the bags of tourists would be ignored is uncertain, but likely.

As usual, the *Samudra Devi*, the office train that reaches Colombo just after eight every weekday morning, was packed when I boarded it at Bentota. I squeezed into a position by an open door and prepared to pass the whole journey standing in boredom.

Although I don't speak Sinhala, it was easy to guess that the group of commuters around me were talking about the stranger in their midst. They delegated someone to speak to me in English.

'Excuse me,' he said politely. 'Are you a tourist?'

'No, I live here.'

He looked a bit anxious. 'Then you speak Sinhala?'

'Oh yes,' I said with a smile. 'I understand perfectly everything you've been saying about me.'

There was a sudden silence as the people around me tried to recall just what they had been saying.

'It's all right,' I told them. 'That's my joke. I really didn't understand a word.'

They looked relieved and we settled down to a fine discussion — in English — and the 90-minute journey passed very quickly.

Another train, the *Ruhunu Kumari* express which goes to Colombo from Matara via Galle and the beach resorts of Hikkaduwa, Alutgama and Kalutara, looks like a tourist special every morning. Foreigners with their tans and beach shorts and armed with bottles of mineral water pack the 2nd class coaches. The smarter ones have discovered that for Rs15 extra they can travel in the reservation-only car at the back of the train.

One traveller from the UK wrote to the local press recently commenting on the train habits of Sri Lankans. 'They engaged in noisy, heated arguments which disturbed the peace and quiet of the journey. An endless stream of male persons kept moving up and down the aisle holding us in the glare of their stare. If the case was that these persons were going home from work, none had tired themselves working.'

Alas, although that visitor caught the train, he seems to have missed the points and gone off the rails completely. Perhaps he was annoyed his fellow passengers were speaking in Sinhala and he couldn't eavesdrop!

In Sri Lanka, rail passengers don't hide behind their newspapers in stuffy silence, they take the opportunity of getting to know their fellow travellers. So if you can't reserve a seat, then shed your reserve and stand with them. I bet those noisy, curious fellow passengers will be just as pleased as you.

from *Explore Sri Lanka*

Meals on Wheels

Meals on trains where there is a buffet car are generally limited to snacks such as short eats like Chinese rolls (a deep fried, battered length stuffed with fish or vegetable purée) and bread rolls with two incisions, one containg a piece of fried egg and another a slither of lettuce. I have seen lunch packets of rice and curry on sale, too. Tea or coffee is available, as are bottled soft drinks, but not usually mineral water. Up to the mid-1980s beer could be bought on trains but this facility does not exist at present.

Thambili

The golden shelled king coconut (*thambili*) is one of the most refreshing and nutrious drinks, on sale on trains and by the roadside. Experienced customers drink straight from the coconut, but the less adept will need a straw.

There is usually no shortage of snacks to be had on trains as freelance vendors pass along the vestibules selling packets of nuts, biscuits, chocolates, cigarettes and, on some coastal trains, deep fried prawns. Sometimes there is a chance to sip the water of a young coconut (*kurumba*).

Trains usually have the buffet car placed between the 2nd and 3rd class carriages. Purchases are made through a hatch in the glass panelled wall of a display cabinet which is at one end of the kitchen in the centre of the car. There are tables and chairs in both sections for customers, but these are often full if the train is crowded.

Tipping

In a commercial establishment a tip helps to reward and encourage good service; probably up to 5% of the bill (before the service charge and goverment tax are added) but give it directly to the person you want to reward. Three-wheeler and other taxi drivers would doubtless have overcharged you so there is no need to tip them at all, unless the fare is metered. Where a tip would be appreciated for a service rendered without a fee, generally Rs20 should be sufficient (but see page 88 about porters).

Opportunist characters and professionals such as snake charmers will expect a tip if you want to photograph them. Arrange the price first, like a modelling fee, but usually people are happy to pose and would not expect a tip.

It always amazes me how — when I'm standing in a crowded bus clutching a brief-case — a Sri Lankan sitting down will offer to hold the bag, and nurse it quite happily for the rest of the journey.

This respect for the luggage of other travellers led a Sri Lankan acquaintance of mine (we'll call him Nimal) into a curious situation recently.

Nimal was sitting in a train at Fort station waiting for it to depart when a young man placed a holdall on the empty seat next to him. He mumbled something which Nimal didn't hear — and disappeared.

Nimal assumed the man had used his bag to bag the seat as the train was crowded. The train started, but there was no sign of the bag's owner. Like any good Sri Lankan, Nimal kept his eye on the bag in case someone tried to remove it and claim the seat.

But then the ticket checkers came along and demanded to know where was the owner of the bag and did he have a 2nd class ticket. Nimal felt a little peeved, especially as he didn't know the man and it was 20 minutes since he had seen him. He explained what had happened.

'I know,' said one of the checkers. 'The fellow probably has a 3rd class ticket. He is waiting for us to pass through 2nd class and then he'll nip in and sit here.'

A checker stationed himself in the corridor, muttering threats of what would happen to the cheeky passenger when he returned. But he didn't come back.

Nimal was getting worried now, wondering what was in the bag. He expressed his concern to the patrol of ticket checkers when they returned form checking the whole train.

'It could be a bomb,' said a bright young spark.

Several passengers offered advice. 'Throw the bag out,' said one. 'Hand it over at the next station,' said another. Finally, the checker who thought it was a bomb decided to open it.

Gingerly he drew back the zipper. The more nervous passengers moved out of the carriage. Others craned forward to see. The checker reached in and drew out a pair of slippers. There was a collective sigh of relief.

But then he pulled out a package which, as he opened it, revealed a solenoid with red and black wires sticking out of it. Panic! People dashed from their seats and the ticket checker froze with this suspicious object in his hand. Nimal wished he had caught a bus instead.

'Hey,' said someone pushing past the people trying to leave. 'What are you doing with my bag?'

The man explained he had been in the pantry car having a tea and met some friends. The solenoid was part of the mechanism to light up a Buddha statue. And yes, he did have a 2nd class ticket.

For the rest of the journey, Nimal wondered why people were laughing at him. Hadn't they been scared, too? And he vows never to look after a stranger's bag again.

from *Explore Sri Lanka*

STATION FACILITIES

At major stations there are snack bars, usually run by independen
contractors who have leased them from the railways. At some stations
such as at Nawalapitiya, the service and the food is better than at others
Most of the snack bars are very basic. None of the licensed bars a
stations are functioning.

Some Stations with Snack Bars

Alutgama	Madawachchi
Anuradhapura	Maho
Badulla	Mihintale
Batticaloa	Moratuwa
Colombo Fort	Nanu Oya
Colombo Maradana	Nawalapitiya
Galle	Nugegoda
Gal Oya	Polgahawela
Gampaha	Polonnaruwa
Hatton	Rambukkana
Kandy	Trincomalee
Kekirawa	Veyangoda
	Wadduwa

Most stations have a lobby which is open to the station forecourt and
drive-up area, and the lobby gives access to the ticket window. Some
stations have their ticket counters on the central, island platform which
is reached by a footbridge over the lines. In many stations the ticket office
is also the stationmaster's control room and you can glimpse wonderfu
ancient contraptions through the counter window, like the red painted
box that controls access to the line and the corroded ticket dating machine

There will usually be a barrier and a gate on to the platform, where a
staff member will punch a passenger's ticket or collect tickets from
arriving passengers. Many stations have Gentlemen and Ladies
lavatories (so-named) in separate locations, sometimes with separate
lavatories for 1st or 2nd class and 3rd class passengers. Rest rooms do
not necessarily have toilets attached, since this is the local term for
waiting room rather than the American name for toilet. Rest rooms are
usually available for 1st or 2nd class passengers with a different one for
3rd class travellers, with a different standard of seating. There are also
separate rest rooms for men and women. Some of them have huge tables
which are used for sleeping on.

Platforms are usually quite long and the major stations have lots of
offices on the platforms for their various officials. Most stations have a

large signboard showing its name in Sinhala, Tamil and English. On longer platforms, these signs are placed at right angles to the track, with lettering on both sides, so they can be read by passengers in approaching or departing trains. Some show the station's height above sea level in metres and feet.

The beauty of a station depends on the stationmaster's enthusiasm and the support of his staff, and the passengers who use it. Some stations are pictures of charm, with potted plants, vines trailing along the roof, antique furniture and even a fish tank or an aviary. Others are desolate. From time to time there are projects to beautify stations and award prizes to the prettiest. One such project identified 147 station gardens.

The major stations have bookstalls, either on the platform or in the ticket lobby. Local papers can be bought there and student texts, but not much in the way of the latest paperbacks, so bring your own with you.

Stations with Bookstalls

Ambalangoda	Matara
Anuradhapura	Moratuwa
Batticaloa	Panadura
Colombo Fort	Polgahawela
Colombo Maradana	Polonnaruwa
Galle	Ragama
Gampaha	Trincomalee
Hatton	Vavuniya
Kalutara South	Veyangoda
Kandy	

Retiring Rooms

The institution of retiring rooms such as exists in India is not a feature of rail travel in Sri Lanka. In India, the railway retiring rooms are the first choice of rail passengers for a place to stay when arriving in a strange town, as rooms with clean linen and attached shower/toilet are available at remarkably low cost.

In Sri Lanka there are only a few stations with retiring rooms and they do not match their Indian counterparts in popularity or desirability. Rates are from Rs300 for a double, Rs150 single.

Stations with Retiring Rooms

Anuradhapura	Mihintale
Batticaloa	Polgahawela
Galle	Trincomalee
Kandy	

Porters

At Colombo Fort station there are some old chaps in black jackets and sarongs who scurry after any tourist they spot with luggage. Actually, they can be very useful in guiding a stranger to the right platform and they know every trick about getting a seat on what looks like a standing-room only train. There are also men in a uniform of khaki shirts and shorts who are genuine railway employees looking for some extra rupees by carrying luggage or advising travellers. I have found them very helpful; one even dashed out of the station and bought me a flask of brandy when I realized there was no bar on the night mail.

There is no official rate of payment and porters will probably ask for double what you give them. Try Rs10 or Rs20 according to what they have done for you. At other stations you will be lucky to get anyone to help you with luggage, unless someone is touting for a guesthouse.

COMPLAINTS

If you have a complaint, bring it to the notice of someone on the spot, the guard on the train or the stationmaster. For a major complaint, contact the Commercial Superintendent, General Manager's Office, Railway Headquarters, Maradana, Colombo 10; tel: 320109.

If you have something stolen, inform the railway police either on the train or at the next station where the train stops. They will advise about what to do. Report it to the local police, too, and get a copy of your entry if the item is insured so that you can support your claim.

SIGNALS

When the railways began in Sri Lanka, timetables were organized so that trains were run at long intervals to make sure they were kept well apart. Hand signalling with flags by day and with lamps by night was sufficient. Then Morse code was used to send messages about trains, especially those coming in the opposite direction on the single track.

The Tyer's Tablet Instrument introduced over 100 years ago has remained on single lines as an unchallenged safeguard against accidents. The line is divided into sections, known as blocks, and two instruments, one at each end, are electrically connected. The one at the start of the block releases the starting signal for a train only when the all clear is received from the instrument at the other end of the block.

The chief stationmaster at Nanu Oya, Mr P A Perera, demonstrated the method for me. At his station, the 'Tyer's Patent Train Tablet Apparatus', two bright red boxes with brass fittings, is linked with the neighbouring Ambala and Great Western stations. Mr Perera pushed a bell plunger on the box, spoke into the telephone (an old wind up one with mouthpiece, fixed to the wall and with a separate earpiece). He gave four beats with the plunger and asked for the tablet (the solid token). To acknowledge he gave four more beats which completed the contact, and then removed the tablet.

The tablet is placed in a leather pouch which is attached to a hoop. This is scooped out of the stationmaster's hand by the driver of the train as it races through the station. Before doing so, though, the driver drops off the tablet he received from the previous station. This is put by the stationmaster into the box for re-use. The train cannot move from the station without the tablet and the driver can only take the tablet if it has been released by the box: and that is only done when the block section is clear for the train to proceed.

Both the apparatus and the change over of tablets as a train passes through a station are impressive rail sights.

Also still in use are the semaphore signals connected by wire to the signal box, although colour light signals have been introduced in busy sections. When the semaphore signal is horizontal it means 'Danger' or 'Stop'; at a diagonal it means the line is clear. Two hands raised in the air by a railway worker also indicates danger; a single raised arm shows all is well.

LEVEL CROSSINGS

Very few level crossing gates are automatically operated. Most are bars — some made of bamboo — lowered in front of road traffic by gatekeepers. There are about 4,000 gatekeepers keeping vigil. When a train stops in the middle of nowhere, it could be because the gate has not been closed so the signal to proceed has not been given. There have been many accidents at level crossings.

DEATH BY TRAIN

The suicide rate in Sri Lanka is very high and placing one's head on the track in the path of an oncoming train frequently happens. So, too, do deaths through inattention. Since the track is used by many as a path or a short cut, and it takes a moving train a long time to brake to a complete halt, strollers on the line are often struck down when they do not heed the warning that a train is coming. Elephants, too, are occasional casualties.

Derailments are frequent although minor and usually without loss of life. Figures for the period 1977 to 1986 show an average of 300 derailments a year. In the same period, 32 elephants were killed by trains.

Chapter Five

Past, Present, Future and Steam

History of the Railways

The idea of building a railway to Kandy was first mooted by the newly formed Ceylon Railway Company in 1845. Then a bullock cart averaged almost 12 days to make the tedious journey of 115km (72 miles) from Colombo to Kandy, climbing from sea level to 488m (1,602ft). It was estimated in 1847 that about 79,000 cart trips were made on the journey, evidence of how a railway could find traffic, mostly carrying coffee to Colombo and consumables, such as rice, to Kandy.

The colonial planters wanted the railway but the company was a private one and, without government support, was unable ro raise the finance. It was not until 1856 that the planters' pleas were successful. The government's attitude changed, and an ordinance was passed in September 1856 for the construction of a railway between Colombo and Kandy. Since part of the cost was to be met out of an increased export duty, there was great opposition from planters elsewhere in the island who would have no access to the railway but would still have to pay the tax. Nevertheless, six routes were surveyed and on August 3 1858, the governor, Sir Henry Ward, cut the first sod, proclaiming grandly: 'As educators, railways supersede roads in oriental lands.'

The first casualty was the Ceylon Railway Company itself. It was dissolved in 1860 causing the island a loss of £243,275 without a line being laid. By 1863, the government had taken over the project and contracted with the Briton W F Faviell (who had already brought railways to India) to build the line.

In that year, 3,000 men began working on the project although malaria and cholera, together with monsoon rains, floods and landslides, frequently slowed progress. In the low country, the building of embankments on marshy lands was done by laying the tracks on beds of screw pines to support the ballast trains that conveyed the heavy stones and earth needed for proper foundations.

From the 53rd to the 65th mile was the most treacherous, with gradients as steep as one in 45 for 12 miles. Nine tunnels were cut, the longest being 1,095 feet. The death toll through malaria was heavy and labour was hard to find; workers had to be brought from southern India.

With most of the railway material imported from Britain, there were many unforeseen delays and increases in costs.

Despite the difficulties, the first section was opened in October 1865 when a train steamed to Ambepussa, 34 miles from Colombo. A year later the line reached Polgahawela. The heavy rock cutting through the hills, especially at Sensation Rock, was completed by December 1866 and, as soon as the bridges over the Mahaweli Ganga and Maya Oya (rivers) were in place, the line was opened for passenger traffic in August 1867, and for goods (the main reason for its construction) in October that year.

The first engine to steam into Kandy was manufactured in England by R Stephenson & Co and went on to serve the Ceylon Government Railway (CGR) for 60 years. The passenger coaches were uncomfortable, four-wheeled carriages, the only luxuries being projecting sun shades, bonnet-type side ventilation, glass drop windows and a double roof with coconut oil lamps.

Faviell, the contractor, had completed the job but not within the terms of his contract. There was a delay of six months and an excess over the estimate (£873,039) of £201,044. This was due to unanticipated difficulties in construction and the cost of labour, increased to 15d a day, and the higher than estimated cost of materials imported from Britain. Faviell was supposed to pay the government £2,500 for every month of delay. However, the government not only understood the problems and absolved Faviell from his obligations but also awarded him £58,202, while the public presented him with a gift costing £600 'as a mark of high appreciation'.

The railway in Sri Lanka opened 11 years after the first line in India. The rolling stock at the time consisted of 15 goods engines (cost £2,909 each) with 65 coaches and 200 goods wagons. The journey from the seaport to the former capital had taken a total of 22 years, and it had come just 52 years after the once unconquerable city had fallen to the British.

A correspondent of the *Observer* newspaper was an eyewitness. 'When the locomotive appeared,' he wrote in 1867, 'there was a tremendous excitement and the mob . . . cheered most lustily and vociferously, trying with might and main to drown the shrill scream of the iron horse whose wild and unearthly snortings were echoed and re-echoed in the surrounding hills.'

Steam locomotives came to be known as *yakada yaka*. Although the words mean 'iron devil' in Sinhala, they are also onomatopoeic, capturing the sound made by the engine as it gathered rhythm and rattled over the points: *yakada yaka . . . yakada yaka*.

With the opening up of the hill country by planters, who turned to tea when the main crop of coffee was stricken by blight, there was a demand for the railway to be extended to keep pace with development. The line from Peradeniya was cut through to Gampola by 1873 and on to Nawalapitiya by 1874. Two years later it reached Hatton and Talawakele and, in 1885, Nanu Oya.

The grade was one in 44 and involved five chain radius curves around the hills and boring through tunnels, climbing to a height of 1,898m (6,226ft) above sea level at the summit just beyond Pattipola station. It was an incredible feat of construction a hundred years ago, which is when the line reached Bandarawela. That station was to remain the terminus of the line for nearly a quarter of a century. It was not until the 1920s that the line was extended through Ella and Demodara to Badulla. The station buildings and fittings on that section still convey a feeling of the 1920s.

Despite there being no lobbying by the plantation community for a railway along the coast, the government saw the advantages in building a line to Galle and Matara in the south. The simplest route out of Colombo was along the Galle Face Green, but a deputation representing the ladies and children of Colombo informed the governor that they refused to allow the Green 'to be desecrated and rendered unsafe by the snorting and rattling and smoking vapours of a railway train'. That is the reason for the abrupt curve in the railway line away from the coast as it approaches Colombo and swings inland behind the Galle Face Hotel to meander through Slave Island to Fort station.

Meanwhile the railway was branching out all over. The line from Kandy to Matale was completed in 1880. From Polgahawela a thrust was begun to the north, reaching Kurunegala in 1894 and the ancient city of Anuradhapura ten years later, making the area easily accessible for the first time to masses of pilgrims. Commercial considerations led to a link up with the northernmost part of Sri Lanka, reaching the Jaffna peninsula in 1905 and Talaimannar in 1914. The connection with the ferry service to India cut down the cost, and the time, of importing Indian labour for the burgeoning tea industry as well as for rice and other commodities.

The Puttalam Line branched out from Ragama in 1908 and took eight years to reach Chilaw and another ten years before it was laid up to Puttalam. Narrow gauge lines were introduced on the Kelani Valley Line (opened in 1902) to Avissawella to serve the rubber plantations east of Colombo, and on to Ratnapura in 1912 and Opanaike in 1919. Upcountry, another narrow gauge line was cut through difficult terrain from Nanu Oya to the hill station of Nuwara Eliya and on to Ragalla in 1903. The line was closed in the late 1940s but traces of it can still be seen, and the bar in Ragalla was formerly the town's railway station.

The next stage was to extend the railway to the east, an idea given impetus because of the strategic importance of the natural harbour at Trincomalee. The line was built from Maho via Gal Oya (1926), reaching Trincomalee in 1927 with a branch to Batticaloa (1928). The rails used were light, hence the railway was called the Batticaloa-Trincomalee Light Railway.

Commenting on the tortuous routes taken for the laying of the lines, a general manager wondered if it was due to construction costs being paid for on a mileage basis. He is quoted as saying that the railway 'followed the path of an intelligent cow' and went round every obstacle in its way.

By the end of the 1920s the total network consisted of 1,530km and it was making a profit. However, competition from road transport began to make an impact and no new lines were built, although an extension of the line along the coast from Matara to Hambantota was considered in the 1920s. By the end of the 1930s the railways were losing money, a trend which, apart from a profit during some years of the Second World War, has continued.

In 1964, one hundred years after its inauguration, the rolling stock had expanded to 225 steam engines, 120 diesel-powered locomotives and rail cars, 1,022 coaches and 3,200 goods wagons.

No new lines were built (although the Matara-Hambantota idea was looked at again in 1977) until this decade, which has seen the new branch from Anuradhapura to Mihintale being opened and the broad gauging of the narrow gauge Kelani Valley Line. Work has commenced on the extension from Matara to Hambantota, Tissamaharama and Kataragama, with a possible link up to Badulla. Plans have also been announced for an extension along the east coast from Batticaloa to Pottuvil and there is talk of a railway link again from Nanu Oya to Nuwara Eliya. Meanwhile, up to 1994, the line to Talaimannar Pier from Madawachchi Junction (north of Anuradhapura) and through Elephant Pass to Jaffna and Kankesanturai remain closed.

The first locomotive to run in Sri Lanka was of the 4-4-0 type, two-wheel coupled, with tender, which arrived by sea in January 1864. This locomotive hauled the train from Colombo to Ambepussa to inaugurate the service. Not a trace of it remains. Records show that the oldest steam locomotive still in existence, and undergoing repairs and restoration, was built by Dubs in 1898. This is number 93, Class E1, 0-6-2T type.

The development of Sri Lanka owes a debt to the coal-fired steam engines that pulled and pushed freight and passenger trains for over a century until finally being phased out on the broad gauge line in 1969 for diesel traction. Actually, diesel made its first appearance in 1933 and diesel locomotives were also introduced on the Kelani Valley Line. The first fleet of diesel electric locomotives for main line service were imported in 1953. Some of the M2 class locomotives given to Sri Lanka by the Canadian government in 1954, with names like Montreal and New Brunswick, are still to be seen in daily use.

Now, like the elephant, steam engines have been recognized as an endangered species, and enthusiasts and dedicated railwaymen have been making attempts to rescue them from junk heaps. At the same time, feasibility studies are underway and plans are being made for the electrification of the busiest lines to and from Colombo.

Steam in Sri Lanka *by Hugh Ballantyne*

The design of locomotives for the Ceylon Government Railway, as it was called, has never been influenced by, or followed the practice of, the large railways operating in its near big neighbour, India, despite the same broad gauge. There were distinctive types of their own, starting with 4-4-0 classes for passenger and mixed traffic work and built by a variety of well-known English locomotive builders. Eventually a classification system was introduced in 1937 using a letter of the alphabet to indicate wheel arrangement such as A for 4-8-0, B for 4-6-0 and V for narrow gauge railcars, with a number to distinguish types and often a suffix letter to differentiate the construction series. A very pleasing feature in the pre Second World War era was that some of the passenger engines were named, mainly after prominent people or governors of the island.

The railway also became a user of railcars, both steam and petrol/diesel, and of diesel shunting locomotives after the war. Three diesel electric, four-car trains built by English Electric entered regular service in 1938 so it was not surprising that during the late 1960s the steam fleet was steadily replaced by diesel traction. A few locomotives lingered on, working odd pick-up goods or engineering trains through the 1970s, but finally the last broad gauge steam on shunting work finished at the end of 1981.

Fortunately for posterity not all the engines were sold for scrap or cut up; some just languished out of use at the main shed in Colombo at Dematagoda. Credit for the idea of persuading the Sri Lanka railway administration to restore some of these locomotives for use on special trains goes to an English travel agent, Clifford Jones from Eccles near

Manchester, who saw the derelict engines whilst on a visit in 1985 and later, in conjunction with a local travel agent, Hemasiri Fernando, managed to obtain the interest of Mr G P S Weerasooriya, the then general manager. He gave the authority for locomotive restoration and the introduction of a special steam-hauled tourist train called the 'Viceroy Special'. The first working of this train took place in 1986.

Another important factor which has enabled this far-sighted scheme to become a reality is that the railway has retained its turntables at termini and main junction stations and water columns at virtually all the places originally provided, which means steam locomotives have the ability to travel over the whole island network. Trains can therefore be readily chartered to suit customer destinations and itinerary requirements. The other vital factor in this scheme is that the railway administration has some dedicated locomotive staff at Dematagoda who have expertise and enthusiasm to maintain and operate these locomotives in service.

At the present time there are four 5ft 6in gauge locomotives available for service:

4-6-0 class B2B 213 built by Vulcan Foundry, Newton le Willows, England in 1922. This was one of six unusual tender tank locomotives, designed for weight distribution, and having a tender with one rigid axle and a four-wheel bogie, thus giving the engine a most striking appearance. These engines were regarded as useful banking locomotives.

4-6-0 class B8C 240 built by Hunslet, Leeds, England in 1927, the survivor of 18 lightly built locomotives with very small boilers.

4-6-0 class B1A 251 'Sir Thomas Maitland' built by Beyer, Peacock, Manchester in 1928. This is a very attractive main line passenger engine in the classic British overseas locomotive style of the 1920/30s. Forty-two of this class were built in batches by Beyer, Peacock during 1927-30 and one group of 12 by Armstrong Whitworth at Newcastle upon Tyne in 1929.

4-6-0 class B1D 340 'Frederick North'. Passenger-engine type built by Robert Stephenson & Hawthorn at Darlington in 1945, and almost identical in appearance to No 251.

In the railway workshops at Ratmalana near Colombo, a superb class C1A 2-6-2+2-6-2 Beyer Garratt number 347, built by Beyer, Peacock in 1947, is undergoing long-term restoration. The Ceylon Garratts were used on the hill section, based at Nawalapitiya for use on the formidable steep grades through breathtaking scenery to Nanu Oya on the line to Badulla. This restoration will be a long project as extensive work is required, but once this powerful locomotive is returned to service it will immediately become an unusual and much sought after engine.

2ft 6in Narrow Gauge Line

Previously narrow gauge, the Kelani Valley Line, which runs east southeast from Colombo Fort to Avissawella is being broad gauged. Steam is sometimes engaged in shunting or occasional relief work to cover a diesel failure. One of these 4-6-4Ts, class J1 220 (built Hunslet 1924), was serviceable in 1994, and was available for use.

The pièce de résistance in Sri Lanka is the beautifully restored steam **Sentinel railcar No 331**. This priceless vehicle was renovated in 1990 to working order. It is classified V2 by the railway and is one of three built by Sentinel Wagon works, Shrewsbury, England in 1928, then used mainly on the passenger train service between Ratnapura and Opanaike. It is immaculately restored in maroon livery with yellow lining and Sri Lanka railway emblems on the body and panels. It is unique in that it is the only steam powered Sentinel railcar at work anywhere in the world today. It is also available for hire, and visitors or groups have a wonderful opportunity for a fascinating ride along the narrow gauge part of the Kelani Valley Line.

The loco shed at Dematagoda at Colombo, besides being the base and servicing facility for all the broad and narrow gauge locomotives described above, houses a number of other locomotives in varying stages of disrepair but worthy of a visit because of the variety, including an E1 class 0-6-2T/93 and a number of narrow gauge 4-6-4Ts. Adjacent to the shed are the steam locomotive workshops which have an abandoned steam powered traverser used as recently as 1993 to gain access to the repair bays. It is a wood fired vertical boilered machine built by Ransome & Rapier in 1912 with power through two cylinders. Also kept and maintained at the loco shed is a 35 tons steam breakdown crane built by Cowans Sheldon.

Outside Fort station on static display on the south side is 4-6-0 class B9 135 which was built by Hunslet at Leeds in 1908.

Finally, but not least, there are small industrial locomotives still to be seen. The Sri Lanka Ports Corporation at Colombo Docks once used delightful little shunting engines, all seven survivors being built by Hunslet but sadly now out of use. Some remain in their shed at the docks but four have been brought up to Dematagoda shed where they are packed together, making them difficult to photograph. Also at Dematagoda shed for safe storage are two small industrial locomotives of the Oil and Fats Corporation at Seeduwa, north of Colombo.

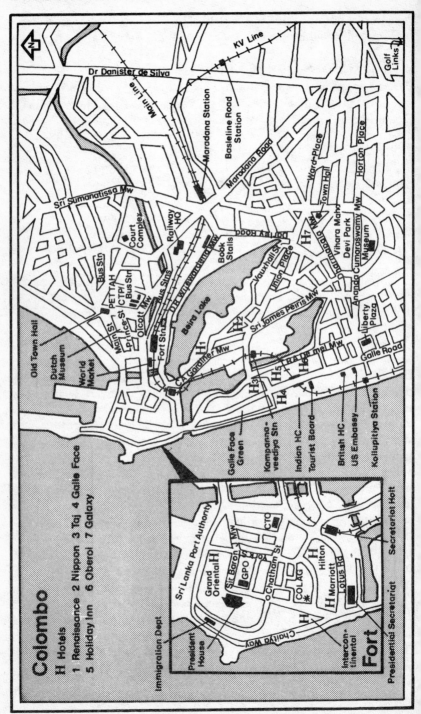

Chapter Six

Colombo

There are two major stations in Colombo: Colombo Fort (known as *Kotuwa* in Sinhala) and Maradana. Trains for the south (except those from Kandy or Anuradhapura) start at Maradana, while trains for the north (unless they have come from Matara in the south) start at Fort. The majority of Sri Lankans, as well as visitors, whether they are going north or south, board their trains at Fort station.

Like Maradana, Fort is actually a through station, and has only two platforms (numbers 1 and 2) which are terminuses; these are used by trains on the Puttalam Line and the Intercity Express to Kandy. Trains originating at Fort station come in empty from the yard, which is actually at Maradana. You cannot board them at Maradana – they usually do not stop – but local travellers in the know use this knowledge somehow to secure a seat before it gets to Fort station.

Colombo Fort Station

If you insist, the three-wheeler taking you to Fort station can actually drive into the forecourt and drop you in front of the ticket booking counters. Entry is blocked by a pole suspended across it but there is a gateman in the crowd who will open it for a genuine passenger with luggage. Otherwise you walk across the busy road to gain access.

Considering the traffic which flows around it, and the people who lurk in its environs, Fort station is kept very clean. With its wooden-faced awning stretching its length to give waiting passengers shade and shelter, it has a traditional railway station ambience.

As you stand facing the station, its facilities taken from right to left are as below. (By the way, if you stand for more than a couple of minutes, someone is bound to come up and offer to help you, or to beg.)

At far right is the first of the ticket halls, containing windows 11 to 15, for 3rd class:

11 Season tickets
12 Railway workers only
13 3rd class tickets from Fort to Matara, Peralanda to Puttalam and

on the KV Line. Open 24 hours a day

14 3rd class, as number 13, open 1300-1930

15 3rd class, Fort to Rambukkana, 1200-2000.

Next is the Multifoods snack bar, open 0500-2000. Always busy and packed with crates of soft drinks, the servers are the bustling youths in sarongs. Find a space at a shared table and one will take your order. Short eats (stuffed buns, and various fried rolls of fish or egg – no meat here) will be served by the mixed plateful. You will be charged only for what you eat. Plain tea (impossible to get without sugar) is recommended. Eat, or buy, snacks here, in preference to the gloomy snack bars on the station.

The Railway Tourist Information Office is next along the station's length; this is where tours can be arranged for independent travellers. It is not the enquiry office but the staff will help if they can.

Ticket counters 1 to 4 are in the next hall, with a confusing arrangement of metal bars to control queues but inevitably leading to bottlenecks as people walk out of the one you are trying to enter.

1 3rd class. Thalawattegedara to Thandikulam (Vavuniya). Open 24 hours.

2 3rd class. Rambukkana to Badulla (and Matale). Open 0400-2130.

3 3rd class. Koonwewa to Trincomalee, Gal Oya to Batticaloa (also Ragama to Polgahawela in peak hours). Open 24 hours.

4 2nd class. All major stations (and reservations on some trains on day of departure). Open 24 hours.

All counters, except number 17, are supposed to sell platform tickets.

This ticket-selling block is the nerve centre of the station, with the stationmaster's office in the centre (entrance is by wooden cowboy style swinging half doors off the forecourt). It is between two closed ticket counters, 5 and 6. Behind the office, on the platform side, sit various station officials. In the same complex is the railway enquiries counter (tel: 434215) which has only limited information, and enthusiasm, about trains. It has a counter open to the platform as well, and inside it a sign which says 'When all is well, who cannot be wise'. It is supposed to be open 0500-2100.

Opposite the enquiries hatch are ticket counters 7 to 9 which deal only with warrants, privilege tickets for certain government and railway employees, and others. Counter 10 is closed.

At the corner is counter 17 for reservations for the Intercity trains to and from Kandy, open 0600-1700 every day but no advance booking between 1430-1530. Counters 18 and 19 are closed. These counters are part of the Berth Reservations Office (open 0830-1530, Sunday

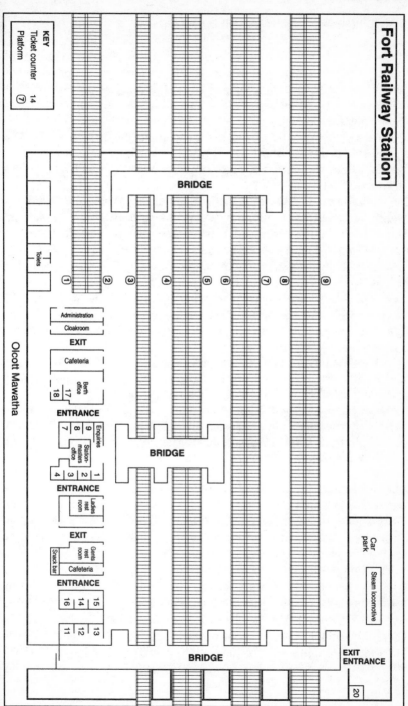

0830-1200; lunch 1230-1300) which comes next.

Access to the cloakroom for leaving luggage is at the far left hand side of the station. There are wooden lockers upstairs which can be rented for Rs7.50 a day. Usually there is a spare one, although in the peak tourist months these are popular. Outside is a letter box for posting late fee letters (cost Rs2.50 instead of Rs1) for sending on the mail trains, with collections from the box for Galle at 1845 and for Badulla at 1945.

The road at this side of the station leads to the Bastian Road bus station (about 200m) and there is also a retail liquor shop. Lingering in this area of the station at night could be hazardous as beggars doss down there.

Counter number 20 is on the other side of the station, over the foot-bridge, where there is an entrance/exit linking with D R Wijewardene Mawatha (Avenue). Only 3rd class tickets can be bought there, to Rambukkana, Matara and Avissawella, and platform tickets, necessary if you want to make a short cut across the station to the main ticket offices.

An old steam loco is permanently parked on this side of the station. Painted black and maroon with some yellow strips, it is a cheerful sight for commuters. Built by Hunslet in 1908, this is a 4-6-0 class, number 135.

Fort station also has other bygones of the steam age. Hanging by the stationmaster's office on platform 3 are ancient wooden frames containing photographs of views of the railway of long ago. Platform 3 becomes platform 2 on the left after entering the station, where it forms a terminus with platform 1. There is a single track served by platform 3 and by platform 4 the other side of it. The main line upcountry trains usually leave from platform 3.

Platforms 5 and 6 are served by the coastal line service. Trains for the KV Line usually leave from platforms 8 or 9. Platform 10 used to be for narrow gauge trains.

Passenger facilities are confined to platform 3 with a newspaper kiosk, two snack bars (the one on the right of the entrance is better than the grubby one near platform 2), and waiting rooms. There are toilets at the head of platform 1.

A huge board and television screens give details of current departures but if you want to check the platform number, you could ask the ticket nipper at the entrance, or try the office adjoining the enquiries counter. There are announcements about trains in English, Sinhala and Tamil, and a recorded one about the Intercity Express.

Times of major train departures from Colombo Fort Station

Time	Train		Destination
0515	81		Trincomalee (with connection to Batticaloa)
0545	77	Yal Devi	Anuradhapura/Vavuniya
0555	05	Podi Menike	Kandy/Badulla
0645	50		Galle/Matara
0655	09	Intercity	Kandy
0830	40		Galle/Matara
0945	15	Udarata Menike	Badulla
1015	19		Kandy
1015	86	Rajarata Rajini	Galle/Matara
1245	23		Kandy
1300	60		Galle/Matara (Friday only)
1335	54		Galle (Saturday only)
1335	56		Galle/Matara (not Saturday & Sunday)
1405	85	Rajarata Rajini	Anuradhapura/Vavuniya
1500	62		Galle/Matara (Friday only)
1535	29	Intercity	Kandy
1545	58	Ruhunu Kumari	Galle/Matara
1620	35		Kandy
1650	760	Samudra Devi	Galle (3rd class only)
1720	39		Kandy
2015	45	Night Mail	Badulla
2230	89	Night Mail	Anuradhapura/Vavuniya with connection to Polonnaruwa

MARADANA STATION

Since all trains that serve Maradana station also call — or originate — at Fort station, Fort, not Maradana is the station usually used by visitors. Maradana is located away from the main area (and bus stations) in Colombo 10, but is by no means quiet. Maradana Road and the road junctions close to the station are clogged with traffic. A system of elevated walkways with shops on one side, and footbridges over the roads, helps passengers gain access without having to dodge through the traffic.

The station building retains its colonial lines even though it is hemmed in by footbridges. The main entrance faces Maradana Road with a small courtyard in front, behind railings. As you enter the station a grim snack bar is on the right, with the booking counters grouped in a semi-circle ahead of you. The fares to all stations are posted on a noticeboard outside, on the left of the station, next to two letter boxes.

Window number 1, on the left of the semi-circle, is for 1st and 2nd class tickets to all destinations. At counter number 2 you can buy 3rd class tickets to Colombo Fort and all stations to Matara. Counter 3 is for 3rd class tickets to Dematagoda and all stations to Polgahawela. At counter 4, tickets are sold for stations from Peralanda to Puttalam, Rambukkana to Badulla, Peradeniya to Matale and to all stations to Vavuniya and Trincomalee and Batticaloa.

The entrance to the platform is on the left with a ticket nipper on duty. On the far wall is a noticeboard clearly displaying the departure platforms, with wooden signs and numbers which may well date from colonial days, painted in brown and gold. There is also a noticeboard giving the times of all trains departing from Maradana on all lines, a facility that could be copied at Fort station.

There are more footbridges to walk along after passing the ticket nipper. Ahead is a long walk down a closed aerial corridor, in front of the Maradana railway operating headquarters building. This leads to platforms 7, 8, 9 and 10. Platform 10 still has a narrow gauge track, a relic of when the Kelani Valley Line trains used it.

The bridge to the left leads to platforms 1, 2, 3, 4, 5 and 6. The usual platform for trains to the south is 5. There is a snack bar on it with the grubbiest walls I have ever seen, which makes one wonder about the tea cups. Short eats and soft drinks are available. The platform has separate waiting rooms for ladies and gents. The guards' lounge and dining room is also on this platform, behind the book kiosk at the foot of the access steps.

There is another entrance to the station on the platform 1 side, opposite the Elphinstone Theatre. This is railway headquarters territory, with the main administration offices and workshops further along Maradana Road. The main yard, where rolling stock and locomotives are to be found, is about 1km along the track, at Dematagoda. As trains to the north pass the sheds you can see the abandoned steam locomotives peeping out from where they await restoration.

If you can arrange a visit to the shed at Dematagoda, some fascinating remnants of the steam age are to be seen, including a Dubs engine (number 93, class E1, 0-6-2T) built in 1898, which the locomotive foreman and his dedicated team are hoping to restore. On the run between Maradana and Fort stations, on the left as you head south, can be glimpsed an open-sided building once intended as a rail museum. A Hunslet steam engine (number 237, Class B8C, 4-6-0) is preserved there.

There is another station in Central Colombo where some trains from the south stop, just outside Fort station. **Secretariat Halt** is so named as it is the station serving the Presidential Secretariat that overlooks the Indian Ocean. It is very convenient for the Colombo Hilton and Marriott Hotels, but usually only the commuter trains stop there. Sometimes the morning inbound *Ruhunu Kumari* slows as it passes through which enables passengers to jump off. There are no facilities at the station.

Special Interest

Pettah

Colombo Fort station is ideally located for strolling (without luggage though) to places of special interest to the rail traveller, and those keen on the off-beat.

For shopping, if you have your wits about you, you can dive into the World Market which adjoins the station, on the left after you negotiate your way through touts and three-wheeler drivers. It is a hectic place for leather bags, T-shirts and clothes of all description. For cooler shopping and less hassle head for Liberty Plaza (you will need a three-wheeler), three kilometres south of the station, where there are two air-conditioned floors of shops (including one with gourmet teas), and a supermarket in the basement. This is actually within walking distance (ten minutes) from **Kollupitiya** (Colpetty) station.

Opposite Fort station is the area known as **Pettah**, Colombo's haunt of the streetwise, a bazaar spreading over several city blocks where everything you have ever wanted, and most things you will never need, can be found. Pettah was a select residential area during the Dutch and early British periods, although later British inhabitants regarded it as 'the native quarter'. A jungle of streets are jammed with bargain hunters, herds of trucks, cars, bullock carts and the ubiquitous three-wheelers. The contents of hardware shops, garment stores and groceries flow over onto the sidewalk.

The road facing the station is Olcott Mawatha, named after Henry Steel Olcott, an American-born Buddhist crusader whose statue stands in the station car park. Cross the road to step into Pettah and you will find down Maliban Street running parallel to Olcott Mawatha (*mawatha* means avenue or street), the Philip Neris church, 1859. The candy-striped

Jami-Ul-Alfar Jummah Mosque deeper in Pettah dates from 1909.

In Prince Street, parallel to Maliban Street, is a 17th century colonnaded Dutch townhouse that has survived the gutting of progress around it. In its time it has served as an orphanage, a private residence, a hospital, the headquarters of the Ceylon Volunteers, a police training school and a post office. Restored in 1980, it is now a museum devoted to the Dutch period 1658-1796. Open 0900-1700 except Fridays; admission is Rs25, cameras Rs100.

Continue northwards up to Main Street and turn right. About 50m from the old town hall junction stands a restored belfry, complete with bell and crows nesting in it, a forgotten link with Pettah's past. The bell is believed to have been salvaged from the ruins of a 16th century Portuguese church. It is all that remains of Kaymans Gate and is placed where crocodiles from Beira Lake once scavenged for food. Public executions were held at its foot; now electricity board transformers block access to it.

The old town hall is almost submerged by the waves of vendors of vegetables and machine spare parts surging around it. Its yard has been turned into the unexpected: an unknown municipal museum featuring bygones of city life — cast-iron water pumps and drinking fountains, a manhole cover, a signpost, a city father's robe, bits of machinery, a massive steamroller and an ancient steam lorry emblazoned with the council's crest. Potted plants brighten the exhibits. Built in 1873, it was the seat of city government until 1928, when the yard became a public market before being turned into a museum in 1984.

The next wonder is down St John's Road where the wholesale fish market is straddled by a shopping complex. Gabo's Lane, not marked on the maps, is a street of remarkable shops specializing in the ingredients of *ayurvedic*, or herbal, remedies. Outside the New Royal Fireworks and Medical Store and its neighbouring ayurvedic merchants are sacks of twigs, strips of bark, dried herbs and leaves that, properly mixed, offer an age-old alternative to modern medicine. Sea Street, close by deals in gold and jewellery.

Back along Main Street, in the direction of Fort, you come to a clock tower in the centre of a roundabout. This commemorates the life of one Framjee Bhikkajee Khan and was erected in 1923 by his sons on the 45th anniversary of his death. It marks the division of Pettah and Fort.

COLOMBO FORT

Not many visitors would admit to Colombo being their favourite city, but it is mine. Facing the Indian Ocean and stretching 14km along Sri Lanka's western shore, it has within its boundaries an astonishing variety of people, historical sites, simple temples, gleaming hotels, tree-lined boulevards, mysterious lanes, old and new markets, even skyscrapers. It never disappoints, although on a hot, hectic day it is certainly tiring.

It is not a city of romance like Paris or of ruthless commerce like Hong Kong, nor is it dedicated to progress like Singapore, or fun like Bangkok. Colombo has no such pretentions, being simply an ancient maritime city burgeoning into a modern metropolis.

In the 1920s it was known as the Garden City of the East and visitors stayed for weeks. Now most visitors stay only for a day, yet even that is enough time to discover Colombo's charms.

Colombo was used as a port in the 8th century by Arab traders. In 1330, a Chinese traveller referred to it as Kao-lan-pu, and the Sinhalese today call it Kolomba. The settlement was fortified by the Portuguese in the 16th century with a wooden stockade and was improved by the Dutch. The British, who came in 1796, extended the city south and east

---

Ayurveda: Care and Cure Nature's Way

Ayurveda (pronounced like ae-uraveda) is the natural medicine of Sri Lanka, an alternative to western medical lore, which has an efficacy proven by 3,000 years of care and cure. It is nature's way to good health because of its reliance on natural plants, herbs and oils. Visitors can undergo a course of treatment by licensed ayurvedic physicians, either by consulting village practitioners or as part of a stay at a holiday resort, such as at Robinson Club by the beach at Bentota, where there is an ayurvedic treatment centre. There are also ayurvedic hospitals which take paying patients from abroad.

Treatment comprises not only potions which are made from fresh, natural ingredients, but also oil massages, steam baths and bathing in herbal waters. Treatments are particularly beneficial for patients suffering from migraine, insomnia, arthritis and gastritis but can also help in cases of paralysis and practically any affliction. The *Panchakarma* method has a great distinction in ayurveda as it uses the five elements of medicinal herbs: leaves, flowers, barks, roots and berries, to cleanse the blood and the body's system of impurities.

Ayurvedic treatment not only cures, it provides immunity, too, so patients are both those in need of a cure for a particular ailment, and those who want to follow a course to stimulate and maintain good health. Treatment by ayurveda cannot be hurried — it is not nature's aspirin.

beyond the fort's limits, leaving a legacy of wide streets and spacious buildings, as though they knew that a century later they would be required to accommodate far more traffic and people than existed then. The fort itself has vanished completely. Colombo's population has grown to nearly one million, with commuters from as far away as Kandy and Galle adding to the throngs of people every weekday. At weekends and at night, the crowds and their cars disappear and you can stroll the streets and stand and stare without disrupting the flow of pedestrians and traffic.

It is best to tour the city early before the sun has a chance to raise temperatures too high and while the streets are still empty. From Pettah, across a bridge where ships' masts peep over the tops of shops hiding the harbour views and the portside freight railway line, the road forks. To the right it leads past the entrance to the harbour, to the left it brings you to the shopping and commercial area of York Street.

Colombo's oldest department store, Cargills, established in 1844, with its broad, puce stone walls, is a contrast to the façade of more modern architecture. Looking up you can see the balustrade typical of Colombo's older buildings, and the plaster horns of plenty bursting with bounty that decorate its walls.

Take the road westwards alongside Cargills and you arrive at Janadhipathi Mawatha (once Queen Street) with the splendid colonial general post office; opposite is Presidents House. Built in the 18th century by the last Dutch governor, it was formerly known as King's or Queen's House. It is the official residence of the President, hidden behind a wealth of trees and guarded by soldiers in scarlet tunics. Changing of the guard takes place every 70 or 80 minutes, depending on the roster, when a quartet of soldiers march from one gate to the other along the pavement in front of the balustraded wall.

Almost hidden by the trees that shade him where he stands permanently on guard is the statue of Sir Edward Barnes, which bears the inscription 'Erected by the European and Native inhabitants of Ceylon and Friends in England and India to testify their respect and affection for this person'. Barnes, governor from 1820 to 1822, and 1824 to 1831, was responsible for much of the development of the island, including its roads. All road distances from Colombo to the outstations are measured from this statue.

Where Chatham Street intersects Janadhipathi Mawatha stands a city landmark, the clock tower, visible not only from parts of Fort but also from the sea. It served as a lighthouse until the 1950s, perhaps the only one in the middle of a city. The tower was built in 1857, although it was not until 1914 that the clock with four faces — to show the time north, east, south and west — was installed.

Walk towards the sea and you will see on the left, by the pavement behind the railings surrounding Ceylinco House, a small, domed cell with a roof of red scalloped tiles. A plaque in English and Sinhala says that Sri Wickrema Rajasinghe, last king of Kandy (1798-1815) was imprisoned 'in this specific chamber'. An effigy of the king behind bars glowers at the passers by who never notice his jail.

Turn right at the roundabout by the Ceylon Inter-Continental Hotel to find the immigration office for visa renewal. Opposite is the lighthouse built in 1951 to function instead of the one in Chatham Street. Below it is a natural sea-water swimming pool in the rocks where colonial governors and their ladies were wont to bathe. Known as the Governor's Bath, it was restored in 1991 and is open to all.

At the other side of the roundabout is the former parliament building, now the Presidential Secretariat, its forum-style brownstone lines an anti-dote to the brightness of the mirror-glass skyscraper of the headquarters of the Bank of Ceylon and the new towers behind the Colombo Marriott Hotel. The Secretariat stands at the northern end of Galle Face Green.

Despite being a bare brown instead of green, Galle Face Green is a popular promenade at dusk, with the venerable Galle Face Hotel commanding the southern end where the road and railway head down to Galle. When the sun and heat have gone, it is fun to stroll along the waterfront, as the citizens of Colombo do, enjoying the breeze, the camaraderie and the night-time hawker snacks. A stone at the sea's edge tells you Galle Face Walk was commenced by Sir Henry Ward in 1856, completed in 1859, and 'recommended to his successors in the interest of the Ladies and Children of Colombo'. The original stone is in the old town hall museum in Pettah.

MARADANA

Emerging from Maradana station, you will probably wish you hadn't when you see the traffic. There are some pedestrian bridges and the one to take is directly outside the station forecourt, behind the pavement paper seller at the entrance. Use it to cross the main road and follow the walkway as it leads you above the main road opposite the station. There are some fascinating shops on this aerial path. When you reach the street, about 400m ahead on the opposite side of the road is the junction with D J Wijewardena Mawatha. Here are Colombo's secondhand book shops, a trove of magazines, paperbacks, and even some rare volumes on Celyon. Books can be borrowed against a deposit and a reading fee.

Where to Stay

Colombo boasts six five-star hotels, all offering luxury at much lower prices than in neighbouring capitals. For a few dollars less there are some hotels of character worth staying in for their link with the past, but only a few economy hotels that could be recommended. I consider that, for the first night in a strange city, the expense of a reliable, top-grade hotel is worth it. In Colombo this is especially so because the room rates, by international standards, are low, and the city can be enervating, and exasperating after stepping off a long-haul flight. A reliable, comfortable, friendly hotel is essential to start with; you can cope with the cheapies later on.

Fortunately, the luxury hotels do not duplicate each other's ambience and all are distinctive. For access to Fort railway station, the closest is the efficient and plush Colombo Hilton. The Colombo Marriott is next to it with a business-like atmosphere and useful shops, including airline offices and a bank. Across the road is the Ceylon Inter-Continental, clublike and compact.

On its own, and with a view of passing trains and the Beira Lake, is the Colombo Renaissance Hotel with a gloomy lobby of sombre, polished granite. The Taj Samudra is at the southern end of Galle Face Green with an appealing informality and lots of action. Further south, opposite the Ceylon Tourist Board office in Galle Road, is the opulence of the Lanka Oberoi. Colombo's Holiday Inn, tucked behind the Taj, is not five-star, which means it sets its own rates; it is popular with British and other tour groups.

Across the road is the seaside Galle Face Hotel, opened in 1864, one of the world's unique hotels of which legends are made and where non-smokers qualify for a $5 a day discount. From the same era, but with a different style, is the Grand Oriental Hotel at the port gates. Another hotel with character (with flowers hanging from its wrought-iron balcony it looks like a New Orleans bordello) is the restored Nippon Hotel (economy).

The Hotel Galaxy is also in the economy class but has a swimming pool on its roof and rooms with all the frills of luxury properties including a minibar and multi-channel television. Lake Lodge, behind the Lanka Oberoi, is the nearest guesthouse to Fort railway station, although it is a three-wheeler drive away. There are cheapie places to stay in Pettah and some better ones off the Galle Road where it heads south through Kollupitiya, Bambalapitiya and Wellawatte.

Where to Eat and Drink

Colombo's restaurants offer lots of variety, with the cheaper eateries being in the Chatham Street area. For a special lunch at less than a dollar more than hotels' coffee shop buffets, there is a salad and dessert buffet with a choice of four main courses served to the table in the splendour of the rooftop Palms Supper Club of the Ceylon Inter-Continental. Views over the Indian Ocean and Galle Face Green match the superb food.

Across the road, the Colombo Marriott's pastry shop is a great place for upmarket snacks and coffee at lower than usual hotel prices. For pub drinking with expats the Hilton has its Echelon Pub and draught Lion and Carlsberg beers. In the Ceylinco building close to the Marriott is a pub known only to locals, the Spotted Deer. Another respectable spot for low-priced drinking is the first-floor bar of the Galaxy Hotel. Like a rural tavern is the bar of the 128-year old Castle Hotel in Slave Island, by the Kompanavidiya (Slave Island) railway station. You can see it on the right as the train from the south approaches Fort station.

The terrace and veranda of the Galle Face Hotel are popular for dining and sundowners mixed with nostalgia. The Galle Face Green at night is the haunt of evening picnickers. Behind, at the Taj Samudra is a distinguished Indian restaurant, the Navaratna. If you crave western food and kingsize portions, and draught beer, the Alt Heidelberg German restaurant is close by in the Galle road. For Sri Lankan food in a better atmosphere than a greasy spoon, there is Ginza Araliya, ten minutes' walk further along the Galle road, or try the genteel Hawker Street in the garden of the Colombo Hilton.

Colombo is not a city for organized nightlife, although there are discothèques at the hotels and at the Saxophone Club and Santa Fe Disco opposite the Lanka Oberoi. Casinos, which flourished for a few years until 1991, added glitter to the city which new nightspots have yet to recapture.

There are plenty of places to discover for yourself in Colombo, and every Sri Lankan has his favourite watering hole, some fascinating in both facilities and clientele. A list of restaurants appears every month in *Explore Sri Lanka* magazine.

Chapter Seven

On the Move

The main line was the first to be built and is probably the most used by visitors since it gives access to Kandy and the scenic grandeur of the hill country. There two pairs of trains (05/06 and 15/16) a day to and from Badulla, and a night mail (45/46). Six major trains a day link Colombo with Kandy and an extra train (65/66) at weekends also serves Matara. A daily service (39/40) via Colombo links Kandy and Matara.

There are over 80 stations on the 290km route from Fort to Badulla. For the run from Peradeniya to Badulla, brace yourself for at least 29 stops at stations and also when the train has to pause for breath. But scenically it is so enjoyable, you won't really mind the dawdling pace.

THE MAIN LINE
Colombo to Kandy

Kandy is not officially on the main line at all, but on the Matale line. But since it is always included in the main line timetables, I have followed that practice.

The opening of the line to Kandy in 1867 was the culmination of years of speculation, negotiation and ingenious engineering, a feat that was considered a masterpiece of railway construction. The line reached Ambepussa in 1865 and up to Polgahewela in 1866. Then heavy rock cutting, especially at Sensation Rock, was carried out for the line to top the incline to Kadugannawa by March 1867. Ten tunnels were built in 19km on a steady gradient of 1 in 44. It was this pioneering enterprise by the railway that opened up the country to change and prosperity.

The well modulated voice over the loudspeaker — 'The train now standing on platform two...' — announces the departure from Colombo Fort station of the Intercity Express for Kandy every day. The excitement rises as the late arrivals hurry to board the train. Although the guard does not shout 'All-abooooard!' as he would do in the USA, he blows his whistle and waves his green flag vigorously, and the train pulls out on time.

The train is scheduled to take 150 minutes for the 119km journey with one stop at Peradeniya Junction. On paper it does not seem very fast but

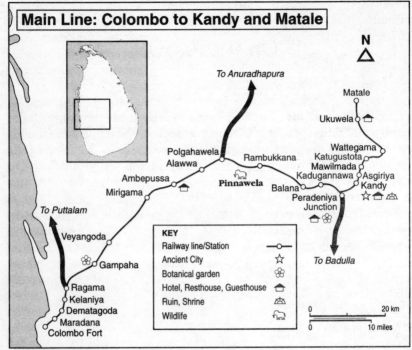

Main Line: Colombo to Kandy and Matale

N

To Anuradhapura

Matale
Ukuwela
Wattegama
Katugustota
Mawilmada
Kadugannawa
Asgiriya
Kandy
Balana
Peradeniya
Junction
To Badulla

Polgahawela
Alawwa
Rambukkana
Ambepussa
Mirigama
Pinnawela

To Puttalam

Veyangoda

Gampaha

Ragama
Kelaniya
Dematagoda
Maradana
Colombo Fort

KEY
Railway line/Station ──○──
Ancient City ☆
Botanical garden ✿
Hotel, Resthouse, Guesthouse ⌂
Ruin, Shrine ⌂
Wildlife 🐘

0   20 km
0   10 miles

on board the train, it certainly does. The carriages sway and the clatter as the train rushes along the track laid over the concrete sleepers makes conversation impossible.

The spectacular scenery is a blur as the train speeds through the mainline stations until it slows for the climb after Rambukkana. The stunning views of distant hills and terraced paddy fields at the base of lush valleys enthral those passengers who are not asleep, although how they could sleep when the train's progress makes such a howling racket baffles me.

On another trip I took an ordinary express, with the journey beginning slowly as the train found its way out of the web of lines surrounding the abandoned rolling stock on the station's outskirts. Just outside Maradana station is **Dematagoda** running shed and workshop, before reaching the Dematagoda railway station (1.76km from Maradana). There are intriguing glimpses of ancient steam locos peeping out of the shed, and of busy Hunslet shunting engines tootling around the yard. A Briton who was working as an executive chef in a Colombo hotel told me how, in 1990, he strolled along the tracks from Maradana station to the yard with his six-year-old son and had a grand time poking around. It is, of course, strictly prohibited.

The scenery assumed a vintage older than the railway, with silhouettes of women bent parallel to the earth, ankle deep in water, planting single blades of paddy by hand. Farmers used oxen to plough. Bullock carts laden with firewood jingled along jungle trails, past mud-walled dwellings thatched with palm fronds. A white-bearded man in a loincloth stood motionless as the train clattered by.

Some trains make a stop at **Ragama**, one of the earliest stations, originally built in 1866. It is an important junction where stopping trains heading northward to Negombo and Puttalam branch off. The station has two island platforms and is always busy, being a dormitory town for Colombo. **Gampaha**, the next major station, is the stop for the Henaratgoda Botanical Gardens, the closest (32km) gardens to Colombo.

Outside the main entrance is a spectacular statue of a group of volleyball players, erected in 1951. But if you want to visit the botanical gardens, cross over the footbridge to the other side of the railway line where buses, or three-wheelers, are available for the short run. Located at Asgiriya down a signposted road to the left of the bus stop (ask the conductor to drop you off; you need a bus headed for Minuwangoda), the gardens are a contrast to the paddy field plains of the area.

Opened in 1876, the 36-acre gardens at 11m above sea level are a well-cared for combination of imported exotic trees, a fernery (where the toilets are hidden) and a plant nursery. The island's first rubber plantation was begun here. Cars and pedal bikes are allowed, but it is small enough to make strolling pleasant; a haven for courting couples, few tourists. Open daily 0730-1700, admission Rs50. There is a snack bar at the entrance.

At **Veyangoda** station (35km from Maradana) express trains connect with the locals running from there to Polgahawela and back, good for a glimpse of lowland rural life. The stationmaster at **Mirigama** (48km) kept rabbits in a cage built around the trunk of a great shade tree on the platform when I stopped there. Golden husks of *thambili* (king coconuts) drained of their water by thirsty travellers, littered the track.

Few trains stop now at **Ambepussa** (54km), the halt for the first train which reached there in 1865. There is an enjoyable resthouse at Ambepussa, on the Colombo-Kandy road, just by the turn off to Kurunegala. One of the oldest hostelries in Sri Lanka (originally built in 1828 when Sir Edward Barnes was opening up the interior with roads), it is British bungalow style with columns and a veranda overlooking the road. New rooms have been built in a garden block; good value economy grade.

Alawwa is a small station with access at the Kandy end of the platform to the town on the left or to the main road where buses can be picked up for Polgahawela or Colombo and easy access to the Ambepussa resthouse. An auction of betel leaf (*piper betel*) is held in Alawwa in a vacant lot behind the bus station every Tuesday and Friday morning, from about 0630. Betel is the heart-shaped leaf traditionally used in offerings and, wrapped around slithers of areca nut, as a jolly good chew. Vendors on trains and at fairs sell a gaudy confection made out of a cone of green betel leaf stuffed with pink, yellow or purple desiccated coconut and spices.

Polgahawela is a junction station where trains to the north leave the line to Kandy and the hill country. It is a major station with spasmodic activity but is otherwise rather dreary. The exit, over a bridge and through the booking hall, leads to the wrong side of town. It is more convenient to walk the platform's length to the level crossing at the end to reach the town. At the other end is a resthouse with a veranda view of the track, but not much else to recommend it.

The station has retiring rooms but these seem to be allocated to railway staff, and the restaurant and bar on the bridge has closed down. There is a snack bar on platform 4, and a newspaper kiosk. The station has five platforms and marks the end of the double track from Colombo.

The excitement of the ascent through the hills begins at the next station, **Rambukkana**. Some trains to Kandy have an extra engine attached to them at Rambukkana to push them up the climb from 116m to Kadugannawa station, 517m above sea level. Maximum speed on this stretch is 32km/h and the trains seem to dawdle along, but fortunately the view of lush vegetation, deep valley and mountain streams is spectacular. The best view is to be had from the right side of the train, facing the engine.

Rambukkana station is a simple one with wooden armchairs set out for passengers and a small hut selling soft drinks, etc. The old entrance hall across the bridge has a wooden roof and is like a Buddhist preaching hall. A colourful vegetable market is held in the access road. Buses (to Kegalle) can be taken from here to the Pinnawela elephant orphanage about five kilometres away.

Hanging on one wall in the station is a brilliantly coloured painting of the Viceroy Special, which makes Rambukkana one of its regular stops. The artist, Upali Jayaweera, is from Balana, the station just before Kadugannawa, and his cheerful paintings of the Intercity and other trains hang at Ihalakotte (a station in the midst of misty hills and valleys), Balana, Kadugannawa and Peradeniya.

The banker engine that has pushed the train through a warren of tunnels and a tangle of tropical jungle is uncoupled at **Kadugannawa** station, as the journey from there to Kandy is actually a descent (from 517m to 488m). The column like a pencil-slim lighthouse which can be glimpsed from the platform is a monument erected in 1832 to Captain W F Dawson who built the Colombo to Kandy road and died in Colombo in 1828.

As befits the station closest to the Botanical Gardens at Peradeniya, the platform is attractively disguised by potted plants. From this junction (see page 119) trains go either to Kandy or continue the long run to Badulla.

The last lap is a run of six kilometres through rural suburbs and stations into the terminus of **Kandy**. The line running from platform 1 is the branch to Matale. The station has four platforms and is bright and clean. There are various restrooms and toilets on the main concourse as well as a fish tank. The kiosk selling refreshments and newspapers (and mineral water!) is pleasant for a snack before departure. The engines which pull trains in are detached here and manoeuvre to the other end of the train for the return, or onward, journey.

On the left after the exit is a bookshop and the ticket windows in a semi-circle. The window where Intercity bookings are made is on the right of the exit, open 0530-1600. Two other windows sell tickets for 1st and 2nd class, and 3rd class journeys. Stairs to the left lead up to the restaurant and defunct bar and also to the retiring rooms, where a double costs Rs300.

The station is not the original 1880 building but has charm with its mock Kandy-style architecture. There is even a clothes/souvenir shop in its lobby. Entrance to the car park (there is another snack bar there) is restricted and taxi drivers are more laidback than their colleagues in Colombo. It is possible to walk to the Temple of the Tooth, and it is an enjoyable stroll through the bustle of the town. Kandy is many people's favourite town in Sri Lanka because of its lake, temple, colonial and Kandyan buildings and genial atmosphere. The bus station is close to the railway station.

Kandy is the ancient capital, the last stronghold of the Kandyan kings before the British conquest, and is also the venue of the world-famous *Perahera* (parade of parades), held annually, in July or August. The chance of finding walk-in accommodation then is negligible since hotels and most guesthouses are booked up in advance. The nightly parade of caprisoned elephants, drummers and dancers is spectacular as it builds over ten days to the climax on the night of the full moon. Special trains are run during this period.

Queen's Hotel is among the best located hotels in the world: on one side of the square in front of the Temple of the Tooth, at the head of the main street, and overlooking the lake built between 1810 and 1812 by the last king of Kandy, Sri Wickrama Rajasinghe. An authentic 19th century hotel which is recovering from neglect, it has 100 rooms in its various wings that surround its new swimming pool. The refurbished rooms, in the standard price range, have retained the antique feel (polished wooden beds and floors), while adding contemporary touches (glass shower cabinets) to the bathrooms.

The Victorian counter, mirror and shelves in the pub bar at one end of the hotel (with access from the lobby through the kitchen) conjures up visions of tea planters at leisure. There are many good hotels in Kandy but because of its atmosphere and location (although it is not always easy to find your room in the hotel itself), Queen's is one of my favourites and somehow characteristic of Kandy. For staying above the town in a hotel that has fabulous views from its swimming pool, the Hotel Thilanka is a charming extension (it grows a little every year) of an old mansion with a richly tiled, and original, parlour. Economy to standard rate according to season.

For unbelievable luxury at a lower rate than Colombo's five-star hotels, in the middle of hills smothered in tea bushes and with a waterfall tumbling into its private lake and out again, make a journey to Hunas Falls Hotel. It is 27km from Kandy so you will have to hire transport to get there or take a local bus. Its bedrooms and bathrooms equal, and even beat, Colombo's luxury properties for comfort. With a swimming pool, the lake, a billiard table, an ornate, clublike bar and a boldly decorated restaurant it is slightly 'over-the-top' in contrast to its natural surroundings, but that makes its isolation bearable, as well as worth the effort to get there.

Main train departures from Kandy station

0130	to Fort (night mail)
0440	to Badulla (slow)
0500	to Matara via Fort (No 40)
0630	to Fort (Intercity)
0645	to Fort (No 36)
0905	to Badulla (Podi Menike)
1000	to Fort (No 24)
1015	to Badulla (slow)
1310	to Matara via Fort (No 66 Sunday only)
1500	to Fort (Intercity)

1530   to Fort (No 20)
1700   to Fort (Podi Menike)
2255   to Badulla (night mail)

Peradeniya Junction to Badulla

Podi Menike (Little Menike) and *Udarata Menike* (Upcountry Menike) are two daytime trains linking Colombo with the hill country and beyond to Badulla. There is also a night mail which is suspended periodically due to track subsidence, making night travel hazardous. Track conditions can also cause delays to the Menike trains and it is not unknown for them to be late and even to be cancelled completely, or to be curtailed halfway through the journey.

However, they do provide the rail traveller with one of the most spectacular journeys in Sri Lanka, especially when viewed from a seat in the observation car. Although there is 3rd class, it is only kind to everyone, including yourself, to avoid that on this line — standing for 290km and through 44 tunnels for 12 hours is not the way to make the most of this wonderful ride — and you'll be taking up the space of someone, especially rural passengers going from one village to another, who cannot afford another class.

You may be lucky enough to bag a seat in 2nd class at the outset of the train's journey from Fort station, but do not even try if you plan to travel during April (when it is the season in Nuwara Eliya) or during the January to February pilgrimage season to Adam's Peak, reached by rail to Hatton station. Better to pay the extra at all times of the year for a reserved seat and travel in the observation saloon. It is the view that makes the main line so attractive and the best place to appreciate the magnificent vistas of the hill country is by the window in your own seat.

There is a snack bar on the train but the train will usually be too packed for you even to edge your way along the vestibule through the crowds to it. Take a picnic lunch — plus alcohol since none is available on the way — to add to the enjoyment of the ride. Sometimes you will be able to buy peanuts and *wade* (fat lentil cookies) from vendors, and in season such delicacies as guava and avocado pear.

Although a train journey of 290km (181 miles) from Colombo to Badulla may not seem long (especially after India) do not be surprised to feel the train equivalent of jet lag, especially on the way back. Not that the train goes slow (which it does in the hills, restricted to 16km/h), but because it goes fast, particularly from Kandy. You will be bounced about rather a lot. It is probably better, as well as giving you a chance to see more of Sri Lanka without pain, to break the journey, perhaps at Kandy, rather than try the whole trip in one day.

The *Podi Menike* which leaves Colombo at 0555 makes stops at Ragama, Veyangoda, Polgahawela, Rambukkana, Kadugannawa, Pilmatalawa, Peradeniya Junction and Sarasavi Uyana before putting into Kandy. There the locomotive changes ends and the observation car which was at the front of the train becomes the rear of the train, with uninterrupted views of the route dashing past you as you gaze spellbound during the ascent to the summit of the railway line just after Pattipola station.

The *Udarata Menike* leaves Fort station at 0945, stopping at Ragama, Veyangoda, Polgahawela, Rambukkana and Kadugannawa before branching off at Peradeniya Junction (without going into Kandy) for the journey uphill. The night mail makes the same stops, and adds a lot more (almost every station) after Peradeniya Junction.

Peradeniya Junction has been rebuilt since it opened in 1867 but the original station building has been carefully preserved opposite the new one. It is an interesting, well-kept and pretty station, with its island platform being built as a triangle. One side is for trains to Kandy (or back to Colombo) and the other for trains to the hill country (or Colombo). The base of the triangle has park bench seats for passengers to watch what is happening. Invariably trains pause here to wait for the single line to clear so that they can proceed safely to the next station crossing.

The Royal Botanical Gardens can be reached by Kandy-bound bus from the main road, two minutes walk out of the station. Opposite the gardens entrance is the Peradeniya Resthouse, run in the resthouse tradition with economy rate accommodation and rice and curry lunches.

At **Gampola** (125km from Colombo, built in 1873), the levels reached by various floods of the Mahaweli River are recorded on the wall of one of the station buildings with an extension on a pole showing where a flood in 1947 completely submerged the station and buildings. There is a small resthouse by the station and the bus station is opposite the station entrance. As Gangasiripura, Gampola was capital of the country about 1344-1408. A flourishing town, it is the gateway to the tea districts of the hill country.

Ulapane is an undistinguished country town where *Podi Menike* stops before reducing speed gradually to cope with the winding track for the 15-minute run to **Nawalapitiya**. This station, built in 1874, 139km from Colombo, has real railway atmosphere with lots of offices for officials (together with Colombo and Anuradhapura, it is one of the railway's three transport division headquarters), a mail room and a rather gloomy

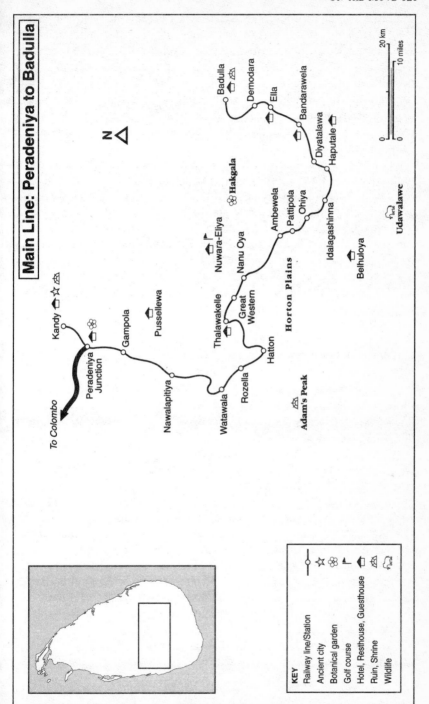

Main Line: Peradeniya to Badulla

KEY

○ Railway line/Station
☆ Ancient city
❀ Botanical garden
⚓ Golf course
◧ Hotel, Resthouse, Guesthouse
🏛 Ruin, Shrine
🐾 Wildlife

but large restaurant room. Vendors hawk rice and curry lunch packets from plastic buckets. There are restrooms, with seats, for ladies and gents. Train crews change at this station; lots of coaches are marshalled there, too.

The bus station is across the road from the station entrance. It is possible to get a Colombo-bound bus from Nawalapitiya which stops on the way at Avissawella. This is an alternative route for returning to Colombo on the way back from the hills. After staying at Avissawella (see page 154) you could take a train on the narrow/broad gauge Kelani Valley Line down to Colombo.

The station booking office is open to the forecourt and nobody seems to hassle strangers since very few tourists alight here. I did once because the *Podi Menike* could go no further due to a landslide at Watawala. When that happens, take a bus to Hatton at the other side of the landslide to pick up a train there. (On the return trip, the process needs to be reversed). There are also three-wheelers available; in 1993, we paid Rs375 from Nawalapitiya to Hatton.

A bell is rung to warn of the train's imminent departure and then it ambles through the outskirts of the town with road and shops beside the line until climbing into the wooded hills. **Inguruoya** (145km from Colombo) has a small 'general waiting hall' and a pretty platform with flowers, befitting the landscape of wooded hillside and some tea gardens. **Galboda** retains its water tank for steam engines, which are rarely seen on this line except for special charters by enthusiasts. By a level crossing is a sign giving rise to fantasy: 'Beware of the Menikes — Podi and Udarata'. They sound like fairies of the hills lurking to spirit unsuspecting passengers to their hideaway behind a waterfall. Oh, those naughty Menikes at it again!

There is more danger of being swept away by a landslide. Between Galboda and **Watawala** the floods of 1947 resulted in a serious landslide which was still causing trouble 45 years later. The track was washed away in June 1992 and was just being restored again when rains in June 1993 resulted in yet another landslide. The scar in the forest torn by the avalanche of soil can be seen during the road trip from Nawalapitiya to Hatton. You will know when you have reached the danger spot by the encampment of huts and the train's reduction to a walking pace.

Signs urging slow speed because of 'weak sleepers' are not to prevent disturbance to those in 1st class taking a light nap, but because of the condition of the track, and this causes the train to dawdle all the way to Badulla.

The track is patrolled daily by linesmen on the watch for obstructions or dangers. They carry a rod with a cloth head and a small bucket containing lubricant, which they apply with the mop end of the rod to the curving bends of the track. Each man also carries a log book which he exchanges with the linesman coming towards him, whom he meets at a certain point before beginning his journey back to base, twice a day. Inspection of this line, and of the men working on it, is also done by a foreman riding on a trolley, pulled uphill by the Menike trains or allowed to freewheel down.

The ruling gradient of the line is 1 in 44, and there are actually 44 tunnels (total length 5,850m) between Colombo and Badulla. The majority of them at this stage of the journey are still to come.

The scenery changes from canyonesque to fir forest according to which side of the hill the track is climbing around, until the tea gardens take over after the tiny station of **Rozella**, 165km from Colombo. The hillsides are dotted with the bright colours of the plastic capes worn by the tea pluckers.

Hatton (1,271m above sea level, 173km from Colombo and built in 1884) is the centre of the tea-growing area. The most popular route to Adam's Peak, via Maskeliya, starts from this station, which is thronged with pilgrims and tourists during the climbing season (January to March). Special trains serve Hatton during the 'Peak' season.

Adam's Peak

A visitor to Sri Lanka, Lucille Weinberger, reports: 'There are two colonial-style bungalows near Hatton which are ideally located for would-be dawn climbers of Adam's Peak. Facilities at Upper and Lower Glencairn (Dickoya) are old fashioned but very clean. Adam's Peak is an hour's drive away. We left Upper Glen at 0100 and were back ready for breakfast by 0930. During the season, the pilgrimage route up Adam's Peak is lit and from a distance the twinkling lights spiralled around the mountain look enchanting. But don't be fooled. The climb is seven kilometres and the last half consists almost entirely of continuous steps cut into the mountainside, some a foot high.' You climb at night because it is cooler, and to see the sun rise.

Hatton station has a frontier look with operations and ticket sales combined in the same office. The restaurant has obliging staff and tasty, crispy vegetable patties.

Poolbank tunnel (at 560m, the longest in the island) comes next, an excuse for kids of all ages on the train to erupt into shrieks of mock horror as the train ambles through it. **Kotagala** interrupts the idyllic scenery of dells and brooks with its fuel tanks at the Ceylon Petroleum Corp bulk terminal. Then, with squeaking wheels, the train lurches past the swoop of St Clair Falls.

Talawakele is 185km from Colombo, 1,200m above sea level and was built in 1884. Today the building is colourful, with lime green shutters, yellow ochre walls and maroon trimmings. It has a turntable overgrown with weeds, and glimpses of muddy waters winding their way through mountain gaps. There is a rural resthouse by the river where the welcome for foreigners is genuine and does not lead to an increase in price. It is within walking distance of the station.

After **Watagoda**, the train's wheels squeal and squeak and it slows to a walking pace through the broad hills and neat tea gardens. Then comes the grandly named **Great Western** station at 1,614m above sea level, 197km from Colombo. This is little more than an isolated granite hut in a blissful misty setting, with a panorama of tea bushes below and Adam's Peak in the distance. The train's progress through the hills is so slow and stately, you feel you can reach out and pluck tea yourself.

Radella is a small station dedicated to tea, and then the train heads through tunnel number 17 and across bridges over twin waterfalls and past the tea factory of Glassaugh Estate before stopping at **Nanu Oya**, built in 1885. The main platform is the island one and if you peep into the operations room, you can see the Tyer's Patent Train Tablet Apparatus, probably there since the station opened, and still used for controlling a train's progress. Without a token (tablet) from the apparatus, signifying the line ahead is clear, no trains can proceed.

You alight here for Nuwara Eliya and transport waits in the forecourt across the track to take passengers there. There is a bridge over the line and the ticket office is at the entrance to the station, not combined with the operations room. Vans can be hired to go to Nuwara Eliya for which you will be asked upwards from Rs200. There are buses but they do not wait for the train if it is late.

A pleasant surprise in Nanu Oya is the presence of licensed guides (call them touts at your peril), who wait on the platform to meet tourists. While I cannot recommend them all (you'll judge their degree of shiftiness yourself) there is one whose courteous, obliging and honest service is recommended not only by tourists but by hotel managers as well. Ask for Selvam; he is short and wiry and always helpful, knows everybody and seems positively surprised when you tip him. (Many men claim to be Selvam or his brother, so ask for his guide licence if you are in doubt).

Trains with observation saloons are scheduled to leave Nanu Oya for Badulla at 1329 (*Podi Menike*) and 1538 (*Udarata Menike*), but are usually delayed. Bound for Colombo, they are more likely to be on time, with departurues from Nanu Oya scheduled for 0931 (*Udarata Menike*) and 1239 (*Podi Menike*); the night mail leaves at 2156. The station-master can help with last-minute reservations.

Nuwara Eliya

Sri Lanka's answer to the more famous hill stations of India, Nuwara Eliya excels in its setting, beauty, and the high standard of accommodation. At 1,898m above sea level but less then six degrees from the Equator, its air is crisp and a welcome respite from the heat of the coast. Invented by the British in the early 19th century, with a lake, shaded avenues, and churches that could be from English shires, it is a favourite overnight stop on coach tours of Sri Lanka's interior.

Real ale buffs delight in the draught beer brewed in Nuwara Eliya with water from Lovers Leap falls, and served at the Beer Shop, a short walk into town from the traditional hostelries of the Grand Hotel and the Hill Club. Another hotel of character is St Andrews, at the other end of the golf course that adds to the town's beauty, emphasized during its April social season by the carefully tended flowers in every garden.

For a Sri Lankan version of an English country manor inn, stay at Glendower, on the road to the Grand Hotel, at standard rate. A surprise is its King Prawn Chinese restaurant, complete with log fire and wooden slab tables.

With a small park, a lake and the Hakgala Botanical Gardens near-by, and surrounded by hills including Sri Lanka's highest peak, Pidurutalagala (2,527m) Nuwara Eliya is a delight for the nostalgic, the nature lover, and those suffering from a surfeit of the tropics and trains. Nanu Oya, the nearest station, is six kilometres by road.

For the next part of the journey, from Nanu Oya to Bandarawela, the train wends its way through, and above, vegetation so lush and scenery so dramatic, it is one of the world's — not just Sri Lanka's — great trips by train. It begins with views of hillside covered with uniformly green, crewcut tea bushes, brightened by women in red, blue and yellow plastic capes nimbly plucking the young leaves, and the heady aroma of tea drying in factories.

Tea

Tea was first grown in Ceylon in 1824 at the Botanical Gardens at Peradeniya when a few plants were brought from China; more were introduced from Assam in 1839. In 1867 (the year the railway line reached Peradeniya), a Scottish planter, James Taylor, planted tea seedlings on eight acres of forest land which had actually been cleared for coffee planting.

Taylor's foresight was remarkable because two years later a blight wiped out the country's coffee crop. The island's planters turned to tea and had 400 hectares flourishing by 1875. In 1965, Ceylon displaced India as the world's biggest tea exporter and tea is one of the major foreign exchange earners for Sri Lanka.

The best Ceylon teas are known as High Grown, from plantations at heights above 1,200m where the climate has a crucial effect on quality. The finest teas from Uva and Udapusellawa districts are produced in the middle of the year when those regions are swept by very dry winds and the teas take on their own characteristic refreshing flavour. Teas from the other, western side of the main range of hills, from Nuwara Eliya, Dimbula and Dickoya, show their best quality in January and February after the northeast monsoon, when dry weather and cold nights predominate. The flavour of Nuwara Eliya tea is quite distinct from Uva, though the two districts are neighbours, which illustrates how sensitive tea is to soil, environment and climate.

Low grown teas, mostly produced on private estates in the Matara, Galle and Ratnapura districts of southern Sri Lanka and bought more for leaf appearance than taste, grow at sea level up to 600m. Medium grown teas, with a rich, mellow taste and good colour, are grown at heights of between 600m and 1,200m

The journey from bush to tea taster's spoon takes 24 hours, although it could be months before the same tea is used to make one of the billion cups brewed around the world every day. The tea bush is actually an evergreen tree called Chinese camellia (*camellia sinensis*) which could grow 10m high if not pruned every two or three years. The pruning encourages the repeated growth of a 'flush' of fresh young shoots throughout the year. These shoots, of two top leaves and a tender bud, are plucked every six to ten days.

On arrival at the tea factory from the field, the leaves are spread out in metal withering troughs until they lose their moisture and go limp. 100kg of green leaf in each trough is reduced to 50 or 55kg during this period.

The withered leaves are fed into a rolling machine which crushes their cell structure, releasing the natural juice and enzymes which give tea its flavour. The leaves emerge from the rotorvane machine in twisted, sticky lumps. Oxidization, not fermentation, takes place there in about three hours, changing the pulverized green leaf into a light, coppery shade through the absorption of oxygen. Firing (or drying) in a hot air chamber for about 20 minutes halts the 'fermentation', kills off any bacteria, dries the tea and preserves it, further reducing the original 100kg to 24kg.

The fired leaf is left to cool naturally before being sifted. The main commercial leaf grades are Orange Pekoe (OP), Pekoe (Pek) and Flowery Pekoe (FP). Broken leaf grades are Broken Orange Pekoe (BOP), Broken Pekoe (BP), Fannings (F) and Dust. Leaf and BOP grades are used in traditional packet blends while fannings and dust find their way into teabags.

Tea auctions are held on Mondays and Tuesdays at the Ceylon Chamber of Commerce building, 50 Navam Mawatha, Colombo 3; tel: 421745; fax: 941 449352.

Parakumpura is a small halt after which the mist-shrouded tea gardens begins to give way to vegetable patches between forests of fir and ferns. **Ambewela** still has the infrastructure for steam amidst tall, straight fir trees, ferns, glades and babbling brooks. Hills shorn of trees for cultivation jerk you back to reality and the air turns crisper.

Pattipola, at 1,891m above sea level, is 223km from Colombo, close to the railway's summit. It is not a particularly pretty station, unless you are lucky enough to encounter a flock of red-sweatered schoolgirls chattering excitedly at the sight of the train, but it is Sri Lanka's highest station. It also marks the beginning of the remainder of the tunnels with the next one, number 18, being bored through the mountain range dividing the Central and Uva provinces. This is the second largest tunnel and is renowned because the concrete lining in it collapsed in 1951, blocking the tunnel with loose material pouring from the hillside above. The holes were patched up with a steel shell but the tunnel was not fixed permanently until 1981.

A mixed passenger goods train also runs on this line and sometimes it will cross with the passenger train at Pattipola. The locomotives used for it were given to the railways in the 1950s and 60s by the Canadian government, hence the names of provinces in Canada, and they ushered in the dieselization of the railways and the demise of steam. These diesels are still used on the upcountry line because their extra adhesive weight makes them ideal for the steep gradients. Only senior drivers operate locomotives on this line since it requires considerable experience when the rails are wet and the wheels cannot grip; and because of those weak sleepers, speed has to be kept to 16km/h.

The summit comes one kilometre after Pattipola station, marked with a signboard. It is 1,911m (6,266ft) above sea level. Another sign says 'Beware of rock slips'.

Ohiya (1,774m, 229km from Colombo) is the station for the trek to Horton Plains and a signboard announces the distance to Farr Inn as 11km. Then the train dives in and out of more than a dozen tunnels, the scenery changing with each gap from cloud-shrouded mountains to forest copses. After yet another tunnel comes the incredible station of **Idalgashinna** (1,615m), amazing because of the deep, stunning views on both sides as it sits atop a ridge in the mountains, overlooking a lunar landscape and the formidable, scalloped hills of Uva. No trains are scheduled to stop at the next station, **Glenanore**, and it is not in the timetable, but it exists as a charming tea garden halt with a lived-in look.

It is worth getting down at **Haputale** (1,431m, 246km from Colombo, built in 1893) for several reasons. It is a pleasant market town with a couple of offbeat places to stay; it offers the unexpected view of its major street apparently disappearing over a cliff to plunge thousands of feet to a low-country plateau below; and it is good for a breakfast break.

Once, on a ride from Badulla to Colombo on the *Udarata Menike*, I stopped off at Haputale at 0755 and had my ticket endorsed by the stationmaster and went to the resthouse opposite the station for breakfast, western style with a mountain of toast. After a stroll around the town I resumed my journey on the *Podi Menike* at 1052.

Highcliffe is a guesthouse in a British-built granite block villa that has seen better days; charming host and hostess, but basic dormitory accommodation, economy rate. But a real find, if you want to wallow in a somewhat sanctimonious ambience totally at odds with life in the tropics, is Adisham.

Hardly a hotel, Adisham certainly has character, much of which it seeks to impose on guests with pithy slogans such as 'You can't do anything about the length of your life, but you can do something about its width and breadth', posted on signs in its gardens. Adisham is a Roman Catholic monastery (actually a novitiate) with three somewhat spartan rooms and cold water showers fed by a mountain stream, for paying guests.

Rooms are in the former chauffeur's quarters, remaining from the days when this mansion of grey granite blocks and turret windows with teak frames was the home-from-home, built in 1931, of retired planter Sir Thomas and Lady Evelyn Hope Villiers of Adisham, Kent. Their library and drawing room are preserved as they were in the 1930s. The monastery is in the middle of a bird sanctuary, superb for energetic walks through the countryside (Haputale is 3km away) and, of course, for meditation. April to October (it's warmer then) is the best time to visit. Economy grade and advance booking is essential. (Father Superior, Adisham, Haputale; tel: 057 8030.)

If you fancy renting a tea planter's bungalow on the edge of the most spectacular view above hills and valleys stretching 40km to the coast, ask for Kelburne Mountain Resort, 2km walk from Haputale. With your own houseboy and an old cook who conjures up dishes mother must have taught him, you can sample the gracious life of colonial days, with plenty of vigorous walks through the tea-clad hills. There are three bungalows, each with two bedrooms (sleep four) and two bathrooms (with hot water!) costing from Rs1,500 per bungalow per day, meals extra. (Reservations through Mountain View Resorts, 282/8 Galle Road, Colombo 3; tel: 575644; fax: 941 575408; resort telephone 057 8029).

For a moment after leaving Haputale you feel the train has taken the wrong turning as it seems to wander down the middle of the main street, with market stalls overflowing on to the main line. Then it recovers to meander through strictly ordered tea terrain. The station at **Diyatalawa** (1,331m) is spanking clean, with a pleasant forecourt and almost a military appearance: not surprising since Diyatalawa has been a military and naval training centre since British times, and also something of a health resort. There is an old cemetery there of Boer prisoners of the South African war.

The train arrives at **Bandarawela** (1,221m, 257km from Colombo) almost before you are ready. It is a favourite hill station for those who find Nuwara Eliya too cold, too difficult to get to or just too expensive. Ask at the station for a taxi to town and you will be told you have to go into the town to get the taxi. Turn left at the station exit and you will find a tunnel under the track about 150m down the road. This leads to the town where you can find a three-wheeler taxi to drive back to the station to collect your luggage and fellow travellers. The road to town is on the right of the station exit.

Unfortunately the town is rather lacking in charm when compared with Nuwara Eliya, but there are some wonderful places to stay, including tea plantation bungalows nearby. One of my favourite hotels in Sri Lanka, the Bandarwela Hotel, is next to the post office, superbly located on a bluff above the town so you escape the dross and have only the bliss of its garden setting, perfect for afternoon tea. In 1993 it was 100 years old but it seems rooted in the 1930s with its glassed-in terrace lounge and deep chesterfields, dining room with mixed grill fit for trenchermen, and atmosphere of a health resort. The beds have brass knobs on the ends, the furniture is practical antique and the whole place is designed for informal relaxation on the lines of a tea planters' club, which is what it used to be. Standard rates, and worth it.

To stay in a tea planter's bungalow, try Kirchchayn bungalow on the Aislaby Estate, which has been taking paying guests for more than 30 years. Agents are John Keels Hotels (PO Box 1048, Colombo 2; tel: 439049). There is no host and you are left to your own devices, which means you will need transport since it is a 30-minute drive along a torturous and bumpy track from Bandarawela. You will feel you have stumbled into a time-warped tropical Surrey where the butler, summoned by a handbell placed at your elbow when you relax on the terrace, asks 'Would master care for peaches for tea?'

The main line was built as far as Bandarawela in 1894 and for 30 years the station served as the terminus. Now it is rather sleepy with a booking office (1st and 2nd class tickets from a separate counter) which opens 30 minutes before a train's departure. If you do not have a reservation in the observation saloon for the trip back to Colombo, you will have to wait until the train comes in, and space is checked, before being able to buy a ticket. This is because, although there might be seats available, these may have been sold in Nanu Oya.

Kinigama is reached after the train runs through the outskirts and scrubland of Bandarawela's suburbs. Close your eyes for **Heeloya**, a nasty, recently built station set in paddy fields where everyone seems to be hard at work. Cauliflowers are also grown close to the line as the train descends carefully, coming to the much lovelier station of **Ella** (built in 1918 at 269km from Colombo) — if you ignore its asbestos canopy in front of the granite, cottage-like station building. Look out for the wooden rickshaw used to carry the mail to the post office, usually chained to a station post, and still used.

The delightful resthouse (ten minutes' walk, economy) once a private bungalow, affords an excellent view of the low country through the Ella Gap. Some bedrooms are actually under the lawn and seem to be suspended over the view. The rice and curry is good here. Part of the Ceylon Hotels Corporation group, booking can be made through the Colombo office (see page 166).

Now some fun. It begins with the trains easing over a bridge of nine arches (known locally as Nine Hearts) and then, at **Demodara**, where the station was built in 1921, the train turns kittenish and chases its tail. The Demodara Loop was constructed to avoid a gradient steeper than the ruling 1 in 44 so the train actually burrows almost under itself down the tunnel under the station. You will see this oddity better from the rear seat of the observation saloon on the way back (from Badulla).

The scenery opens up as the line follows the curve of the river to the tiny hamlet of **Uduwara**. After the high bridge by Rosette Estate, the train comes to **Hali Ella** where the station building, with its flowers and fir tree look like a cottage transported from the Yorkshire Dales. The final descent brings you to **Badulla** which, being 3,000 feet lower than Bandarawela, seems to have a sluggish air after the vibrancy of the hills.

At the station, built in 1924 and characterized by a liberal use of dark green paint, people queue for tickets in a cattle grid of guard rails until the booking office opens 30 minutes before a train's departure. There is a small lobby with park-bench type wooden seats and ornate wrought-iron railings and gates. It is all very relaxed and you suspect it has not changed much since the 1920s. There is a shed selling short eats and soft drinks.

Badulla has a resthouse managed by the Urban Development

Authority, in the centre of the town, 800m from the railway station, with rooms built around a central courtyard. Economy.

Departures of trains from Badulla are at 0555 (*Udarate Menike*), 0850 (*Podi Menike*) and 1745 (night mail), with arrival in Colombo at 1523, 2000 and 0540 respectively.

THE COAST LINE
Maradana to Matara

The line running southwards along the western coast to Galle and then eastwards along the southern coast as far as Matara is understandably popular with travellers. It serves the beach resort areas and the journey does not take very long. If you plan your trip properly, you will even be able to get a seat.

If possible, travel against the regular flow of passenger traffic, for this is a commuter line with office workers coming into Colombo every morning on working days from as far away as Matara and Galle. Thus the early morning trains into Colombo are standing room only, especially the all 3rd class *Samudra Devi* which leaves Galle at 0440, arriving Colombo Fort at 0831. This is also the train to avoid when leaving Colombo (it departs from Maradana at 1642). Even the seats which appear to be empty at Fort have 'owners' whose friends vigorously defend the territory until their cronies board to claim them.

The best train in both directions is the fast express, *Ruhunu Kumari* (58/59), which leaves Matara at 0540, stopping at Galle, Hikkaduwa, Ambalangoda, Alutgama and Kalutara, arriving at Fort at 0912, thence to Maradana. This daily train leaves Maradana at 1535, Fort at 1545, stopping at the same stations on the way back before arriving at Matara at 1910. It has a reservation-only 2nd class car as part of the guard's van, and if there is a seat and you do not have a reservation, you can pay the fee of Rs15 on board. Advance reservation on the day of travel from Colombo can be done at counter 4 at Fort station.

The car is attached to the rear of the train for the journey to Colombo and at the front of the train, behind the engine, for the trip south from Colombo. For both journeys, the best seats are the window seats on the coast side, numbers 1, 5, 9, 13, 17 and, if there is one, 21. However, these seats are hit by the sun on both inbound and outbound journeys.

The other train on which you might get a seat during the journey is the popular *Galu Kumari* (56/57), with 2nd and 3rd class. This leaves Matara at 0730, arrives Fort at 1125; for the return, it leaves Fort at 1335, reaching Matara at 1735.

When catching a train to the south from Colombo, it is easier to get a seat at Maradana station where the train originates. You can get to Maradana from Fort station by taking one of the local trains or by three-wheeler. For the best coastal views, sit on the right, facing the engine. From Colombo the 2nd class carriages lead the train; they are at the rear of the train on journeys into Colombo.

While most visitors prefer to gaze at the beach and the sea, which starts about ten minutes after the beginning of the ride, a seat on the other side of the carriage gives views of town and village houses and glimpses of Sri Lankans at ease.

It took 19 years after the signing of the contract in 1875 for the line to be laid all the way to Galle. But by 1877, the line reached Moratuwa, arriving at Kalutara two years later. Alutgama, which is now a turn-ing point on the line for local slow trains, was opened in 1890. The line reached Matara five years later. The west coast was a well-populated area even then, and one of the attractions of the ride now is the views of grand, century-old mansions nestling among tropical foliage, facing the sea.

The journey begins with the train creaking slowly out of Fort station, allowing late comers to scramble aboard. Then it turns southward, passing the bilious green waters of the Beira Lake and the shanties on its embankment, with Taj Samudra Hotel in the distance on the right. On the left comes the Castle Hotel with its Victorian façade.

Kompannavidiya (Slave Island) is a commuter halt, a grim looking station. Passing under the Galle Road bridge, with the Lanka Oberoi Hotel on the left, the train reaches the sea. The view here, up to Mount Lavinia, is of couples courting under the shade of umbrellas in crannies in the rocks, and of rubbish dumps at the sea's edge. Litter is scattered willynilly for this is the backyard of the southern edge of the city.

Kollupitiya (Colpetty) has a wall obscuring the sea in front of the platform; it is the closest station to the US Embassy and British and Indian High Commissions. The ticket office is on the island platform, reached by a bridge from the entrance, 100m from the Galle Road. Next is **Bambalapitiya** station, another charmless one with concrete pillars and asbestos roof and a vast wall preventing a view of the sea. The ticket office is on the island platform and this is a major halt for commuters. The Majestic City shopping and entertainment complex is between the station and Galle Road.

Wellawatta and **Dehiwela** come next, both stations serving the busy commercial and residential areas. After Wellawatta, the beach scene improves with fishing catamarans drawn up on the sand. The stretch

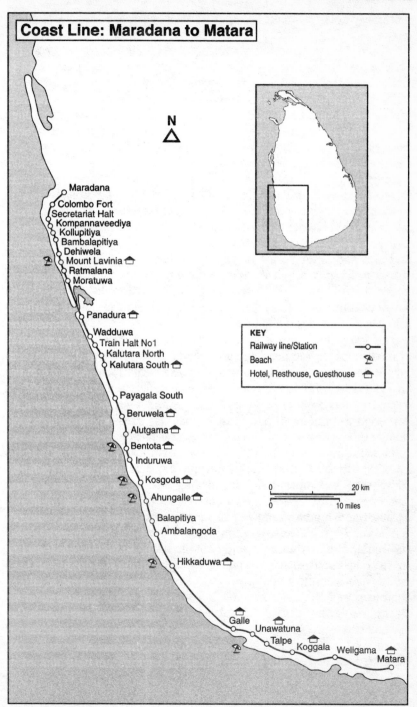

from Dehiwela to Mount Lavinia has thatched beach huts between the railway line and the beach, serving as snack bars.

Mount Lavinia station has an old-style booking office, spacious, with wide arches and a high roof. Train times are chalked on a blackboard, giving arrival and departure times from Fort station. From its exterior it is like a rural station, tucked away down a leafy lane and beside the Mount Lavinia Hotel. There are four platforms to serve the double track (the line becomes a single track after Panadura) with a linking footbridge. The view of the beach is blocked by a wall running the length of the platform, and by the back of one wing of the Mount Lavinia Hotel.

The hotel is a combination of colonial charm (dating from 1877) and modern monstrosity (the 1983 wing). Look carefully and you can see where the old has withstood the new. Some rooms in the lower-priced Governor's Wing overlook the railway line. The hotel is in both the standard and luxury price range and is really rather splendid with its many restaurants and deck-style swimming pool with a view along the beach to Colombo. The beach south of it is carefully maintained to restrict disturbances to sunbathing guests, although sometimes it erupts into carnivals and beach parties.

The domestic airport is located at **Ratmalana** whose station is in the typical suburban mould. The carriage and locomotive repair workshop is at Ratmalana, where the country's newest steam locomotive was built in 1990. It is a miniature one of 2.28m in length and draws four open compartments on a special narrow gauge line. Only local raw material was used in building it and most of that was salvaged from the scrap dump at the workshop. It is used for special fairs.

The next major station is **Moratuwa**, 20km from Maradana. It has its booking office off a busy forecourt and a snack bar on the main platform (there are four). Furniture making is a thriving industry in this heavily populated town. Bolgoda Lake is part of the waterway embracing Moratuwa, extending from Mount Lavinia to south of Panadura.

The station at **Panadura** is similar to Moratuwa and marks the end of the double track. After it, at Talpitiya, the line crosses a bridge, donated in 1991 by the British government to replace the old one (to be seen at the river's mouth) which proved too narrow, claiming the lives of footboard travellers.

The tourist strip begins at **Wadduwa**, another charmless station with an asbestos roof and small package hotels between the railway line and the sea. Three kilometres further down the line is what has been described as the only railway station in Sri Lanka without a name. In

1953 the station was dubbed *Train Halt Number One* because the people of the area it serves (Potupitiya and Waskaduwa) could not agree on what it should be called.

Kalutara North is easily recognizable by the vines trailing over its roof and the potted plants along the platform, an example of how a little-used station can be brightened up to delight passengers. **Kalutara South** is the main station for Kalutara, just after crossing the Kalu river and passing the modern — and hollow — *dagaba* (stupa). Do not be alarmed at the sight of passengers tossing coins out of the window. It is customary for Buddhists passing the *dagaba* and the Bo tree by the road to make an offering of money to ward off bad luck during their journey.

The district is known for its basketware, for its rubber plantations and for its mangosteens (a delicious seasonal tropical fruit). The main toddy-tapping and arrack-distilling area starts here, which is why many of the coconut palm trees alongside the railway line right up to Hikkaduwa have no nuts. The line crosses the main road to Galle at **Payagala South** station to wend through palm groves alongside the road which runs beside the rural belt of the south as the scenery takes on a greener hue.

Beruwela station is inland where package tourist hotels line the beach. Beruwela began as an early Moorish settlement and has a 1,000-year-old tomb of a Muslim saint overlooking its harbour. There is a fish market held on the beach at the southern end of the harbour every morning, 0600-0800. Fishermen auction their catch, which is transported often on the backs of pedal and motorbikes, to inland villages to be chopped into pieces and sold for lunch.

Alutgama was an important station in the past. Today it consists of a single, long island platform with a bridge connecting it to the roadway entrance. The ticket office is on the platform, and there is a small fish tank as well. Slow trains both from Galle and Colombo terminate and turn around here. The station still preserves facilities for steam engines with a water tower and a turntable. It is the starting point for the Viceroy Special departures to Kandy.

From the station there is access to the independent small hotels to the north of Alutgama (walk through to the main road and turn right) which have sprung up to cater for the refugees from mass tourism. The bus station is at the end of the station access road. You have to turn left to walk through the town to reach Bentota, or walk off the platform (at the Galle end) and trek along the railway track to the level crossing where you can join the road. This will bring you to the bridges across the Bentota river.

A neat guesthouse (upper economy range) is located on the Alutgama side of the bridge, right on the river. Called Terrena Lodge, it is renowned locally for European-inspired food. Enquire at the Rainbow Boat House (good for lagoon watersports and river cruises) on the left for how to get to Susantha Guesthouse, a gem of a place hidden up a country lane but only five minutes from the beach.

Having crossed the bridge, you are now in Bentota with its package hotels and broad (in October to April) beach. It is a National Tourist Resort which means infrastructure for visitors (bank, post office, souvenir shops) as well as some repectable restaurants and guesthouses. Opposite the Bentota Beach Hotel is Aida's Gem and Jewellery shop with a pleasant roof-top restaurant with views of river and sea.

Behind the **Bentota** railway station with access from the sole platform is the Susantha Palm Restaurant, where there are a dozen well-appointed rooms in the upper economy range. On the other side of the platform is the beach. Not all trains stop at Bentota, so sometimes you will have to get down at Alutgama. From Maradana the 1325 departure of the *Galu Kumari* is the best train, reaching Bentota at 1510. Coming from the south, *Galu Kumari* stops at 0956 and there is another train (number 39) from Matara to Kandy which stops at 1459.

The stations get prettier after Bentota with nothing much happening to them since they were built a century ago, apart from the addition of a roofing of asbestos over the platforms. **Induruwa** is particularly pretty (it does not have the dreaded asbestos canopy) since the station staff have added potted plants and creepers. It is sometimes used as a backdrop for German fashion photographers. Along the coast near Induruwa, before **Kosgoda** station, are a few turtle sanctuaries.

Turtle eggs

Turtle eggs are collected from the beach by local people who sell them to the sanctuaries instead of eating them. The eggs are buried in the sand at the sanctuaries until they hatch. After the young turtles have grown sufficiently they are returned to the sea, often sponsored by tourists paying to release them to celebrate an occasion, such as 30 turtles on a 30th birthday.

If you are bound for Sri Lanka's first five-star beach resort, the Triton **Ahungalle** is the station but it is served only by slow, local trains and is rather lacklustre. The next station, **Balapitiya**, retains the railway atmosphere of its British styling, enhanced by potted plants and its location on the bank of a broad river. Watch carefully after the station for the train to cross the river. You are now on an island with no road access, only the railway bridges at both sides. It has several houses, most of which get flooded when the river rises. It takes about two minutes to cross it by train, then more palm groves and houses of red-tiled roofs until the train reaches **Ambalangoda**.

The station has the familiar look of its late 19th century origins. An attraction of the town, as well as the brightly painted wooden masks produced there, is the number of antique shops. The reproduction of antique furniture using aged wood and old methods is quite an industry. Other old items can also be picked up here but you need an expert's eye. By law, antiques cannot be exported without official permission; an antique is regarded as an object over 50 years old.

Hikkaduwa is the station for beggars to get on or off — they know that's where the tourists are. Exit at the southern end of the platform for quick access to the bus station and three-wheeler park. Known as 'Hippy-kaduwa' in the past, this former sleepy fishing village is now Sri Lanka's seaside Soho: all the sleaze you want, as well as low-cost guesthouses and a main road lined with restaurants offering ersatz Italian and Chinese cuisine as well as 'live lobsters'. It has sprung up in response to the younger visitors' demand for action during their vacation — and because it provides super surfing. It is part of Sri Lanka's formula of offering something for everyone, even though it wasn't planned that way, or any way.

There is a range of places to stay, from the upmarket luxury category such as Coral Garden Hotel which looms over the town like a fortress, to the usual package hotels and guesthouses in the palm groves beyond the beach. A pleasant oddity is Nippon Villa (economy grade), newly built with miniature gardens in the bedrooms and Japanese food prepared by its Japanese-trained Sri Lankan owner.

Galle is 20 minutes run from Hikkaduwa and you know you are getting there when the palm trees give way to suburbs. It is the terminus, although some trains do reverse out to continue to Matara. There are four platforms, with rest rooms on the right of the ticket barriers, alongside platform 1, and a huge table in the gents' rest room on which a score of passengers could sleep overnight. The cafeteria is best avoided. Tickets are collected as you leave the platform, or clipped as you enter.

There is a kiosk selling newspapers in English in the booking hall. A plaque commemorating the laying of the foundation of the new railway station in 1965 is by the ticket office. Train departure times are shown on clocks and there are loudspeaker announcements. The railway retiring rooms are up a flight of stairs on the left of the booking hall, eight double rooms with attached shower and toilet at Rs300. If open, there is a snack bar on the same floor with a terrace overlooking the town, playing field and the ramparts of the fort only five minutes' walk away.

The fort was begun by the Portuguese in the 17th century and was completed by the Dutch, and then the British in the 19th. It is a residential area with government buildings and red-tiled cottages and villas huddled together. It is a magic, mysterious place to wander through, especially at sunset, or to stroll along the ramparts. The tallest building is the New Oriental Hotel, built in 1684 to house the Dutch garrison and turned into a hotel in 1865. It has declined gracefully since its heyday when Galle was Ceylon's main port and is now a hotel of character and charm not to be missed.

Rooms are great fun, including 12 massive suites furnished with pairs of four-posters, 1930 period chairs and junk. A swimming pool with a notice warning guests not to spit in it is hidden by a delightful walled garden. Prices are in the upper economy range and the rice and curry lunch at one (screened off) end of the old ballroom is memorable.

The bus station adjoins the railway station. Down the street running alongside the canal and railway line are two Chinese-type restaurants and a Bottle Shop, which is the local off-licence.

Major departures from Galle to Colombo Maradana are at 0600 (Monday only), 0634 (*Ruhunu Kumari*), 0810 (Saturday only, to Kandy), 0840 (not Saturday or Sunday), 1115 (to Anuradhapura and Vavuniya), 1400 (to Kandy), 1500 (Sunday only) and 1640.

To Matara there are through trains from Colombo at 0942, 1120, 1320, 1557 (Friday only), 1630 (not Saturday or Sunday), 1815 and 1840 (Sunday only).

The through train to Matara stops for about ten minutes in Galle while the engine is detached from the front and, if no other engine is available, reverses to the other end of the train. So if you want to keep on the sea side, it is time to cross over the vestibule and sit on the other side, so you are still on the right of the train, facing the engine. Sometimes an express becomes a slow train between Galle and Matara, stopping at every station. Even for the enthusiast of train journeys (the track bashers) and of rural scenes, this can become wearying since there are 12 stations, and sometimes long waits in sidings (for incoming trains to cross) before reaching Matara.

First is a tunnel after Galle as the train assumes a leisurely pace through coconut and palmyrah groves with only occasional glimpses of the sea. **Unawatuna** station gives no hint of the delightful beach within

15 minutes' walk (across the main road), and is not particularly attractive. The train times are prominently displayed since this is a major halt for independent tourists seeking the sun and fun of this romantic cove.

The booking office at **Talpe** is built of granite and since it has no awning it is easy to imagine how it looked a hundred years ago when the line was built. Gradually the scenery from there changes to flat scrubland and then to the industrial landscape of the Free Trade Zone at **Koggala**, with lagoon, airstrip and new factories waiting for future development. A succession of halts consisting of concrete huts and a brief stretch of platform come next until the scenery grows lusher and the line wends inland and comes back to reach **Weligama**.

All the platforms on this line are single ones on the southern side of the track. A surprise is the sight of verdant paddy fields as the train approaches **Walgama**, which makes it resemble mainline scenery. Then there is a gentle build up of houses and the train comes to the end of its journey, entering **Matara** station.

This station, marking the current end of the line, is a step back in time. It was built in 1895 and the bullock carts with their polished brass fittings which meet passengers seem to date to then. There are Morris Minor taxis, too, as well as the ubiquitous three-wheelers. You will need some form of transport to get to the bus station; in 1993 the asking price was Rs50 (for tourists) or Rs30 (for locals) by hackery (bullock-drawn trap) or Rs20 by three-wheeler. Bargaining over fares is good natured.

The station has the air of a frontier, with booking office open to the forecourt, and the leisurely ambience of knowing that train journeys begin or end there and no trains race through. Although it is planned to extend the line to Kataragama, at the time of writing the only way to continue along the south coast is by bus or some kind of taxi. By the end of 1994, though, the first section of the new line was scheduled to be opened.

The three-wheeler drivers have fixed fares to south coast towns and will willingly agree to take you even the 115km (72 miles) to Tissamaharama (3½ hours). If you want to see something of the coast, perhaps stopping at a resthouse for lunch on the way, a three-wheeler for two can be a good deal. Buses originate and terminate at Matara and are as crowded and as crazily driven as most.

If you are catching a train at Matara, allow time to buy the ticket as there is sometimes a queue and you may want to get a window seat ahead of the others. Sit on the left side facing the engine for the run along the coast to Galle, but switch seats when the engine is put at the other end of the train to leave Galle for the run up the west coast.

Most trains to Colombo are supposed to be through trains but if the incoming train is delayed, you may have to take a special local train (3rd class only) to connect with the Colombo-bound train at Galle. There is a daily train from Matara via Colombo to Anuradhapura and also one to Kandy. The station has a bookstall but the only reading matter in English seems to be the morning newspapers. There is a snack bar, a waiting room and toilets.

To visit Matara's petite Star Fort, dating from Dutch days, you could ride a bullock buggy. The resthouse in the main fort has an extensive menu of dishes to appeal to visitors but the quickest and tastiest meal is rice and curry. The resthouse is on the sea front and is an attractive place to stay (economy rate).

Main train departures from Matara station

0450   to Maradana (No 55) (Monday only)
0540   to Maradana (*Ruhunu Kumari*)
0700   to Kandy (No 65) (Saturday only)
0730   to Maradana (*Galu Kumari*) (not Saturdays/Sundays)
0950   to Vavuniya via Colombo and Anuradhapura (*Rajarata Rajini*)
1255   to Kandy (No 39)
1530   to Maradana (No 51)

Matara to Tissamaharama

In the next edition, this section should be about the rail journey. If you go by road there are stalls selling the best (ie: thickest) buffalo curd in Sri Lanka, a variety of fruits (check the watermelon) and vegetables, and garishly painted clay moneyboxes and gaudy figurines.

Buildings of the Ruhunu University dominate the hillside and then, just before **Tangalle**, down a track that gets progressively narrower, is a beachside fishing village called Hoo-manaya. Pay a few rupees to a lady who claims to be custodian of the narrow path leading up the hillside, through villagers' gardens, and you can scramble up to discover a blow hole. From a fissure in the rocks of the cliff overlooking the idyllic fishing cove, sea water fumes and spouts with a mighty roar some 20m into the air.

Tangalle itself climbs around a beach and looks a very orderly resort with thatched roundels as restaurants and several administrative buildings, including a navy base. The charm of the resthouse, reputed to date from Dutch days, has been overwhelmed by annexes. The landscape levels out to saltpans afterwards, with Ambalantota being a commercial town, and then you reach Hambantota, from where buses are available for the hill country — but it is a dreary ride.

As soon as you reach the outskirts of Tissamaharama, dashing young men in jeeps chase after you to offer safaris to the Ruhunu National Park at Yala (see page 173). If you have your own vehicle you could drive yourself the 12km to the park and even inside it, as long as you have an official tracker from the park office with you.

There are guesthouses in Tissa, as well as Sri Lanka's most upmarket resthouse which has rooms on three floors overlooking a swimming pool and a lake. Rates in the upper economy range.

THE NORTHERN LINE

Polgahawela to Anuradhapura, Vavuniya and Mihintale

The original extent of the Northern Line was 412km from Colombo via Jaffna to Kankesanturai. At present, rail passengers can travel only as far as Vavuniya, 252km from Colombo, but the line is mostly used by passengers bound for Anuradhapura. There is even a through train (*Rajarata Rajini*) once a day from the southern terminus of Matara. In distance (410km) this is the longest through train ride in Sri Lanka. Another train, *Rajarata Charika*, operates between Galle and Anuradhapura on special weekend holidays.

The Northern Line begins at Polgahawela (on the main line to Kandy). It first reached Kurunegala in 1894 and on to Anuradhapura in 1903. Building was started on the station and track at Kankesanturai in the extreme north in 1902, continuing southwards to meet the new track at Anuradhapura.

The *Yal Devi* (number 77) train leaves Colombo Fort at 0545 and leaves Vavuniya (as number 78) for the return trip at 1230 every day. It has the luxury of a 1st class air-conditioned carriage with 32 seats in a 2 × 2 layout. Seats 7 and 8 face seats 9 and 10 with a table in between, and seats 23 and 24 face seats 25 and 26, also with a table. All other seats have drop-down tables from the seat back in front. They recline and are comfortably padded with cloth upholstery. There are two toilets (both in need of a good scrub) and sealed windows which also need a clean, and window blinds to keep out the sun.

This air-conditioned accommodation is perfect if you want to sleep your way through the scenery but isolates you from the real world of rail travel. No breeze nor vendors penetrate. It is best to use this carriage as a base during the journey, wandering through the train when you get bored, although if it is crowded you would be better off enjoying what you have paid for.

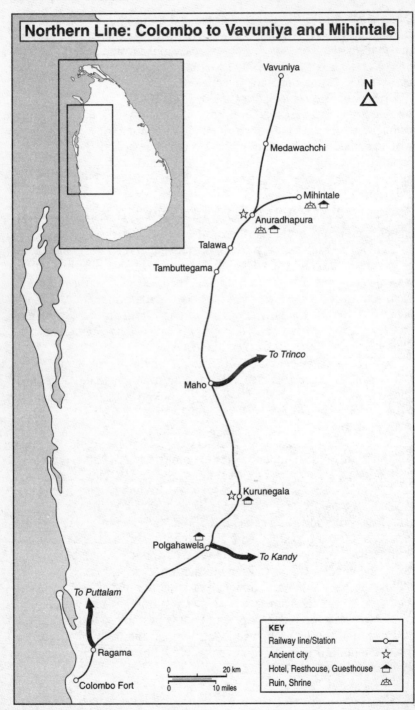

Northern Line: Colombo to Vavuniya and Mihintale

N

Vavuniya

Medawachchi

Mihintale

Anuradhapura

Talawa

Tambuttegama

To Trinco

Maho

Kurunegala

Polgahawela

To Kandy

To Puttalam

Ragama

Colombo Fort

| 0 | | 20 km |
| 0 | 10 miles | |

KEY

Railway line/Station	—○—
Ancient city	☆
Hotel, Resthouse, Guesthouse	⌂
Ruin, Shrine	灬

Other types of accommodation are 2nd and 3rd class sleeperettes, ordinary 2nd class (no reclining seats) and 3rd class bench seats for two and three passengers, sometimes wooden but more often the rexine-covered version of the new coaches. The night mail (89/90) has 1st class sleepers and 2nd and 3rd class sleeperettes.

After branching off the main line at Polgahawela the train speeds for 30 minutes to **Kurunegala** (93km from Colombo). Once a capital, now a bustling agricultural town, its station is 15 minutes' walk from the town centre, which is represented by the bus station and resthouse. Formerly the abode of the colonial administrator, the resthouse has suffered from neglect but, according to James Fraser Darling writing in a letter to the *Daily News* in July 1991, it is 'an architectural jewel which if protected . . . can still lend serenity to Sri Lankans and world travellers alike'.

The huge rock looming over the town can be climbed for a magnificent view of the countryside and the lake. Rocks are a feature of the landscape and are named after animals — elephant, tortoise, etc — which they resemble, as can be seen when the train leaves Kurunegala.

After Kurunegala you begin to understand the magnificence of Sri Lanka's rural heartland. The train speeds through coconut plantations ringed with hills and past phantom stations which are no more than a nameboard and not in the timetable. You will glimpse lily ponds blinking in the early morning sunlight on one side of the line and brilliant green paddy fields on the other. When the train does stop, the platforms are not long enough and the atmosphere is overwhelmingly relaxed. At **Timbiriyagedara** (131km from Colombo) you discover from the station signboard that it is only 79m above sea level, yet you feel it should be higher.

Maho, five kilometres further on and built in 1899, is the Crewe of Sri Lanka, the junction for trains heading north, east and south. It is modest considering the number of trains it deals with. Prettier, and a prize winner, is the next station on the northern line, **Ambanpola**, while the one after it, **Senarathgama**, is lent charm by the temple trees (frangipani) on its platform. The lushness of the scenery begins to evaporate to dry zone forest and scrub, but watch out for the colonial stations of **Tambuttegama** and **Talawa** in the midst of trees.

A contrast comes with the cowshed architecture of **Anuradhapura New Town**, 200km from Colombo. Don't get down here but continue to the main station of **Anuradhapura**, originally built in 1904. All that remains from that period are the colonnaded railway cottages that house the colony of railway residents surrounding the station. The new station opened in 1963 and has a façade, painted white, built to resemble the temples of the ancient city with all its pillars. It has an island platform reached by a tunnel, as well as a main one.

There is a snack bar at the station with a succinct notice: PARTAKING OF MEALS FROM OUTSIDE PROHIBITED WITHIN. There are what the stationmaster describes as 'spacious' retiring rooms with rates in 1994 of single Rs150, double Rs300. For more fun — even if double the cost — head for the queen of Sri Lanka's resthouses: the Tissawewa.

It stands in what, 2,000 years ago, was the Royal Pleasure Garden, within 15 minutes' walking distance of the oldest (at least 2,200 years) documented tree on earth, the Sri Maha Bodhi, or sacred Bo tree. The resthouse was conceived in the early 1900s as a grand hotel with spacious rooms, high ceilings and broad verandas. Managed since 1967 by a private company, Quickshaws, every room has hot and cold showers (and large bath towels) with furniture that is heavy and traditional. With five rooms leading off the teak boarded gallery on the first floor, a sun balcony on the roof of the entrance porch, 15 rooms downstairs opening on to the garden, monkeys popping in and out, and country-style cuisine utilizing local vegetables, this is a place to linger, especially at its economy rate.

Alcoholic drinks are not served at the Tissawewa Resthouse but you can buy them at its sister, at the other side of town, the Nuwarawewa Resthouse. With 60 older rooms and 11 newer ones, all with air-conditioning, and a swimming pool, this resembles a resort in facilities and being in the upper economy bracket is ideal if you want a holiday atmosphere instead of a colonial one.

Anuradhapura rates its own chapter in most guidebooks because of its importance as an ancient city (one-time capital) and for its religious edifices. The best way to explore the ruins of the ancient city (the modern town is not up to much) is by bicycle, available for hire from the resthouses, but make sure you have a viewing permit (obtainable from the Archaeological Department for the entire cultural triangle sites, if you do not have one). You can buy a map of Anuradhapura in the town.

Part of the ancient religious circuit is Mihintale which, according to Buddhist traditions, is the place where Prince Mahinda, son of the Indian emperor Asoka, came in 307BC to preach Buddhism. A new railway line, opened in 1993, serves Mihintale from Anuradhapura main station.

The train — usually a thrice-daily local power-set but with extra services during the pilgrimage season of *Poson* (in June) — starts by following the line to Vavuniya. Then at the inaptly named **Mihintale Junction** station (which is not in Mihintale but 13km from it), it branches off, cutting through flat, sparse jungly vegetation with scarcely a house or a person to be seen. Of course this will change as the line, which cost Rs151 million to build in a period of six months, leads to the region being developed.

The journey takes 35 minutes. **Mihintale** station has been designed with flair, with linking pavilions making it look like a new beach hotel, not a railway station. On one side are shelters and toilet facilities for pilgrims while at the end is the retiring room complex: two family rooms and six doubles, all with toilet facilities and fans in a modern village villa setting; economy rate.

The station is so aesthetically pleasing, I did not want to throw my rubbish on the platform and looked in vain for a litter bin. The stationmaster noticed and beckoned me into his office to toss my sandwich wrapper in his own wastepaper basket.

Trains to Mihintale from Anuradhapura connect with arriving trains from Colombo and those from Mihintale are timed to arrive in Anuradhapura to connect with Colombo-bound trains. Tickets to any station in the railway network can be bought at Mihintale, which has six ticket windows to cope with the Poson crowds.

The run to Vavuniya from Anuradhapura is not scenic as the train scythes through scrubland and plains, passing the occasional *cadjan* (thatched) roof mudhouse. The platform at **Parasangahawewa** is not much longer than its name, but it has an upturned train lying in the brushwood beside its loop line.

Madawachchi Junction (229km from Colombo and built in 1905) is a neat island station where the ticket checkers get down to wait for the train to make its return journey. Moden buildings are used instead of the old ones, which still remain. Although still out of operation in 1994, the line to **Talaimannar Pier** (335km from Colombo, built in 1914), from where train passengers used to be able to take the ferry to India, begins here.

Although a sign by the track says 'Beware Floods' it is arid and dusty in the dry season. At the halt of **Poonewa** the station offices are housed in a lone goods wagon on the short platform. The train picks up speed for a final sprint. Parkland and paddy characterize the area and sweet oranges are grown there, too. The railway line up to 1994 terminated at **Vavuniya** and passengers were subjected to security searches as they filed out of the station.

The train goes a few kilometres up the line for the engine to change ends and then it returns to Vavuniya to commence its journey back to Colombo. If you are waiting for it, there is a pleasant local bar reached by walking to the road end of the platform and turning left into the town, about 300m towards the post office. The Empire Hotel and Bar has a streetside veranda, protected by chicken wire, and little parlours for drinking or snacking in private.

There are two trains a day and a night mail from Vavuniya to Colombo. When passengers come through by road from Jaffna, the train can get very crowded.

	Read down			Read up		
	77 Yal Devi	85 Rajarata Rajini	89 Night Mail	86 Rajarata Rajini	78 Yal Devi	90 Night Mail
Colombo Fort	0545	1405	2230	1015	1825	0420
Anuradhapura	1002	1852	0355	0505	1332	2315
Vavuniya	1135	2020	0505	0315	1230	2145

BATTICALOA AND TRINCOMALEE LINE

Maho to Gal Oya and Trincomalee

What used to be known as the BTLR (the Batticaloa-Trincomalee Light Railway) begins at Maho, the junction where the Northern Line has a branch to the east. Although **Maho** station was built in 1899, it was not until the 1920s that it was considered worthwhile to build a rail line to the east. The BTLR opened for traffic to Trincomalee in 1927 and to Batticaloa in 1928.

The section from Maho was first constructed with light rails and with earthwork kept to the minimum, to reduce costs, so the track followed the natural contours, skirting hills. It was strengthened to allow greater speeds by 1960.

A night mail used to make the journey but in recent years service has been restricted to day trains and even these change schedules according to demand.

At Maho station, all trains making the BTLR journey stop for at least ten minutes while the engine changes ends. The sellers of the thirst-quenching *thambili* coconuts are well organized, crouching on the platform every few yards as the train draws in, to leap on it to sell their wares. There is a ticket counter on the island platform with a blackboard showing the expected times of arrival and departure of the various trains

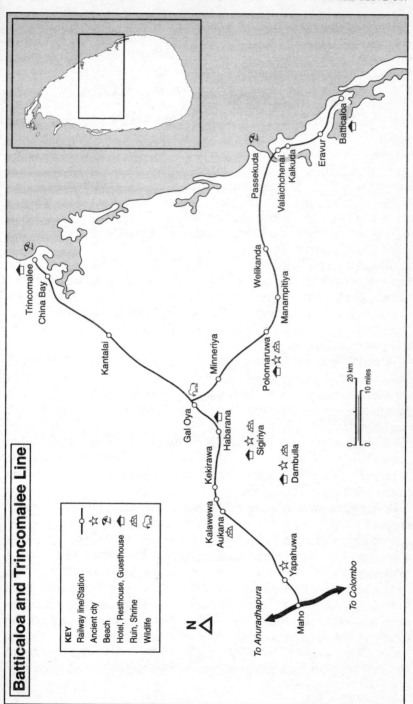

Batticaloa and Trincomalee Line

north, south and eastwards. This is a rural station and the only activity seems to be train arrivals. There is a snack bar counter fenced in with chicken wire. Yapahuwa, a rock fortress that was the capital of the island 1271-1283, is five kilometres from the station. There is, in fact, a train halt at **Yapahuwa**, but the major trains sail right through.

The scenery here is typical of *chena* (slash and burn) cultivation with the occasional hillock and mud hut in the plains. **Moragollagama** station has retained the old-style stationmaster's quarters above the booking office and has shade provided by trees instead of asbestos sheeting. A leafy lane and a new road glimpsed from the track make you wonder where you are, and then there is the halt of **Aukana** (174km from Colombo), with its new shed. You can walk from there into the scrub to view what is described as the most magnificent undamaged ancient image in the island, the Aukana Buddha, dating from the 5th century. A modern brick canopy has been added.

Women do their laundry in the drain-off from the tank (*wewa*) by the line just before the train reaches **Kelawewa**, a stop for all trains on this section. (Aukana can be reached by road from here, since not all trains stop at its station.) The ancient tank is over 4,400 acres in area. This is chilli growing country and you will see flashes of red where they are laid out on rocks to dry in the fierce sun.

Train vendors turn up with all sorts of fare, including limes and oranges, after **Kekirawa** station. Built in 1925, it serves a busy town among the paddy fields. Buses are available here for the ancient cave temple of Dambulla and thence to the rock fortress of Sigiriya (see page 157).

The train slows to a jog past **Horiwila**, a halt in the midst of red earth, then on through dry scrubland where the monotony is relieved by temple trees (frangipani) abloom at **Palugaswewa** station, 201km from Colombo.

Habarana is next, a halt with one small room as its office; it is about three kilometres from the town. It is tempting to get down here as the nearest station to Sigiriya, but you will have to walk to the town to catch a bus or taxi. The scenery is jungly and a trackside sign warns of elephants. In 1994 at **Hathareskotuwa**, another small halt in the middle of nowhere, the train I was on was boarded by a posse of police. They carried out a thorough security check of passengers and luggage while the train waited outside Gal Oya station and an ice-cream salesman did a brisk trade pedalling his bicycle along the side of the train selling cornets.

Gal Oya station (224km from Colombo) was built in 1926 and the line bifurcates here for Trincomalee. A mark on the wall of the gents' toilet shows the level reached by flood water in December 1957. Station staff and 400 passengers were marooned then but salvaged provisions, including a case of whisky, from the goods wagons and survived on that and food drops until rescued. The new station building was built in 1970.

The train to Trincomalee waits at Gal Oya for the train from Trincomalee to arrive and they swap engines. Then it resumes a staid and steady pace through dry flat lands as it heads northeastwards, passing several stations on its way. **Agbopura** has its ticket office in an abandoned goods wagon. The view as the train approaches **Kantala** is of the *bund* around the 4,725 acre Kantalai Lake, the source of water for Trincomalee. Curd in clay pots and peanuts are offered for sale by vendors on the station. The plains are swept by a cool breeze blowing in from the sea as the train creeps into **China Bay** for a short stop. From its window you can glimpse first a temple, then a church and then, of course, comes a *kovil* (a Hindu temple) and a mosque. In season (May to October), the sea shimmers like the Caribbean and the barren hills surrounding the bay make you feel you are in the Virgin Islands. Five more minutes to go before the train reaches **Trincomalee**, at the end of the 295km journey from Colombo.

The new station building was opened in 1970 and has recently undergone renovation. There is only one platform and that is kept clean and has plenty of potted plants, demonstrating the staff's pride in its maintenance. There is even a cage of lovebirds at the exit. There is a modest snack bar open to both the rail and land side. The ticket office is open 0730-1430, with advance reservation available up to ten days before a train's departure, from 0930 every day.

Above the station offices is a retiring room complex with a central sitting room and a view from its balcony of the station forecourt. Six rooms all have shower, toilet and fan; some have mosquito nets and a writing desk. Rates Rs150, single; Rs300 double.

Dozens of Morris Minors and three-wheeler taxis meet the train on its arrival at Trinco (as Trincomalee is known) and it is easy to bargain for a good price. The town has a laidback atmosphere containing the feel of the Caribbean. Fishing boats are hauled up on the beach behind the fish market in the centre of the town by the clock tower and the abandoned watering hole of yore, the Trinco Hotel. Opposite is the compound containing the daily market. Emerge from the main road side of the market and opposite is the bus station, where drinks made of lurid bright orange, green, blue and yellow water are sold from vendor's colourful stands.

The gate of Fort Frederick bears the date 1676 above its arch. Inside, you can climb the summit of the hill for a view of the natural harbour and, behind the temple, is the Swami Rock (121m high) and the ruin of the monument to the Dutch girl who is supposed to have flung herself into the sea from the rock as her lover sailed away. There is a telecommunication tower here, deer cared for by the army, and a *nuga* tree under whose shady branches an old sage with a flowing white beard sits, having lived in the fort for more than 50 years.

For refreshment, head for King's Hotel in the town, a bit seedy and threatened with being smartened up, a warren of rooms with tables and a courtyard for serious drinking. You might be the only foreigner there so try the *kotu roti* (chopped mix of meat, vegetables, egg and roti pancake) for something different and delicious with your beer.

There is a clean, modern-style resthouse in Trincomalee with a VIP toilet ('paper on request') and ten small but adequate rooms with fan and attached bathroom, economy rate.

Beachcombers rave over Pragash French Garden, off the road to Nilaveli, which I was amazed to see is not only still open after all the troubles, but has not changed much since I stayed there when I first visited Sri Lanka in 1980, except that all the rooms now have their own shower/toilet. There are mini-cottages (about Rs250 a night) on the beach and rooms from Rs100.

Even the 80-room Nilaveli Beach Resort Hotel has room rates in the economy range yet it is far superior in comfort and ambience (and fun) to many of the expensive beach hotels on the west coast, and the beach and sea (in the season) are perfect. There is a swimming pool, a good bar and the informal atmosphere of a place trendsetters adore before the hoi polloi hear of it. With ten miles of beach, watersports, angling and trips to the deserted twin Pigeon Islands (a delight for nature lovers, with hundreds of nesting birds), it makes a visit to Trinco by train especially worthwhile.

The daily service (train 81) leaves Colombo Fort at 0515 with 2nd and 3rd class sleeperettes, arriving Trincomalee at 1245. For the return journey, as train 82, it leaves Trincomalee at 0900, arriving Fort at 1645, although times are expected to change.

Gal Oya to Polonnaruwa and Batticaloa

The journey to Batticaloa is not quite so easy or rewarding. At the time of writing there were five services a week which consisted of through carriages attached to the daily train to Trincomalee (departing from Fort station at 0515). At Gal Oya these carriages are connected to a train bound for Polonnaruwa and Batticaloa.

A new daily service was also introduced in March 1994 to Polonnaruwa, which entails taking the night mail bound for Vavuniya (leaving Fort at 2230). At Maho carriages are detached and form a separate train, arriving at Polonnaruwa at 0545.

The new schedules allow passengers from Trincomalee to change at Gal Oya for Batticaloa and vice versa.

The Batticaloa correspondent of the *Daily News* reported in March 1994: 'From Trincomalee nine carriages and from Batticaloa four carriages go to Gal Oya. These 13 carriages are shunted at Gal Oya and go together to Colombo. The Batticaloa carriages are fully packed. From Batticaloa railway station itself more than 500 passengers begin their journey where the capacity of the carriages is 448 passengers... More than half the passengers go only up to Polonnaruwa and take the bus from there to Kandy.'

It is hoped that as the need for security decreases the service will eventually return to the three trains a day, including a night mail, which used to run between Batticaloa and Colombo.

With a nightly service linking it with Colombo, and its thrice a week daytime link, **Polonnaruwa** is actually only 33km by rail from Gal Oya. It can also be reached by bus from Kandy and Anuradhapura, as well as from Colombo. The Polonnaruwa station is actually at Kaduruwela, a few kilometres southeast of the ancient ruins which draw visitors.

In Polonnaruwa the resthouse is built next to the Sea of Parakrama, 2,400 hectacres of water created in the 12th century by King Parakramabahu. Managed by the government-owned Ceylon Hotels Corporation, it has ten rooms (five are air conditioned) in an idyllic setting by the vast spread of water, with the great Polonnaruwa ruins lying just behind. The building itself is not pretty: bedroom windows which should allow you to see the lake and the rolling hills beyond have been painted black and covered with chicken wire.

Breakfast and lunch are served in a restaurant built out over the lake; the newly caught freshwater fish is delicious, although the steward will apologize for it not being sea fish. Local lads bathe and frolic all day in the lake's clear water, unconcerned about the tourists who read their guidebooks in the shade of trees in the lakeside garden.

Batticaloa station is 347km from Maradana, reached after a journey of nearly ten hours. The 89/79 service to Polonnaruwa and the 90/80 from Polonnaruwa have 2nd and 3rd class sleeperette accommodation.

Station	Read down				Read up			
	81	87	89	79	82	88	80	90
Colombo Fort	0515		2230		1645			0420
Maho	0749		0142	0220	1332		0027	0054
Anuradhapura	↓		0355	↓	↑		↑	2315
Gal Oya	1028	1125		0448	1105	1024	2216	
Polonnaruwa	↓	1225		0545	↑	0918	2110	
Batticaloa		1450				0700		
Trincomalee	1245				0900			

(All times subject to change)

THE KELANI VALLEY LINE

Colombo to Avissawella

This is a railway in transition, from a sleepy narrow gauge (2ft 6in wide) line with a couple of trains a day through cluttered suburbs and tranquil byways, to a broad gauge service with regular commuter trains clattering through the landscape.

A survey for the railway was carried out in 1896 with the result that a break in gauge (all other lines then were broad gauge) was introduced

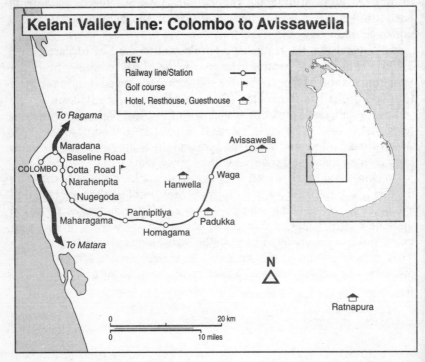

when the narrow gauge line was laid to Avissawella in 1902. The service was extended further inland to Yatiyantota in 1903, then to Ratnapura in 1912 and to Opanaike in 1919. Because the extensions were not 'economically viable' they were dismantled in stages, beginning in 1942 and ending in 1977.

In 1938 the whole line was recommended for closure and in 1975 it was decided to run a passenger service only to Homagama, but somehow the link to Avissawella survived, although by 1990 it was reduced to one train a day in each direction. This was hauled by a diminutive steam loco (No 220 class J1, type 4-6-4T Hunslet built in 1924) or a 1949 diesel. When the line served Ratnapura, it was used by pilgrims bound for Adam's Peak, and three Sentinel steam railcars were put into service in 1928. One coach long, with a tiny coal boiler at one end and capable of being driven from either end, one of those Sentinels (No 331 V2) is still in operation for special hires, the only narrow gauge steam railcar running anywhere in the world.

Unique, too, is the current dual track, capable of taking both broad and narrow gauge trains. Work started in 1991 and in October the section from Maradana to Nugegoda, a busy suburb, was opened to broad gauge trains. The track has been broadened by the addition of a third rail, keeping the two rails of the narrow gauge track in place. This was done so the regular narrow gauge service could continue to run while the line was being converted.

The dual gauge track was claimed to be an engineering first but in a letter to the *Daily News*, Mr A F Dunster of Dehiwela wrote: 'the three rail system existed in the UK during the transition of broad gauge to narrow gauge about the latter end of the 19th century'.

At present there is a broad gauge service to Homagama (24km from Maradana) with eight trains a day serving this heavily populated district. Eventually, the broad gauge line will reach Avissawella; at the time of writing the dual gauge line had been laid as far as Padukka, 35km from Maradana.

Departures from Fort station to Homagama are at 0540, 0610, 1000, 1200, 1345, 1625, 1645 (not Saturday and Sunday), 1708, 1735, 1825 and 2025; there is also a departure from Maradana at 0845. Trains from Homagama to Fort depart at 0420, 0600, 0655, 0710, 1000, 1214, 1322, 1505, 1755, 1850 (not Saturday and Sunday), 1910 and 1955, taking about 70 minutes for the journey. Times will change as the broad gauging of the line progresses.

At Homagama, at the time of writing, there was a daily connection to Avissawella meeting the 1625 and 1645 departures from Fort, arriving in Avissawella between 1930 and 2000. In the morning, at 0515, a train left Avissawella to connect at Homagama with a train to Fort.

Although it is no longer served by steam and the narrow gauge is broad, the Kelani Valley Line is still a great little trip. To get to Homagama in April 1994, I took the orange and grey liveried Hitachi suburban power-set which left Fort station at 1625. After a stop at Maradana, the train began its journey by following the single track which detaches itself from the web of main lines to disappear down a narrow funnel formed by two side walls, overhung with trees. This opens out as the train trundles alongside the crowded streets of Colombo's fringes, passing under the eaves of overhanging roofs of houses bordering the track. After a stop at **Baseline Road** the train runs on to **Cotta Road** where flowers entwine the trellis roof shading the old platform.

Then the train emerges from the suburbs into a vast expanse of green, the golf links of the Royal Colombo Golf Club. Regular golfers sigh with resignation as the train cuts across the course while newcomers rub their eyes in disbelief at this unexpected hazard to their play. The scenery between the newly built stations with their raised platforms becomes rural until the palm-thatched cabins beside the line give way to the neat villas of middle-class **Nugegoda**. Yellow and mauve passion fruit flowers still garland the old station building while the new one is a bustling hive of activity by the level crossing. Leave the platform at the opposite end, turn left and walk along the road for five minutes and you will see a narrow gauge loco from 1920 (No 203 L1B, 0-4-2T Hunslet) in a children's park.

At **Homagama**, the new booking office has a sign displaying the times and stops of all trains to and from Colombo. There is a bridge linking the platforms as this station is an important one on the line and many trains will terminate and originate here, even when the broad gauge is completed all the way to Avissawella.

From Homagama, the narrow gauge train, composed of four wooden carriages, dawdles across shimmering paddy fields which give way to wild orchards of mangoes, breadfruit, areca nut, coffee and cocoa. At **Padukka** most of the passengers alight. The station is close to the centre of the town and there is a typical country-style rest-house with garden and veranda and three basic rooms. A special railcar service operates between Padukka and Avissawella every day except Sundays.

Like a bus, the railcar — a train of three coaches hauled by a diesel — stops at the request of passengers standing at halts by the line. The guard collects fares and issues tickets. The journey is through woods and tea and rubber plantations, with hills in the distance glimpsed through tangled vegetation. Betel leaf and croton (a tropical bush with coloured, skewer-like leaves) grow in profusion by the line and cottages with gardens full of flowers look idyllic.

Many of the halts do not have platforms, while some of the old station buildings have not changed much since they were built with granite blocks 90 years ago, with stationmaster's quarters above the booking office. From Padukka, the railcar service starts at 0837, 1407 and 1720; from Avissawella, there are trains at 0610, 1015 and 1545.

Within five minutes' walk of **Avissawella** station, the line's terminus, is a resthouse with a mixed reputation. It has a good bar and lunch service but the rooms are basic and sometimes without water, and guests who want to leave early to catch the 0515 train to Colombo have been known to find themselves locked in and have to scramble over the wall.

It is expected that train times quoted here will change.

Ratnapura

While there used to be a narrow gauge railway from Colombo to Ratnapura via Avissawella, now the journey must be done by road. There are buses from Colombo, via Avissawella, and it is also possible to reach Ratnapura by road from the hill country, via Haputale (where there is a railway station), Balangoda and Pelmadula.

Most people visit Ratnapura for one thing: gems. Even its name means City of Gems. The land around the town is dotted with thatched shelters over gem pits being mined in crudely built shafts by near-naked miners knee deep in mud at the bottom.

The types of gems found in Sri Lanka include sapphire, garnet, quartz, spinel, topaz, tourmaline, zircon, ruby and cat's eye. No emerald or diamonds (except the Matara diamond, another name for zircon).

Attractions close to the town are its lush scenery, rivers and waterfalls, tea and rubber plantations and wildlife (it is two hours' drive from the 300km^2 Udawalawe wildlife sanctuary, where more than 400 elephants roam.

THE MATALE LINE

Kandy to Matale

Officially, Kandy is not on the main upcountry line at all but forms part of the Kandy to Matale line (see map page 114). This branch of the main line was opened in 1880 and soon afterwards H W Cave in his book *Golden Tips* (actually about tea, not hints on premium travel) commented that Matale 'is the most northerly district cultivated by Europeans and at present the utmost point to which the railway extends in this direction'.

It has remained the utmost point and the traveller has to resort to buses to get to Dambulla and Sigiriya from Matale. There are seven trains a day to Matale from Kandy (at 0425, 0525, 0655, 1005, 1418, 1655 and 1845). The last one serves passengers arriving in Kandy from Colombo if the Intercity (due at 1805) is on time. There is no service on the line on Sundays and holidays.

Apart from the first train of the day (No 231) and number 243 at 1655, which are mixed goods and passenger trains, the service is run by 'Baby Trains'. The passenger carriages are like those of other trains but the train is short rather than babyish and usually only two or three carriages long.

It is scheduled to take 74 minutes to cover the distance of 27km but since this is a rural line in the classic tradition, with landscapes of paddy-fields terraced in curves and richly wooded hillsides, no one expects it to hurry. The train eases slowly out of Kandy station to rattle over the main road and then to plunge into the countryside north of the city.

Three minutes later it stops, at **Asgiriya**, the first of 17 halts on the line. The next station, reached after another three-minute run, is **Mahaiyawa**, built like a pavilion with a colonnaded veranda all around it. **Katugastota** station is also pavilion style. Look up to the left just after crossing the magificent river bridge and you will see, where the road and the track cross at the Katugastota level crossing, a tree weighed down, not with fruit but with fruit bats, also known as flying foxes.

There seems to be no place to buy tickets at **Mawilmada**, which is like a bus shelter on a brief stretch of platform. But then the train guard passes through the carriages selling tickets, as on a bus. Many of the stations on this line have no staff, just a name board.

After the main crossing station of **Wattegama**, the train meanders at much less than the permitted 32km an hour through forests of tall trees. Wheels squeal as it tackles an incline before running into **Ukuwela** station, another colonial pavilion. A trio of halts at intervals of three minutes come next before the train pulls into **Matale**.

Matale, at 369m above sea level, is 146km from Maradana. The outlines of the original station building are still to be seen, despite the ugliness of attempts to close in the archways of the veranda with breeze blocks. The station — and the staff — have the charm of a leisurely, forgotten lifestyle and you get the impression, from the dilapidated condition of the rolling stock, that the line is regarded as a backwater.

Trains leave Matale for Kandy at 0440, 0525, 0655, 1020, 1400, 1645 and 1850.

There is a chance to stay as a paying guest in a hacienda-style farmhouse if you leave the train at Ukuwela or Wattegama and take a taxi for the 5km to Grassmere Farm. It is on a hillside reached by winding track off the main road linking Matale with Wattegama, by the 12-mile post. There are only three guest rooms (with attached bathroom) and guests are welcomed as friends of the owners and looked after by an attentive staff. There are 36 acres of tea, pepper, coffee, cloves and a variety of tropical fruits and plants in a lush setting which even has its own waterfall. Low econmy rate, with free transport from Kandy railway station. (Contact Mr Jayawardena, Grassmere Farm, Alupothuweala, Ukuwela, Kandy; tel: 072 41110.)

Sigiriya

Getting to Sigiriya by train is not easy. The nearest railway station is Habarana but, since that is far from the main road and onward transport, it is not practical. Better to try from Kekirawa station, or from Anuradhapura, Matale or Trincomalee by bus. Coming the 115km by bus from Trincomalee, get out at the Inamaluwa junction before the road gets to Dambulla and wait for a private bus which will take you straight to Sigiriya. From there the hotels (there is also a resthouse) are five minutes' walk.

Sigiriya is famous for its toadstool of golden-hued granite, protruding 183m into the searing blue sky from a hot, flat wilderness of scrubland, which is transformed in the rainy season to a water garden. In the 5th century a king domesticated the Lion rock, as it is known, by building a palace atop its three-acre summit. Only windswept foundations, and a rubbish dump, remain to reward the foolhardy few who climb to the top of the rock's sheer face with the help of narrow, caged-in ladders that must be more than 50 years old.

Frescos from the 5th century of bare-breasted women, acknowledged as art treasures, can be seen on the side of the rock. You reach the viewing ledge by hauling yourself up an iron spiral staircase pegged to the rock's face. The frescos, shaded from the elements by a canvas awning and smeared with cement, look better on postcards than in real life.

There is a car park opposite the entrance to the Sigiriya complex (part of the cultural triangle, so you will need a permit, see page 171), with several stalls selling soft drinks and spices. It is within easy walking distance of the Sigiriya Village Hotel, one of those hotels that is worth the expense (standard grade) just for the experience. Even if you have no intention of climbing the rock you can see how impressive it is from the hotel's gardens. Thirty gardeners tend the trees, plants and flowers of the hotel and have created a virtual botanical park in what was previously scrubland. The trees, representing most of the varieties found in Sri Lanka, bear tags with their Latin and local names, and the gardens are home to over 80 species of birds.

Accommodation is in cottages grouped in clusters; each cluster of ten cottages has a special theme garden (based on river, temple, paddy field, etc) which is followed in the room decor. Cottages are built of concrete, camouflaged to resemble the traditional mud dwellings of villages but with an interior layout like an up-market apartment. The hotel's public areas are based in a central complex with rustic-style furniture and trestle tables in the dining hall.

THE PUTTALAM LINE

Ragama to Puttalam

To take a train to Puttalam is to experience Sri Lanka in a lethargic mood, commuters going lazily home, and the sluggish backwaters of coastal life. If you had to make the long haul to Puttalam regularly, as some local rail travellers do, it would soon lose its magic, but as a journey into the unknown, for the first time, every minute can be exciting.

Rail travel requires a relaxed frame of mind to be enjoyable, and some advance preparation. Since none of the trains to Puttalam have catering — except for itinerant vendors of peanuts and prawn croquettes — take a picnic. It helps pass the time. Only a few of the trains have loos which may mean you will have to break the journey, or dash out when the train is unloading freight, that ranges from clay pots of curd from the south to sacks of seeds.

The line to Puttalam was begun with the building of a branch from Ragama which reached Ja-Ela in 1908. Negombo railway station was originally opened in 1909 and the line reached Chilaw in 1916, then up to Puttalam ten years later. The track from Bangadeniya to Puttalam was removed in 1943 as the rails were needed due to shortages caused by the Second World War. It was re-laid with new station buildings in 1964.

Only slow (sometimes very slow) trains serve the line now, stopping at every one of more than 40 stations on the way. To make the 133km journey from Colombo Fort more fun (it can take six hours), it is

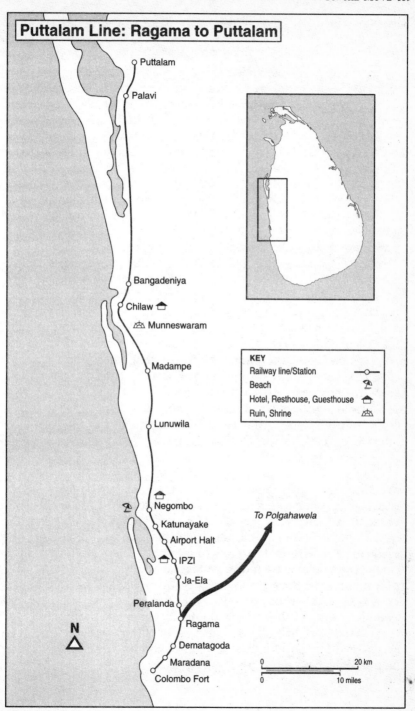

Puttalam Line: Ragama to Puttalam

KEY
Railway line/Station
Beach
Hotel, Resthouse, Guesthouse
Ruin, Shrine

better to stop overnight on the way, either at the beach resort of Negombo or at the fishing town of Chilaw.

The train follows the main line, stopping at every station, up to Ragama where it branches northwards. Three halts and 20 minutes later it stops at the industrial area station of **Ja-Ela** and then passes through the developments leading to the free trade zone at Seeduwa and around the airport. The closest railway station on this line to the airport is the new Investment Promotional Zone halt (IPZ1) but it is a long walk of more than a kilometre from there to the terminal buildings. The morning and afternoon trains to the **Colombo Airport Katunayake** station branch off here, but even that station is about 500m from the terminal.

The train gives a good view of the runway at the main old station of **Katunayake**, where you could be isolated in the rural heartland except for the jets touching down a stone's throw away. Perhaps that is why the security forces are billeted in the station signal box.

Next is Negombo. Attempts have been made at **Negombo** station (rebuilt in 1978) to make it attractive: there are plants in pots and a few lovebirds in a cage. The toilet and waiting rooms, though, are padlocked. Outside is a huge, silver-painted statue of a buxom fishwife, with a fish rampant in her hand. There are a dozen trains a day either northward to Chilaw and Puttalam or south to Colombo. The ticket office is not always manned until a few minutes before a train's departure.

The bus station is a five-minute walk south of the railway station. There are three-wheelers in the station forecourt and you will need one to get to a guesthouse or hotel since these are alongside the stretch of beach to the north, with the main concentration at Ethukala. The leading hotel is the Royal Oceanic (standard) and a popular one with budget travellers is its older sister, Sea Garden, upper economy, also right on the beach.

Negombo is a pleasant cross between the two extremes of its southern counterparts, Bentota and Hikkaduwa. With scores of restaurants, it is livelier than Bentota but not as sleazy as Hikkaduwa. However, the beach is not as clean or as broad and the sea not as blue nor the vegetation as lush as in the resorts of the south. There is a tourist information centre (behind the tourist police station). It is possible to arrange a cruise on the backwater canals as a change from lazing on the beach.

It seems only hardy passengers continue on the train beyond Negombo. Many of the stations on the long journey northwards have managed to retain their original colonial era railway architecture but the few passengers pay no attention to what visitors see as a fascinating glimpse of the past.

The building at **Kudawewa** station (65km from Colombo) has no asbestos canopy obscuring its gracious lines; instead it is wreathed with a picturesque riot of colourful bougainvillaea. At **Kakapalliya**, a few kilometres further on, majestic trees shade the station. Less attractive are the goods wagons left to rot on loop lines at many rural stations.

At **Chilaw**, sea breeze billows over the lagoon ruffling fishing boats moored close to the station. It is a colourful, if sleepy, town and the shore is only five minutes' walk from the station. The resthouse with access on to the beach is low economy grade and does not double its prices at the sight of a tourist. This is not actually tourist country as the beach is a bit bleak. The Munneswaram temple with its renowned Tamil inscriptions is a place for pilgrims who usually walk the kilometre to it from the town.

After Chilaw, the train put-puts merrily to Puttalam, past the lagoon and fishing hamlets up to **Bangadeniya** (89km from Colombo) and the uninspiring, flat countryside beyond. The train seems to delight in the long straight line of the single track, picking up speed and with klaxon blaring raucously as it races through drab, deserted land. After **Madurankuli**'s broad island platform, the train speeds on through windswept flats to the clean station of **Palavi**, and then to Puttalam.

Puttalam is an island station with all its offices on its sole, central platform. It was rebuilt in 1966 and has the air of a forgotten frontier. The line continues to the north, but passenger trains do not. It is possible, instead, to pick up a bus at the town's bus station for the cross-country ride to Anuradhapura, on the northern line.

Chapter 8

Where to Stay

Resthouses

One of the joys of travelling in Sri Lanka is the availability of resthouses throughout the country. As places for travellers to rest for a night, they were developed by the British who extended the network of bungalows for travelling officials begun by the Dutch. They were usually built in superb locations, each within a day's march, or horse ride, from one another. More than a hundred remain, ranging from the luxury of Tissamaharama Resthouse to the basic, cowshed architecture of municipal properties deep in the heartland. Some are charming while some, alas, are not.

Resthouses are government-owned, leased either to urban councils or government organizations to manage or, through the Ceylon Tourist Board, to private companies. A major operator is the Ceylon Hotels Corporation whose resthouses are all run to a high standard and are accustomed to accommodating visitors from overseas.

Some of the municipal resthouses operate a double rate tariff, with higher room charges for foreigners. This is not only annoying, it is often a scam perpetuated by the staff. On the other hand, I have stayed in municipal authority resthouses where the price for room, meals and drinks is lower than anywhere else in the area and is unbelievably good value, with staff keen to help strangers since they rarely come their way.

While some resthouses are not so restful — especially those that function as arrack bars — others are havens of peace and intriguing local ambience. They are usually small hostelries with only a few rooms, although one of the most well known, the Tissamaharama Resthouse near the Yala National Park, boasts 62.

Resthouses are distinguished by the personal service provided by stewards of the 'old school' in their white sarongs and starched white tunics, who treat every visitor as an honoured guest. Many resthouses have a well-deserved reputation for providing authentic, rural cuisine.

If you want to enjoy a meal in a resthouse, here are some hints to make the process smooth and stress free, from the moment a steward greets you on arrival: (1) To save time, order your meal as soon as you sit on the veranda, since it may have to be cooked especially for you. (2) Do not order drinks until after the steward has given your meal order to the kitchen. (3) If you are in a hurry at lunch time, only order rice and curry. This will have been prepared that morning, will be fresh and tasty, and cheap compared with other items on the menu. (4) Do not request chicken curry unless the steward guarantees it is already prepared; it won't be cooked properly in a hurry from a frozen bird. (5) Because you are a foreigner, the curries may have extra coconut milk added to tame them for your palate. If you want your curry local style, insist on the real thing when ordering. (6) If you have a driver he will usually be able to eat free — or at a nominal local rate — with the staff so you don't have to invite him to dine with you at the tourist price for the same food. (7) Some resthouses charge more for foreigners than locals even if you all sit together and eat the same dishes. If this worries you, find out before you order. (8) Beware of the offer of anything not actually presented on the table, such as mango chutney, as this could be an extra over the set fee for rice and curry. (9) Relax on the veranda with a drink until you are called into the restaurant to eat. Then you will find the table set up with curries in different dishes, surrounding a huge plate of rice. The steward will serve the rice, you help yourself, and fellow diners if you like, to the curries. Second servings of curries are not charged as extras. (10) The choice for non vegetarians is usually either fish or beef, rice and curry. For two people dining together, order one fish and one beef as you will usually get more, and certainly a better choice, than ordering two fish or two beef. (11) If you want to eat with your fingers, use only the right hand, but nobody will mind if you stick to cutlery: a spoon and fork is better than a knife and fork. (12) When it comes to paying the bill, most resthouses keep up the old tradition of presenting you with a register in which you are supposed to enter your name, nationality and address. Your name will then appear on the bill which will be large in size (but usually not in amount). Every item, including an occupation (cover) charge, will be itemized with beer listed in millilitres not bottles. A service charge of 10% and the government tax will be added to the bill. Tipping is up to you, but you will usually have had such superb service and a great rice and curry meal so another 5% will seem reasonable.

Guesthouses

There are guesthouses wherever there are hotels. Do not despair if the only information you have before reaching a place is about Tourist Board approved hotels which are either beyond your budget or simply not your cup of tea. You will be amazed at how easy it is to find places that suit both your pocket and your mood — and with tea, too. Obviously, it is better to arrive in a strange town before dark so you have a chance to look around. And if the guesthouse you stay in at first is not really what you want, don't worry. Find another the next day and check out of the first one. The lads who will want to guide you can sometimes come up with a super place you would never find yourself.

When business in a guesthouse is slack, a lowering of the price you are first quoted is possible, but do not make this a condition of your stay in a place if otherwise it is just what you are looking for. You might not find somewhere else as good.

Of the many guesthouses in Sri Lanka, I mention only a few in the accommodation list because I know, and happen to like, them.

Hotels of Character

Most of the hotels in Sri Lanka were built — and cater for — mass market tourism. Older ones survive from the days when travel was more leisurely and the guest was exactly that, not a tour operator's client. Some of the new hotels do have an appeal because they are original and offer something different but generally the independent traveller will be better served by the older hotels that were not created for groups but for individuals. Of course, not all hotels of character are without shortcomings and if you really do want hot water and air conditioning you should stick to the newer properties. Those in this list are my personal choice of places that I enjoy staying in; I hope you do, too!

Price Guide

The simple grading system used in this listing indicates the price range of a hotel for a room (single/double) per night, not the degree of comfort or style. While prices are sure to change, the actual grading of luxury, standard or economy can be expected to remain the same. Based on 1994 listed prices, gradings correspond to the following:

1. Luxury (currently US$50 and above)
2. Standard (currently US$20-$50)
3. Economy (currently under US$20)

Resthouses and Guesthouses

	Telephone	Fax	Grade
Ceylon Hotels Corporation			
63 Janadhipathi Mawatha			
Colombo 1	433291	941 422732	
(Head office of the following resthouses)			
Ambepussa	035 7299		3
Belihuloya	045 7200		3
Dambulla	066 8299		3
Ella	057 2636		3
Farr Inn (Worlds End)			3
Habarana	066 8355		3
Hanwella	036 5042		3
Kitulgala	036 7528		3
Mihintale	025 6599		3
Polonnaruwa	027 2299		3
Pussellawa	08 78397		3
Sigiriya	066 8325		3
Tissamaharama	047 37299		3
Quickshaws (for reservations)			
3 Kalinga Place			
Colombo 3	583133	941 587613	
Tissawewa, Anuradhapura	025 2299	025 3265	3
Nuwarawewa, Anuradhapura	025 2565	025 3265	3
Adisham (Haputale)	057 8030		3
Avissawella	036 2299		3
Badulla	055 2299		3
Chilaw	032 2299		3
Gampaha	033 2299		3
Grassmere Farm, Ukuwela, Kandy	072 41110		3
Highcliffe, Haputale	057 8096		3
Kelburne Mountain View Resort, Haputale	057 8029		3
Kurunegala (Old resthouse)	037 22299		3
Lake Lodge, 20 Alvis Terrace, Colombo 3	326443		3
Matara	041 2299		3
Nippon Villa, Hikkaduwa	09 57429		3
Peradeniya	08 88299		3
Pragash French Garden, Nilaveli Road, Trincomalee,			3
Ratnapura	045 2299		3
Susantha Guesthouse, Bentota	034 75554		3
Susantha Palm, Bentota	034 75324	941 446535	3

esthouses and Guesthouses (cont'd)

	Telephone	Fax	Grade
alawakele	052 8299		3
angalle	047 40299		3
errena Lodge, Alutgama	034 75001		3
rincomalee	026 2229		3

etiring Rooms

	Telephone	Fax	Grade
nuradhapura	025 2271		3
atticaloa	065 2271		3
alle	09 22271		3
andy	08 22271		3
Mihintale			3
olgahawela	037 43271		3
rincomalee	026 22271		3

olombo Hotels

see also *Hotels of Character*)

	Telephone	Fax	Grade
irport Garden	452951-4	941 452953	1
eylon Inter-Continental	421221	941 447326	1
olombo Hilton	544644	941 544657	1
olombo Marriott	544544	941 449875	1
olombo Renaissance	544200	941 449184	1
alaxy			
388 Union Place, Colombo 2	696372		2/3
oliday Inn	422001	941 447977	1
anka Oberoi	320001	941 449280	1
aj Samudra	446622	941 446348	1

ome Hotels of Character

	Telephone	Fax	Grade
andarawela	057 2501		2/3
itadel (Kandy)	08 25314		1
losenberg (Galle)	09 23073		3
alle Face (Colombo)	541010	941 541072	1/2
lendower (Nuwara Eliya)	052 2501	9452 2749	2
rand (Nuwara Eliya)	052 2264		2
rand Oriental (Colombo)	548734		2
ill Club (Nuwara Eliya)	052 2653		2
unas Falls (Elkaduwa, Kandy)	08 76402		1
osgoda Beach (Bentota)	09 54017		2
Mount Lavinia	715221	941 715228	1/2
ew Oriental (Galle)	09 32191	941 932191	2/3
ilaveli Beach (Trincomalee)	026 22071		3

Some Hotels of Character (cont'd)

	Telephone	Fax	Grade
Nippon			
123 Kumaran Ratnam Road,			
Colombo 2	431887		3
Queens (Kandy)	08 22121		2
Robinson Club (Bentota)	034 75167	034 75172	2
Saint Andrews (Nuwara Eliya)	052 2445		3
Sigiriya Village (Sigiriya)	066 8216		2
Suisse (Kandy)	08 32083		2
Thilanka (Kandy)	08 22060		3
Yala Beach Safari	047 20471		2

Chapter 9

Off the Rails

FREE TIME

Colombo has lots of opportunities for cultural pursuits when you want a
break from rail travel. Here are some of the museums, galleries,
libraries, cultural centres and bookshops.

Museums

Dutch Period Museum
95 Prince Street, Pettah
Tel: 448466
Open daily 0900-1700

Municipal Museum
Old Town Hall, Pettah
Open daily

National Museum
Sir Marcus Fernando Mawatha, Colombo 7
Tel: 695366
Open daily, except Friday and public holidays, 0900-1700

National History Museum
(behind the National Museum)
Tel: 691399
Open daily 0900-1700

Galleries

Gallery 706
706 Galle Road, Colombo 3

Lionel Wendt Memorial Art Gallery
18 Guildford Cresent, Colombo 7
Tel: 695794

National Art Gallery
106 Ananda Coomaraswamy Mawatha, Colombo 7
Tel: 693965

Libraries

British Council Library
40 Alfred House Gardens, Colombo 3
Tel: 580301
Open Tuesday-Saturday 0830-1800

Colombo Public Library
Ananda Coomaraswamy Mawatha, Colombo 7
Open daily, except Wednesday and holidays, 0800-1800

National Library of Sri Lanka
Independence Avenue, Colombo 7
Tel: 685199; fax: 941 685201
Open Tuesday-Saturday 0900-1700
(Reference, documents and bibliographic material)

United States Information Service
44 Galle Road, Colombo 6
Tel: 332725
Open Tuesday-Saturday 1000-1800

Cultural Centres

Alliance Française de Colombo
11 Barnes Place, Colombo 7
Tel: 694162
Open weekdays 0900-1300, 1400-1700

German Cultural Institute
39 Gregory's Road, Colombo 7
Tel: 694562
Open weekdays 0900-1300, 1500-1700. Library closed Thursday afternoon

Soviet Cultural Centre
10 Independence Avenue, Colombo 7
Tel: 685429
Open weekdays 0900-1700

Bookshops

Chas Subasinghe
720 Galle Road, Colombo 3
Tel: 502491
also at Ceylon Hotel Inter-Continental, Colombo Marriott, Grand Oriental,
Airport Garden, Sindbad, Riverina, Bentota Beach and Grand Hotels.

Lake House Bookshop
100 Sir Chittampalam A Gardiner Mawatha, Colombo 2
Tel: 432104
also at Liberty Plaza

K V G de Silva
415 Galle Road, Colombo 4
also at Liberty Plaza

M D Gunasena & Co
217 Olcott Mawatha, Colombo 11
also at some railway stations

Vijitha Yapa Bookshop
376 Galle Road, Colombo 3
also in Kandy and Galle

Secondhand bookstalls, some with collector's items, are to be found in D J Wijewardena Mawatha (near Maradana station).

Antiques

Every week there are sales of antiques at halls in Colombo (see notices in the local press) supplementing items on sale in the antique shops of Dehiwela, Mount Lavinia, Panadura, Bentota, Ambalangoda, Galle and Kandy. There are also auctions held occasionally at weekends. A law prohibits the export of antique items over 50 years old.

Some Ruins and Shrines

To visit or photograph the main ancient monuments a permit is required from the office of the Cultural Triangle Fund, 212 Bauddhaloka Mawatha (Bullers Road); tel: 587912, 500733. This can also be obtained at the Archaeological Museum at Anuradhapura and the Archaeological offices at Polonnaruwa and Sigiriya. A single ticket for one month covers viewing of historic monuments in all parts of Sri Lanka, photography of ancient monuments where photography is permitted and entry to all archaeological museums. The cost: $15. The cost of entry tickets to Anuradhapura, Polonnaruwa or Sigiriya is $4 per adult, half price for a child, per site.

(Closest access railway station shown in brackets)
Adam's Peak (Hatton)
Anuradhapura (Anuradhapura)
Aukana (Aukana)
Dambulla rock temple (Matale, Anuradhapura, Kekirawa)
Embekke (Kandy)
Galle Fort (Galle)
Katagarama (Matara)
Mihintale (Mihintale)
Munneswaram (Chilaw)
Polonnaruwa (Polonnaruwa)
Sigiriya (Matale, Anuradhapura, Kekirawa, Habarana)
Temple of the Tooth, Kandy (Kandy)
Tissamaharama (Matara)
Yapahuwa (Maho, Yapahuwa)

Best Beaches

The beaches of Sri Lanka are a golden sand which makes them ideal for sunbathing. But the sun is fierce, even on a cloudy day, so newcomers should begin by gradual exposure; even as little as 30 minutes on the first day is enough. Since beachside hotels have their own swimming pools the beaches themselves are not very crowded and even in season you will find only a few other people sharing the sand with you.

Beaches on the west and south coasts are best from October to April, with the east coast being delightful from April to October. The station closest to each beach is shown in brackets.

West/South Coasts
Bentota (Bentota or Alutgama)
Beruwela (Alutgama)
Hikkaduwa (Hikkaduwa)
Mount Lavinia (Mount Lavinia)
Negombo (Negombo)
Tangalle (Matara)
Unawatuna (Galle or Unawatuna)

East
Arugam Bay (Batticaloa)
Kalkuda (Kalkuda or Valaichchenai)
Nilaveli (Trincomalee)
Passekuda (Kalkuda)

Windsurfing, waterskiing, scuba diving and deep sea fishing are all available at the beach resorts.

NATURE AND WILDLIFE

Sri Lanka's best known national park is Ruhunu National Park, Yala, in the southeast corner, about 305km from Colombo. Access by rail is from Colombo to Matara station and then by road (bus or three-wheeler) for the 115km to Tissamaharama and on to Yala. The best time to go is between December and May.

There is only one entrance to the park, the turn-off being along the road between Tissa and Kirinda. If you do not have your own vehicle, there are plenty of people around with jeeps for hire. Access to the park is only by vehicle and with an official tracker, assigned to each vehicle at the site office. You can use your own vehicle to enter the park if you keep to the 50km of good track, but a jeep is necessary if you want to explore the 43km of rough trails. The park consists of 976km^2 with 140km^2 being open to the public for game viewing.

The terrain is semi-arid thorn brush country and fairly dense secondary forest: there are few plains so elephants are usually to be seen in the bush or ambling along the trails. Leopards are rare, bears even rarer; lots of deer, wild boar and buffalo; peacocks, jungle fowl, waterbirds, crocodiles. Best time is early morning or late afternoon.

Admission for foreigners is US$10 per person, payable in rupees, plus Rs100 for a jeep or Rs75 for a car and US$5 service charge. Rates are lower for residents of Sri Lanka. There is a small museum at the park office, as well as toilets. Maps of the park are on sale. The park is open 0600-1830 every day except during the period September 1 — October 15 when it is closed. Best months to visit are February and March but other months have their attractions, such as bears nibbling fruit in May and June.

The park is bordered by the sea and on the beach is a fishing *wadiya*, a temporary settlement of palm-thatch huts of itinerant fishermen who come from their homes on the west coast during April-October.

The Yala Safari Beach Hotel (reservations through Jetwing Hotels, 457 Union Place, Colombo 2; tel: 698818; fax: 941 314277) is close to the park entrance with 54 twin-bedded rooms in neat, rustic style, overlooking sand dunes and the ocean.There is a pavilion bar and an open-sided restaurant with a lake view where breakfast is served from 0530 to enable guests to go on a daybreak safari. Wild animals, including pangolins, roam the ten acre grounds. Standard rate.

Wildlife and nature can also be appreciated at the Udwalawe Wildlife

Park (the nearest station, Matara, is too far away to be much help) and the Sinharaja rain forest. Trekking to World's End at Horton Plains (nearest stations: Ohiya and Pattiploa) is possible. Orphaned wild elephants are to be seen in the elephant orphanage at Pinnawela, reached by bus from Rambukkana station. The three botanical gardens are the Royal Botanical Gardens at Peradeniya (via Peradeniya or Kandy stations), the one at Gampaha (bus from the station there) and at Hakgala (Nanu Oya via Nuwara Eliya by road).

Also of interest are the National Zoological Gardens at Anagarika Dharmapala Mawatha, Dehiwela (Dehiwela is the closest station; then bus 118). Admission: local adults Rs15, local children Rs5; foreign visitors Rs75, foreign children Rs35.

Colombo's Vihara Maha Devi Park (opposite the town hall) is a pleasant place for a quiet walk in the shade of large trees; open daily 0600-1800.

The Department of Wildlife is at 82 Rajamalwatta Road, Battaramulla. The Wildlife Protection Society of Ceylon is in Chaitya Road (Marine Drive, near the visa renewal office), Colombo 1; tel: 325248.

FEEL AT HOME

With Sri Lanka's mix of western ways and eastern *mores*, visitors quickly feel at home, but if homesickness does creep up, there are plenty of social organizations which welcome visitors, and contact with their members who share your interests will help allay feelings of loneliness.

Association of British Residents of Sri Lanka
(contact through the British High Commission)
PO Box 73, Colombo
(Newcomers group meets monthly)

Buddhist Cultural Centre
125 Anderson Road, Nedimala, Dehiwela
Tel: 714256
(Library, lectures, information and counselling. Nearest station, Dehiwela)
Ceylon Anglers Club
Chaitya Road, Colombo Fort
(opposite the lighthouse; nearest station is Secretariat Halt, or Fort. Free membership for visitors)

Colombo Rowing Club
Sir Chittampalam A Gardiner Mawatha, Colombo 2
Tel: 433758
(By the Beira Lake, entrance opposite the Lake House Bookshop,
nearest station, Fort, back exit.)

Kinross Swimming & Life Saving Club
10 Station Avenue, Wellawatte
Tel: 586461
(Temporary membership, nearest station is Wellawatte.)

Model Railway Club
37 Galle Road, Colombo 4
Tel: 581568; Fax: 941 586977

Nuwara Eliya Golf Club
Nuwara Eliya
Tel: 952 2835
(Temporary members welcome. The course is one of the finest in Asia,
1,890m above sea level; nearest station is Nanu Oya.)

Royal Colombo Golf Club
185 Model Farm Road, Colombo5
Tel: 695431
(Temporary members welcome. The course is in the suburbs, with the
Kelani Valley railway line running through it; nearest stations Cotta
Road and Narahenpitiya.)

Vintage Car Owners' Club
c/o 5 Manthri Road, Colombo 5

Young Mens' Christian Association (YMCA)
Bristol Street, Colombo 1

Young Womens' Christian Association (YWCA)
7 Rotunda Gardens, Colombo 3
Sri Lanka-American Society
120/10 Wigerama Mawatha, Colombo 2
(Contact through Consular Office, US Embassy)

HELP

Fire and ambulance	422222
Police	433333
Accident service	691111
Bomb disposal	434251
Dog pound and rabies laboratory	695139
Flight information	452861
Red Cross	694487
Colombo Fort railway station	435838
	434215
	436900
Ceylon Tourist Board	437055
Tourist police	421111
Department of Immigration	436353/437050

Chapter Ten

Check Out

MIND YOUR LANGUAGE

For many visitors to Sri Lanka, a lot of the charm comes from the kind of English you will hear spoken by both railway staff and passengers. To listen to a mature, well-read Sri Lankan in full flow is to experience a classical English probably seldom heard in England.

At the other extreme is the English that is spoken by beginners, especially in the hospitality industry where the steward might be influenced by tourists whose own English is less than perfect. Sometimes the mistakes, and the accents, of visitors are accepted as correct by Sri Lankans, resulting in a hodgepodge of odd phrases, and strangled vowels.

Hotel staff do try to adapt to the nationalities they are dealing with. They will bid their German clients *Guten Appetit*, the French clients *Bon Appétit* and their English guests *Good Appetite*. Good appetite? Try not to wince, they really mean 'Enjoy your meal'.

For years I was troubled by reading in the local newspapers, the word reputed, as in 'the reputed banker' as it seemed to imply the banker was, in fact, bogus. Thanks to a wonderful book *Words in Indian English* by S. Muthiah, published by Indus (7/16 Ansari Road, New Delhi 110 002) in 1991, I discovered that reputed is not the wrong word because, in Indian and Sri Lankan English, it means 'of repute' (ie: reputable) and not, as in English, that the reputation is questionable.

Some of the many words in Sri Lankan English to watch out for, and their meanings, adapted from the book:

after	having consumed (as in 'after liquor' ie: drunk)
alternate	alternative
anything	whatever you wish to offer (in response to a host's question about what you would like to eat or drink)
backside	located at the rear (of a place)
Baila	Sri Lankan melody and dance derived from the Portuguese
balance	change (the money being returned to you)
bed tea	tea served early morning in the bedroom
before	ago (as in 'I ate two hours before'.)

Bo tres	the sacred *pipal* (*Ficus religiosa*) tree. It was under one of these (a descendent of which grows in Anuradhapura) that the Buddha attained enlightenment
bogie	a railway carriage
boutique	a wayside shop that is part tea shop, snack bar and sales counter for sundries
boy	a male household servant
buck	a rupee, in conventional slang
Burgher	originally the descendent of Dutch-Ceylonese alliances, but now used to describe Eurasians of any descent
cadjan	dried palm leaves used in thatch
cadju	cashew nut
chit	a message-bearing note
coupé	a compartment in a railway carriage with two berths
cousin-brother	male cousin
cousin-sister	female cousin
fired	scolded, rebuked, not sacked as in English
finger chips	French fries
lady's fingers	okra, gumbo
kurumba	a young green coconut sold for its contents to be drunk
lakh	one hundred thousand, in figures 100,000
leaf tea	tea made with leaves, not bags
mango friend	best friend
outstation	a town away from the usual place of work or residence
paddy	unhusked rice, the rice plant
SAARC	the countries of the South Asian Association of Regional Cooperation: India, Pakistan, Bangladesh, Nepal, Sri Lanka, Bhutan and the Maldives. With the addition of Afghanistan and Burma, these countries form the Indian Sub-Continent of British empire days
thambili	a golden shelled (king) coconut sold for its contents to be drunk
VIP	a very important person
VVIP	an even more important person

An inaccurate phrase has crept into the Sri Lankan telephone operators' lexicon. Phone someone in a hotel or at an office and you will be told when you ask for the person, 'You're connected'. Then the phone line goes dead.

Quite clearly, you are not connected. You can only be connected when you are speaking to the person you have asked for. What is really meant is 'Connecting you'.

If you are told that the person you want to speak to is 'not on his seat' it does not mean he is, perhaps, on his desk or on the window ledge. The English equivalent is 'He is in a meeting' — not available to take your call.

To add to the confusion in conversation, you must be careful not to misinterpret body language. You will frequently encounter a waggle or shake of the head in a semi-circular motion. Although this seems like an emphatic 'No!' it actually means 'Yes, I am considering the matter'.

The man, or woman, who clasps your hand too long in a handshake is not being suggestive. It happens due to unfamiliarity with the formal etiquette of shaking hands. Two men walking along a street holding hands are friends, perhaps mango friends, not liberated gays. And if you hear someone apparently blowing kisses at you, it is a way of attracting your attention, not a proposition.

Finally, when strangers ask 'Where are you going?' they are not being nosy. They don't really want to know your destination, they are just being polite and using a popular but oblique form of greeting. The correct answer is something like 'Close by' not 'Mind your own business!'

COCKTAIL CONDUCT

If you are lucky enough to stay on in Sri Lanka for any length of time, you are certain to be invited to a cocktail party.

Of all the courses advertised for young people eager to enhance their career prospects with a diploma, one you never see is that offering a certificate in Cocktail Party Strategy. Yet it could be as useful to the ambitious as a diploma in accounting or computers.

Imagine the young executive starting on the steep trail to the upper echelons of his new company. He has his qualifications, the spark of enthusiasm and lick of dedication that won him the job, and his new tie. His chairman lauds him up-the-ladder and suddenly he is hauled out of the clubhouse circuit where he parties with his batch-mates and into the rarefied circle of the cocktail party power game.

Visitors, too, need to know the rules. Colombo is a sociable city and you are quite likely to bump into VVIPs at parties. What to wear is not a problem, as long as it looks smart. The invitation for the annual reception held by the British High Commissioner to celebrate the Queen's official birthday states: 'Dress: National/Shirt & Tie'.

Actually, a cocktail party is more treacherous than quick sand or a jungle swamp. You never know you are being sucked in until you are head over heels in mud. Your own eyes may be out of focus through having inadvertently chased your scotch with gin, but those of the other guests are not. Your conduct is being observed, by mothers (for themselves or for their marriageable daughters), by company executives looking for a character weakness to exploit in boardroom battles, and by the part-time stewards grading how they will serve you when they see you again at the hotel where they usually work, or at the next party.

A cocktail party is more dangerous than Russian roulette, because you are the one that's loaded and can go off at the wrong moment. I remember the young executive at an embassy party who was asked by an addled lady if he would be a sweetie and get another drink for her. 'But the bar is closed,' he said ungallantly, only to be told it was his hostess herself he was refusing. No visa for him.

Here are some basic rules of survival for the newcomer to the cocktail party circuit.

(1) Arrive one hour late. By that time everyone will be too drunk to remember you or what you say.
(2) Arrive on time, drink only soda water (but say it is gin and tonic) so you remember all the gossip. Leave after one hour and go to the club for a decent drink, and to repeat the scandal.
(3) Eat before you go. Cocktail snacks do not soak up the alcohol fast enough and it is too complicated to hold a plate and a napkin and a glass while you hand out business cards or try to light a lady's cigarette.
(4) Do not tell jokes. You will be interrupted before you reach the punchline and nobody can hear you properly above all the noise.
(5) Do not believe people can't hear what you are saying. The person you are joking about will be standing right behind you at the wrong moment.
(6) Do not stand in the same place all evening. The party bores will find you, but the waiter won't.
(7) Do not move around. People will think you are the host, or trying to get an extra drink.

Actually, perhaps it is better not to go at all... but then you miss all the fun.

SOME USEFUL PHRASES

	SINHALA	TAMIL
	(phonetic pronunciation)	
(Traditional greeting)	Ayubowan	Vanakkam
How are you?	kohomada	eh-pudi
How much is it?	keeyada	evvalavu
Thank you	stuti	nandri
What is your name?	oyaga nama makade	ungada peyar enna
My name is . . .	mage nama . . .	en peyar . . .
Where do you live?	oba koheda innay	enga irrukkureergal
Yes	o-u	ama
No	naha	illai
Go away!	yan-na	po-onga
I don't understand	mata tereney naha	ennakku vilanga illai

SPELLING

Is it Beruwela or Beruwala station? The timetable gives the first spelling but the name on the station platform is spelt the second way. Since many of the English spellings of place names are adapted from the Sinhala or Tamil, inconsistencies are likely. I have tried to use the railway timetable spelling which, rather like the train times it gives, is sometimes more approximate than exact.

SOME MAJOR EXPRESS TRAINS

Number	Name	From/To	Facilities
05	Podi Menike	Fort/Badulla	Observation car; catering
06	Podi Menike	Badulla/Fort	Observation car; catering
09	Intercity	Fort/Kandy	Only 2nd class reserved
10	Intercity	Kandy/Fort	Observation car; catering
15	Udarata Menike	Fort/Badulla	Observation car; catering
16	Udarata Menike	Badulla/Fort	Observation car; catering
19		Fort/Kandy	
20		Kandy/Fort	
23		Fort/Kandy	
24		Kandy/Fort	
29	Intercity	Fort/Kandy	Only 2nd class reserved
30	Intercity	Kandy/Fort	Observation car; catering
35		Fort/Kandy	
36		Kandy/Fort	
39		Matara/Kandy	Catering
40		Kandy/Matara	Catering
45	Night Mail	Fort/Badulla	1st class berths; 2nd & 3rd
46	Night Mail	Badulla/Fort	sleeperettes; catering
50		Maradana/Matara	Catering
51		Matara/Maradana	Catering
54		Maradana/Galle	Saturday only
55		Matara/Maradana	Monday only; catering
56	Galu Kumari	Maradana/Matara	Not Saturday & Sunday
57	Galu Kumari	Matara/Maradana	Not Saturday & Sunday
58	Ruhunu Kumari	Maradana/Matara	2nd class reserved;
59	Ruhunu Kumari	Matara/Maradana	catering
60		Maradana/Matara	Friday only; catering
61		Galle/Maradana	Sunday only
62		Maranda/Galle	Friday only
65		Matara/Kandy	Saturday only; catering
66		Kandy/Matara	Sunday only; catering
77	Yal Devi	Fort/Vavuniya	2nd & 3rd class reserved
78	Yal Devi	Vavuniya/Fort	Air-conditioned 1st class; catering
81		Fort/Trincomalee	2nd & 3rd class sleeperettes; Catering (with through carriages to Batticaloa)
82		Trincomalee/Fort	2nd & 3rd class sleeperettes; catering (with through carriages from Batticaloa on Tuesday, Thursday & Sunday)
85	Rajarata Rajini	Matara/Vavuniya	Catering
86	Rajarata Rajini	Vavuniya/Matara	Catering
89	Night Mail	Fort/Vavuniya	1st class berths; 2nd & 3rd class sleeperettes; catering (through carriages to Polonnaruwa)
90	Night Mail	Vavuniya/Fort	1st class berths; 2nd & 3rd class sleeperettes; catering (through carriages from Polonnaruwa)

All trains, except Intercity, have 2nd and 3rd class unreserved seating All trains, except where stated, run daily.

FURTHER READING

Since this book is intended as a guide to Sri Lanka by rail, and not as a comprehensive general guide to the country, you will need books that tell you about the places and ways of Sri Lanka as well. Many books on Sri Lanka are available only inside the country, not abroad, and a visit to the Sri Lanka books section of the major bookshops will yield books covering various areas of special interest, from identifying Sri Lankan butterflies to appreciating Dutch furniture.

General

Sri Lanka, a travel survival kit, Lonely Planet, 1993
Packed with detail and good on low cost accommodation but misses out much of the interior and less visited parts.

Colombo Handbook, American Womens' Association
240 pages of lists covering almost every question you could have about where to get/do things in Colombo.

Guide to Ceylon by H A J Hulagalle, Lake House, 1969 & 1981

Sri Lanka Insight Guide by Apa Publications
Lots of colour photos and informative essays.

Culture Shock! Sri Lanka by Robert Barlas and Nanda P Wanasundera, Times Books International, Singapore, 1992

Sri Lanka in Brief, published by Ceylon Chamber of Commerce, 1993

The Grand Hotel by Royston Ellis, Colombo 1991

Books on the Railways

A History of the Sri Lanka Government Railway compiled and edited by L S de Silva, published 1992 by the Institution of Engineers, 120-15 Wijerama Mawatha, Colombo 7; price US$40 soft cover, $45 hard cover. A collection of essays by retired and practising railroad men, covering the development of the railways in a technical and anecdotal form, musing on the days of the railways under the first Sri Lankan engineer to be appointed general manager of the (then) Ceylon Government Railways, B D Rampala. Good for the enthusiast.

The Travelling Post Offices of Ceylon by Derek Walker, published in 1990 by the Ceylon Study Circle of Great Britain (Secretary: R W P Frost, 42 Lonsdale Road, Cannington, Bridgwater, Somerset, England) A 40-page history with fascinating details of the development of the travelling (train) post offices, illustrated with postmarks and postcards, issued as one of the Circle's in-depth reports on the philatelic background of Ceylon.

Ceylon Railways, One Hundred Years 1864-1964 published by the Ceylon Government Railway, Colombo, 1964

Ceylon Government Railway by Henry W Cave, Colombo, 1910

The Ceylon Railway by G F Perera, Colombo, 1925

Note: The Ceylon Tourist Board planned, in 1994, to publish a booklet of colour photographs by Gemunu Amarasinghe, with text by Royston Ellis, on seeing Sri Lanka by train. (Colombo, 1994).

UPDATE

The railways in Sri Lanka are expanding, with new lines planned and old lines, which were closed when this book was written, set to reopen eventually. Although the railway system is small, keeping up to date with all developments is not always possible. So if you have any new information, tips for other rail travellers, or reports on new developments (and corrections to any errors), please send them to me:

Royston Ellis, Sri Lanka By Rail, Bradt Publications, 41 Nortoft Road, Chalfont St Peter, Bucks SL9 0LA, England

Contributions which are used will be acknowledged in the next edition, as well as being of great help to other rail travellers.

Appendix

SRI LANKA RAILWAYS TIMETABLE

This timetable has been compiled from the latest information supplied by the Enquiries Counter at the Colombo Fort railway station. (There was no timetable published by the railway available at the time.) It was valid in April 1994 and although major changes are unlikely, do check in advance for the latest information. Only the main expresses are included; services on the Puttulam, Matale and Kelani Valley lines are not given as they are commuter or slow passenger trains and liable to change.

Timetable A traces trains from the main north, northeast and upcountry stations through Colombo to the south. Timetable B shows trains from the south through Colombo to stations in the north, northeast and upcountry.

To use the timetable, consult the map (inside front cover) for the routing and the junction for changing trains (but there might be a through train). Then select your starting and destination points on the timetable and look across the page for times of trains serving both. If you are heading across country, it may be necessary to refer to both south and northbound tables for connections.

As an example, if you want to get from Anuradhapura to Badulla, from the map you will locate the connecting station: Polgahawela. Table A (trains from the north) shows trains from Anuradhapura arriving at Polgahawela at 0815, 1615 and 0245. From Table B (trains from the south to upcountry) departures from Polgahawela to Badulla are shown as 0715, 1105 and 2149. This indicates it is possible to connect at Polgahawela with arrival by train number 86 at 0815 and departure by train number 15 at 1105.

Table A   **Trains from North, Northeast & Upcountry through Colom**

Read down	16 Udarata Menike	06 Podi Menike	46 Night Mail	40	30 Inter-city	36	24	66 Sun only	10 Inter-city
Badulla	0555	0850	1745						
Bandarawela	0724	1020	1917						
Haputale	0755	1052	1959						
Nanu Oya	0931	1239	2156						
Talawakele	1023	1336	2253						
Hatton	1051	1408	2328						
Peradeniya		↓	0212*						
Kandy		1705		0500	0630	0645	1000	1310	1500
Peradeniya	↓	1736	↓	0511	0638	0655	1010	1320	1508
Rambukkana	1347	1824	0330	0621	—	0806	1115	1434	—
Batticaloa									
Polonnaruwa									
Trincomalee									
Gal Oya									
Vavuniya									
Anuradhapura									
Maho									
Kurunegala									
Polgahawela	1400	1845	0348	0639	—	0840	1137	1457	—
Colombo-Maradana	1516	2000	0531	0809	—	1000	1253	1555	—
Colombo-Fort	1523	2010	0540	0830	0900	1005	1300	1615	1730
Kalutara South				0930				1708	
Alutgama				0955				1727	
Bentota				—				—	
Ambalangoda				1033				1757	
Hikkaduwa				1046				1816	
Galle				1120				1850	
Matara				1215				1945	

*Connecting train to/from Kandy available

o the south.

86 Rajarata Rajini	78 Yal Devi	80 Udaya Devi	90 Night Mail	88	82	50	60 Fri only	56 Galu Kumari (not Sat, Sun)	54 Sat only	62 Fri only	58 Ruhunu Kumari
				0700							
		2110		0918							
		↓		↓	0900						
		2216		1024	1105						
0315	1230	↓	2145		↓						
0505	1332		2315								
0622	1515	0027	0054		1332						
0717	1608		0206		1442						
0815	1655		0245		1515						
0934	1817		0411		1636	0625	1245	1325	1325	1445	1535
1015	1825		0420		1645	0645	1300	1335	1335	1500	1545
1112						0750	1403	1435	1435	1605	1633
1139						0822	1430	1506	1506	1630	1658
—						0826	—	1509	1509	—	—
1225						0851	1505	1533	1533	1700	1727
1240						0905	1517	1547	1547	1718	1740
1320						0942	1558	1630	1630	1740	1815
1415						1035	1645	1750			1910

Prepared by Royston Ellis April 1994 for 'Sri Lanka By Rail'

Table B   Trains from the South through Colombo to the North, North

Read down	55 Mon only	59 Ruhunu Kumari	65 Sat only	57 Galu Kumari (not Sat, Sun)	85 Rajarata Rajini	39	61 Sun only	51
Matara	0450	0540	0700	0730	0950	1255		1530
Galle	0600	0634	0810	0840	1115	1400	1500	1640
Hikkaduwa	0622	0708	0832	0902	1137	1422	1522	1702
Ambalangoda	0635	0721	0845	0930	1150	1435	1535	1718
Bentota	—	—	—	0955	—	1459	1556	1750
Alutgama	0701	0750	0923	1000	1220	1503	1600	1754
Kalutara South	0724	0815	0952	1025	1247	1526	1622	1837
Colombo-Fort	0830	0912	1100	1125	1405^d	1715^d	1755	1940
Colombo-Maradana	0840	0920	—	1135	—	—	1800	2000
Polgahawela			1215		1538	1838		
Kurunegala					1615			
Maho					1714			
Anuradhapura					1852			
Vavuniya					2020			
Gal Oya								
Trincomalee								
Polonnaruwa								
Batticaloa								
Rambukkana			1228			1903		
Peradeniya			1349			2011		
Kandy			1402			2025		
Hatton								
Talawakelle								
Nanu Oya								
Haputale								
Bandarawela								
Badulla								

*Connecting train to/from Kandy available
d = departs

Upcountry.

5 ...rata ...ike	45 Night Mail	09 Inter-city	19	23	29 Inter-city	35	89 Night Mail	79 Udaya Devi	77 Yal Devi	81	87
45	2015	0655	1015	1245	1535	1620	2230		0545	0515	
—	—	—	—	—	—	—	—		—	—	
05	2149	—	1139	1405	—	1740	2400		0705	0629	
							0035		0731	0658	
							0142	0220	0829	0749	
							0355	↓	1002	↓	
							0505	↓	1135	↓	
								0448		1028	1125
								↓		1245	↓
								0545			1225
											1450
18	2208	—	1200	1420	—	1756					
—	2324*	0921	1325	1540	1756	1913					
↓	↓	0930	1336	1550	1805	1925					
13	0214										
44	0253										
38	0347										
13	0535										
38	0607										
05	0748										

Prepared by Royston Ellis April 1994 for 'Sri Lanka By Rail'

Other Rail Guides published by Bradt

Australia by Rail by Colin Taylor
Practical and readable information for holders of the Austrail Pass.

Eastern Europe by Rail by Rob Dodson
A practical guide to the areas of eastern Europe which are now covered by a rail pass: Poland, the Czech Republic, Slovakia, Hungary, Romania, Bulgaria and eastern Germany.

India by Rail by Royston Ellis
The second edition of this highly praised guide. 'A practical planner and fuel for the finest kind of armchair fantasy...' *The Times*

Mexico by Rail by Gary A Poole
An indispensable companion to travelling in Mexico, with itineraries, history, walking tours, and what to see in each region.

Spain and Portugal by Rail by Norman Renouf
A guide to the public railway networks of Spain and Portugal, complete with details of major cities and towns, including places to visit and accommodation. Ideal for the rail pass holder.

Switzerland by Rail by Anthony Lambert
Due 1995

Thailand, Malaysia & Singapore by Rail by Brian McPhee
How and where to travel by rail in these popular countries, giving the opportunity to see parts not reached by other forms of transport.

USA by Rail by John Pitt
28 long-distance train journeys, featuring outstanding sites along the route and the main towns or places of interest where the journey may be broken.

For a catalogue of these and other guides to unusual places, contact Bradt Publications, 41 Nortoft Road, Chalfont St Peter, Bucks SL9 0LA, England. Tel/fax: 0494 873478.

NOTES

NOTES

INDEX